TARGETING COMMITMENT

TARGETING COMMITMENT

Interagency Performance in New Zealand

RODNEY SCOTT
ROSS BOYD

BROOKINGS INSTITUTION PRESS
Washington, D.C.

Copyright © 2022
THE BROOKINGS INSTITUTION
1775 Massachusetts Avenue, N.W.
Washington, D.C. 20036
www.brookings.edu

The Brookings Institution is a private nonprofit organization devoted to research, education, and publication on important issues of domestic and foreign policy. Its principal purpose is to bring the highest quality independent research and analysis to bear on current and emerging policy problems. Interpretations or conclusions in Brookings publications should be understood to be solely those of the authors.

Library of Congress Control Number: 2021951982

ISBN 9780815739180 (pbk)
ISBN 9780815739197 (ebook)

9 8 7 6 5 4 3 2 1

Typeset in Adobe Garamond Pro

Composition by Elliott Beard

Contents

Figures, Tables, and Boxes

Figures

Tables

Boxes

Foreword

As the world continues to adapt to COVID-19, social indicators that were worsening before the pandemic will now accelerate at the same time as governments must deal with slowing economies, aging populations, and very high levels of public debt. The hard problems of entrenched disadvantage and public agency silos have been pushed into the background for now but in time will reappear as larger challenges than ever.

The behavior of government and public agencies will influence the long-term effects of these challenges for individuals and households dependent on support. Policymakers need to understand more than ever what they want to achieve, whether they are achieving it and how to organize themselves to sustain success.

For the most disadvantaged, state institutions are too often untrustworthy, threatening, and inflexible. For people with few personal and financial resources, the exhausting processes of dysfunctional public services are part of the pathology of deprivation.

This book matters because it shows a path to overcoming the shortcomings of the universal welfare state. In 2012, New Zealand set out on a system-wide experiment designed to cut through inertia and complexity in the public service. We specified a few numerical results, set up tight accountability and created feedback loops so everyone could learn. We aimed to change the lives of people whose lives needed changing one by one—abused children, habitual offenders, and people waiting too long in the emergency department or too long on the call waiting at a government agency

This book captures the essence of that endeavor. It's a dynamic story of hope and innovation. The authors create a sense of a rich testing experience connecting the sometimes-ethereal world of public administration theory to real people. They capture the grittiness of government work; the tensions in measurement, organization, and decision-making; and the motivations of politicians and public servants. Some of the most satisfying Cabinet committee work I did was to participate in robust, blame-free, highly focused discussions as Ministers and public servants wrestled with transparent accountability for verifiable progress.

Over time, politicians learn how hard these problems are to solve. With their consistent political backing, public servants build confidence to test solutions. Both groups learn that they need to stay focused on people in communities in order to stave off the suffocating effects of institutional interests.

Ross Boyd and Rodney Scott do a marvelous job of charting a pragmatic, agile process and turning it into a unique textbook for policy in these COVID times. Their unique combination of practical experience and intellectual frameworks makes a powerful explanatory tool for probing the strengths and weaknesses of the approach.

Cynicism and hopelessness abound in public agencies. It's easy to say that there is nothing new here and that the demise of the Results program proves it. But the most vulnerable deserve better. Who can argue against working more thoughtfully on reducing misery and improving well-being, even if there's some bureaucratic tension to achieve it? And why doesn't the public service always work like this?

The Right Honourable Sir Simon William English KNZM,
Former Prime Minister of New Zealand

Preface

Rheumatic fever is a disease associated with poverty. Successive governments were both appalled and mystified by its high incidence in New Zealand and for several years had charged the health system with reducing it, but to no avail. Many public servants were equally appalled and mystified when in 2012, the government included a target to reduce rheumatic fever by two-thirds over five years as part of a reform package called the Better Public Service Results. In settling on only ten Results, why did the government choose a problem that affected only a small number of people, one that had proven so difficult to resolve, and set a target that few thought could be achieved?

The New Zealand government ultimately failed to achieve its target to reduce rheumatic fever by two-thirds. Instead, it was only able to cut the incidence of rheumatic fever in half. That is, it was prepared to "fail" at a self-imposed target to create the urgency and commitment needed to implement changes that saved children's lives.

Choosing only a few problems, and defining them quite selectively, provided a focus to the government's efforts and a bias toward action. Rheumatic fever affects only a small number of children, but preventing rheumatic fever required the government to address all the risk factors associated with poverty and inadequate housing that affect many more New Zealand families. While setting an ambitious target to reduce the incidence of a Third-World disease in New Zealand was remarkably successful, it would be misleading to attribute success solely to setting targets in priority areas. What happened here was a change in the way New Zealand's public service operated. Agencies got out of their silos and worked collaboratively to address a significant problem.

Agencies worked in partnership with nongovernmental organizations. People thought about the problem differently and did different things.

This book describes the New Zealand government's efforts to address rheumatic fever, and nine other important social problems, between 2012 and 2017. Along with the ambitious targets, the government used public accountability as levers to overcome the bureaucratic barriers that impeded public service delivery and used data, evidence, and innovation to change practice. New Zealand experimented, failed, succeeded, and learned from the experience over five years. This New Zealand experience demonstrates that interagency performance targets are a potentially powerful tool for improving social outcomes through better public services. This has been described as "the most important change in how public services are delivered" in New Zealand in a generation.

Some of the details of these cases are specific to New Zealand, but some of the lessons are broadly applicable. They present hints as to how policy makers can design programs for generating goal commitment and inspiring public entrepreneurship to solve complex, cross-cutting problems.

Acknowledgments

This book was many years in the making. The original design work to develop New Zealand's Results program was completed in 2011. Then between 2012 and 2017, thousands of public servants worked as part of the program to improve the lives of New Zealanders. Every six months, about a hundred public servants contributed to a report to Cabinet on the lessons that had been learned, and the progress made.

The initial work to evaluate the program was made possible due to an author stipend from the IBM Business of Government series to write a short report on the Results program. Through the various articles published since then, various editors and reviewers have made thoughtful and helpful suggestions on how we were interpreting different aspects of the data and presenting our conclusions. Since then, we benefited from two fellowships, wherein Rodney was able to spend one semester each at Harvard University's Kennedy School of Government (2017) and University of Oxford's Blavatnik School of Government (2018). These fellowships allowed Rodney to meet with academics and practitioners involved in interagency collaboration and performance targets in both the United States and the United Kingdom. Rodney would like to thank both institutions and, in particular, Professor Ngaire Woods (dean, Blavatnik School of Government, University of Oxford) and Professor Anthony Saich (director, Ash Center for Democratic Governance and Innovation, Harvard University) for making these fellowships possible.

In the United States, Rodney visited more than thirty jurisdictions that use a -Stat system, interviewing practitioners and observing performance discussions in action. We have also engaged in long and useful conversations with a wide variety of academics and practitioners with experience in performance targets, horizontal management, or both. A very partial list of people who generously shared their time includes: Kevin Donahue (Washington, D.C.); Matt Malament Matthew Bartleet, and Emily Love (Atlanta, Georgia); Greg Useem (Alexandria, Virginia); Emily Monea (Somerville, Massachusetts); Harry Black, Leigh Tami and Dante Perez (Cincinnati, Ohio); Michael Jacobsen (King County, Washington); David Gottesman (Montgomery County, Maryland); Drusilla Roessle (State of Vermont); Melissa Wavelet (State of Colorado); Kevin Ward (NYPD); Dana Roberts and Tammy Tippie (Performance Improvement Council); Mark Moore, Jorrit DeJong, and Stephen Goldsmith (Harvard University); Beth Blauer (Johns Hopkins University); Lara Benson (University of Washington); Rosemary O'Leary (University of Kansas); John Kamensky (IBM); Matthew Smith (Cap Gemini); and Wendy Korthuis-Smith (Deloitte).

We would like to particularly acknowledge the help of five people: Professors Robert (Bob) Behn, Chris Ansell, Eugene Bardach, John Bryson, and Barbara Crosby. Harvard's Professor Behn is the leading authority on -Stat systems, particularly his book *The PerformanceStat Potential* published by the Brookings Institution Press. While Rodney was completing his fellowship at Harvard University, Professor Behn introduced Rodney to his many contacts who have worked or are working on performance management around the United States. Professor Behn and Rodney discussed and compared US and New Zealand systems over many bowls of New England clam chowder. Without Professor Behn's insights, we would never have understood US practices in quite the same way.

Professor Chris Ansell, from the University of California, Berkeley, has been a leading author on horizontal government, perhaps best known for "Collaborative Governance in Theory and Practice," written with Alison Gash in 2008. Professor Ansell provided feedback on our evaluation of the Results program and helped us to pick out generalizable theory about commitment and accountability.

Professor Eugene Bardach was a coauthor on our comparative evaluation of the Results program. Professor Bardach has been a leading voice in public administration for decades, but of particular relevance here is his seminal 1998 book *Getting Agencies to Work Together: The Practice and Theory of Managerial Craftsmanship*. Professor Bardach challenged us to think not just about the ideal start conditions for horizontal management but also about how public servants were able to adapt to nonideal conditions.

Finally, Professors John Bryson and Barbara Crosby from the University of Minnesota have helped us to think about the informal behaviors behind the program's success. Professors Bryson and Crosby are leading voices on cross-sectoral collaboration and gave their time to discuss the Results program (and its comparison to US programs) during their visiting appointments in Wellington, New Zealand; at a conference in Aarhus, Denmark; and while visiting Atlanta, Georgia.

In the United Kingdom, we are indebted to Professor Gwyn Bevan, Sir Michael Barber, and Sir Julian Le Grand for their generosity in sharing their time. Professor Bevan worked in the National Health Service and has been one of the leading academic authors exploring the impact of the Delivery Unit on the performance of the health system. Professor Bevan worked with us over many months to compare the Results program with the use of targets in the United Kingdom and spent many afternoons discussing the interaction of targets and motivation with Rodney during his fellowship at Oxford University.

Sir Michael Barber was the head of the Delivery Unit from 2001 to 2005, reporting directly to Prime Minister Tony Blair. Barber's 2007 book *Instruction to Deliver* was one of the main inspirations for the Results program. We were able to test the conclusions presented in this book with Sir Michael over cups of tea at Queen's College in Oxford in 2018.

Sir Julian Le Grand was the senior policy adviser to Prime Minister Tony Blair from 2003 to 2005 and author of the influential 2003 book *Motivation, Agency, and Public Policy*. Le Grand is also a professor at the London School of Economics. On one visit to New Zealand, Sir Julian shared his time with employees of the New Zealand Treasury, where both authors were based at the time. We were able to refine the discussion of motivation presented in this book over a long discussion on "knights" and "knaves" with Sir Julian.

Through the feedback and challenge from these people and others, we have formed a view on which parts of the Results program are unique adaptations to the New Zealand context and which are likely to be transferable and applicable elsewhere. Furthermore, these discussions reinforced for us that the Results program brings something distinct and important to share—a different way of looking at target setting and horizontal management that both complement and extend previous and existing programs in the United Kingdom and the United States.

We would like to acknowledge the people involved in producing the book itself, including Eleanor Merton—research fellow at the Victoria University School of Government—for extensive revisions of the manuscript, Christina Marchand at Harvard University's Kennedy School of Government, the book's peer reviewers—Professors Gwyn Bevan and Michael Macaulay—and the Brookings Institution Press.

Finally, we would like to thank all those thousands of public servants who act every day with a spirit of service to the community. This book tells the story of public servants determined to improve the lives of everyday New Zealanders despite any obstacles they encountered along the way. Significant contributions were made to the design of the program by central agency thought leaders such as Peter Hughes, Andrew Kibblewhite, Iain Rennie, Ryan Orange, and Kirsten

Jensen, among many others. Other State Services Commission managers encouraged the authors to write about the Results program, in particular, Dr. Andrew Burns and Hugo Vitalis. The book mentions by name several public entrepreneurs whose contributions were noteworthy—Dr. Chrissie Pickin, Kararaina Calcott-Cribb, Richard Foy, Aphra Green, and Linda Oliver—and also draws on conversations with Dr. Brook Barrington, Paul Barker, and Carolyn Palmer. But the improvements in social, health, educational, and justice outcomes, and the improvements in government interaction with citizens and businesses, were all successes created by many hands.

Introduction

Some of the hardest problems that governments must manage are those in which many agencies will need to contribute to unknown solutions. These include "wicked" problems like crime, family violence, and long-term unemployment.[1] Like most countries, New Zealand struggled to effectively address these problems for many years. Always trying to learn from others, New Zealand public servants tried many of the practices used around the world, with varying success.

In 2012, they tried a new approach: interagency performance targets, which drew on features from prioritization, target, and collaboration practices in other jurisdictions. The government chose ten of the hardest problems—problems that spanned the responsibility of multiple agencies and had been resistant to previous interventions—and declared them to be priorities. They set challenging five-year targets (in this case, a number and a date—for example, reducing the rate of rheumatic fever by two-thirds by 2017) at the edge of what was considered possible to achieve. The targets were set at an "outcome" level, despite issues with attribution and control, and public servants were held responsible for achieving them.

What follows is an account of why interagency performance targets were effective, despite the checkered past of the individual management practices that they combined. In fact, combining performance targets with interagency working helped address some of the limitations of each. Interagency working is slow, but targets gave it urgency. Interagency working is expensive, but feedback systems allowed new solutions to be rapidly iterated and improved. Interagency working is hard to attribute accountability for, but targets provided an expectation of performance for which there was shared responsibility. Inter-

1

agency working is difficult to sustain, but targets provided periodic milestones and continued profile.

This is not to say that the New Zealand experience was perfectly designed or was a universal success. Much of this book focuses on the successes of the program because these will be of most interest to practitioners wishing to replicate or adapt them. But the Results program was of course not without substantial challenges. Each of the gains was hard won, and the successes were accompanied by failures. Ultimately, not all the targets were met. In 2017, the government of the day decided to renew the program for a further five years, but then there was an election and a change of government, and the program was abandoned.

When we talked to public servants involved in the program, their feedback was remarkably similar. They described the work as hard—they had encountered all the challenges and setbacks described in the collaborative governance literature. Making decisions by consensus was slow and frustrating. Coordinating actions by different agencies was inefficient. Agency leaders frequently focused on the outputs for which each was individually accountable rather than on the outcomes that they could influence together. For every example of joint working, there was an example of inward-looking and siloed behavior.

The success of the Results program can be traced, in large part, to the enduring commitment of public servants to achieving the targets. We therefore present this book as a description of goal commitment in action, using the Results program in totality as a single case study. Public servants made progress on solving ten difficult problems because they were all focused on a single target and committed to achieving it. Throughout the book, we distil the experiences from the program into lessons and insights, suggesting how they might be applied by others in different contexts. To draw out these lessons, we attempt to answer how we know that the Results program was effective, how we know why it was effective, and how we know what is useful for others to use.

This book has two authors. Rodney Scott was asked to evaluate the Results program in 2015, to inform the eventual redesign in 2017. Ross Boyd was the Results program coordinator, living and breathing the interagency performance targets from the design of the program in 2011, through its implementation in 2012, until its conclusion in 2017. This cannot be a purely impartial text, because the authors are not impartial. The book combines Rodney's analysis and evaluation that compare New Zealand's interagency performance targets with practices in other jurisdictions and in New Zealand's own past, with Ross's direct experiences and relationships with people involved in the program. The book is structured in four parts, which are each broken into chapters and smaller sections, interspersed with case study vignettes that explore core design principles and aspects of the program in greater detail.

Part 1 brings together discussion of the context for the program—its "supportive architecture" and enabling factors along with the context for the problems that needed to be addressed. New Zealand in 2011 was performing well in problems when responsibility fell to a single agency but struggled with managing across agency boundaries. The aftereffects of the global financial crisis meant that there was no extra money to go around; the government needed to improve performance without extra resources. Financial constraint provided urgency. Solving complex social problems would reduce future demand for public services and was therefore the best way to improve the financial sustainability of New Zealand's public services.

Conditions such as New Zealand's strong institutions and respected, independent, and authoritative data; culture of accountability; and stable government able to credibly set multiyear objectives and to see them through provided a window of opportunity. This lent viability to the political calculus of a government publicly declaring what it planned to achieve and how its success would be measured.

Such political calculus was risky because interagency working has notoriously high coordination costs. It can be slow and expensive and have unclear goals. It's difficult to sustain and difficult to assign accountability for. It is also the only way to address some of the more complex and persistent social problems. Likewise, performance targets are known to be distortionary, demoralizing, discouraging of cooperation, and difficult to sustain. But they are also effective for assigning accountability and driving performance improvements. Combining two fraught practices in one program sounds like an ambitious and unlikely marriage at best and a bad idea at worst. Nevertheless, this is what the New Zealand government did with the Better Public Services Results program (the Results program), staking much of its political capital on the achievement of the ten interagency performance targets. This program was an enormous part of the New Zealand public services reform agenda from 2012 to 2017 in both scope and significance.

In New Zealand's judicious application of an interagency performance target system to a small number of well-defined problems, the country was taking a step into the unknown. But not the complete unknown. Other jurisdictions had solved parts of the puzzle already. New Zealand was able to take from the successes and failures of programs in Scotland, England, the State of Washington, the Commonwealth of Virginia, and the city of Baltimore and to add several unique and novel features to the program design.

In writing this book, our most important motivation, in addition to explaining what happened and why, was to help other people learn from what New Zealand did just as New Zealand had learned from others. The adaptive practice that involved trial and error over the five years from 2012 to 2017 will hopefully allow other jurisdictions to take the best parts from New Zealand's experience and extend the practice further. However, our claim to generalization rests on analytic generalization—the New Zealand experience illustrates phenomena described elsewhere but combines them in different ways.

Part 2 describes the Results program itself, covering its development and the selection of the problems, targets, and measures; discussing features of its implementation such as governance and reporting; and outlining the 2017 re-fresh and renewal of the Results. New Zealand saw the Results as simple mo-tivational statements about things that matter to citizens. This section outlines each of the Results in these terms, briefly summarizing some of the principal areas of interest for each to lay the groundwork for the more in-depth discus-sion in later sections.

Part 3 starts to make some evaluations of the program, drawing on four prior analyses to discuss successes and challenges. One of the more prominent challenges was gaming and cheating, which are an inevitable consideration for any measurement scheme for performance management that includes powerful incentives. While it is important to minimize those distortionary effects, both to generate the greatest true performance gains and maintain the perceived integrity of the program, this should not invalidate the idea of measurement altogether. The appropriate comparison is not whether measurement caused distortions but whether measurement caused an improvement in performance over no measurement at all.

This section also includes specific case studies from some of the Result areas. The authors interacted with hundreds of public servants over a six-year period, drawing out stories from each of the ten Results. The stories describe frequently messy experiences, which preclude neat "best-practice" answers, but also do illustrate performance improvement over time and contribute to under-standing the "craft" of being an effective public servant.[2]

This carries through into part 4, where we more specifically attribute the goal commitment achieved by the program to a combination of several factors. This covers chapters 12–14, which also draw on theory from public admin-istration (as well as psychology and philosophy) to group these factors into a framework of expectancy, instrumentality, and valence.

The section on expectancy explores the relationship between targets and be-haviors. It was important that public servants were confident that the program would continue until its scheduled completion, so targets would become "due." Only ten problems were selected, so each remained prominent and significant. The targets defined the government's level of ambition and were described in ways that seemed manageable in size and delay. They were set at the "edge of possible"—hard enough to maximize effort and urgency but not so hard that they caused despair.

The section on instrumentality illustrates how public servants responded to the challenges before them. Agencies organized themselves into governance groups and shared support functions. This was a great learning period for New

Zealand public servants as they moved through a relationship maturity continuum and learned to work effectively with each other. They encountered tensions: between broad participation and narrow shared responsibility; between individual leadership and joint, indivisible, and equal responsibility; and between developing prerequisite relationships and the need for urgent action. This section explores public servants' different professional, organizational, and social identities and their different sources of felt accountability—to ministers, to parliament, to their employer, to their peers, and importantly to the public, to make a difference for New Zealanders.

The section on valence describes the sense of obligation in mechanistic terms, focusing on reporting documents that measured progress with time-series data (line graphs), judgments (performance ratings), and qualitative human-centered stories and that celebrated that progress. We also explore strong positive and negative reputational consequences for performance, noting the effects of ministerial responses to lack of progress. Mechanisms that contextualized achievement as an improvement from the baseline of the past, rather than the meeting of a somewhat-arbitrary aspiration for the future, ensured that the government was not punished for failing to reach the majority of the targets it had set, in contrast to the experience of other governments using target regimes (which have also been barely acknowledged for the targets they did meet). This success was due at least in part to the interest of the public (via the media) in the program, which mattered to public servants because it mattered to the public. This evidences the relationship between public servants' sense of self or self-esteem and their motivations to help (and to be seen as helping) their community.

Despite challenges, public servants persisted and made progress. What they did to rise to these challenges is described in the following chapters. It is a rich story, told by the practitioners with experience at the cutting edge of the reform. Over five years, they remained committed to achieving the targets and continually innovated new ways around the various barriers they encountered. As with any learning system, it evolved over time—some practices were tried and failed, and others were iterated and improved. New Zealand government agencies progressively learned how to better work with each other and how to work with a data-led target regime. Public servants responded to each of the ten problems with different solutions and learned from each other.

Against long odds, New Zealand's interagency performance targets were an enormous success, associated with improvements in all ten problems to which they were applied. Outcomes for New Zealanders improved in areas that had proven intractable in the face of previous efforts. Even in areas wherein outcomes had been improving slowly before 2012, performance exceeded the trend data. Public servants could see that they were making a difference to New Zealanders. Many described working toward these targets as the most important and rewarding thing they had done in their careers. Agencies worked together in new ways, and a more data-driven and collaborative approach began to infect the rest of the public service. On a systemic level, New Zealand's public service emerged from the experience stronger and determined to apply the learning more widely.

PART I

SUPPORTIVE ARCHITECTURE

Since the 1980s, New Zealand has been regarded as a world leader in public management and in organizing to deliver public services effectively. The New Zealand government went further and faster in implementing reforms known as New Public Management, which have been emulated around the world. While the reforms of the 1980s led to substantial improvements, they also created challenges in other areas. New Zealand now has dozens of separate agencies with strong vertical accountabilities, and it struggles to manage horizontally for problems that fall across or between those agencies.

The authors hope in writing this book is that the experiences from New Zealand will be useful for public servants in other jurisdictions. One of the challenges of translating lessons from one jurisdiction to another is in understanding the local context to adjust and adapt for another context. The chapters in this part describe crucial aspects of the New Zealand public management system and history as context for experiences and lessons illustrated in later chapters.

1

Governance in Aotearoa New Zealand

New Zealand is a small country in the southern Pacific Ocean. Known as *Aotearoa* ("the land of the long white cloud") in the indigenous language *te reo Māori*, it sits between Australia to the west, and the vast Pacific to the east, dotted with small Pacific island nations.

It is a young nation, with the indigenous Māori people arriving from Polynesia in the 13th century. The British colonized it in the 18th century. Representatives of both groups signed a treaty in 1840, one of the founding documents of the nation and that is still referred to throughout the public service and government today.[1] People of Māori and British descent continue to compose the largest ethnic groups, along with other Polynesian groups that have arrived more recently. Aotearoa/New Zealand is neither purely Māori nor purely British and represents a living partnership between both cultures (described in New Zealand as "biculturalism").

New Zealand's system of government appears, on its surface, to have retained much of the British institutionalism New Zealand's colonizers favored. And yet this is tempered by Pacific values of relationships and community. Historian and Professor David Hackett Fischer observed that the central ideal of U.S. politics is "freedom," whereas in New Zealand, it is "fairness."[2] Although New Zealand is undoubtedly both a liberal democracy and a social democracy, public discourse tends to focus on the latter, with an emphasis on equality and egalitarianism.[3]

New Zealand is governed by a parliamentary representative democratic monarchy, closely patterned on the British Westminster system. The government is formed after a democratic election held every three years. Voters elect representatives to New Zealand's unicameral legislature, the House of Representatives. New Zealand uses a mixed-member proportional voting system, which makes it unlikely that any one political party will win a majority of the seats in the House of Representatives. The party with the most votes typically needs to form a coalition or agreement with another party or parties.

Unlike in a presidential system, the government is formed of ministers who are first elected members of the House of Representatives. The government can only stay in power while it has the support of a majority of members in the House of Representatives, known as having the confidence of the House.

The executive branch of government (also known as "the government") is formed of Ministers of the Crown. The government makes day-to-day decisions on how to manage the country, brings proposed laws to the House of Representatives, and decides on policies that government departments implement.

Government in New Zealand is highly unitary, with a significant proportion of services and functions delivered by central government departments and national-level arms-length agencies (although usually through a regional and local presence). Local authorities play a relatively minor role.[4] This makes it feasible for the state sector to conceive of itself as a single "system," in contrast to federalized systems like those of the United States, Canada, and Australia.

New Zealand is a relatively wealthy, developed country, with a high standard of living. It has a population of only 4.9 million people, similar in population and land area to the state of Colorado.[5] With such a small population, a great deal can be accomplished through personal relationships and leadership behaviors. When research was being conducted for this book, it became apparent that many of the lessons from New Zealand might be just as applicable to city, county, province, or state governments in larger federalized countries.

New Public Management Reforms in the 1980s

Although the range of changes retroactively described as New Public Management was much envied and emulated, these reforms emerged from a fiscal crisis facing New Zealand in the late 1980s. New Zealand was in the process of shifting from a closed managed economy to an open one, trading freely with the world. During the transition, the economy experienced several boom and bust cycles, including the crash of 1987 in which the share market lost 60 percent of its value and took years to recover. The government faced declining revenue and urgently needed to reduce public spending, so it searched for ways to deliver public services more efficiently.

Public servants within the New Zealand Treasury recommended radical change. They had been influenced by institutional economists Ronald Coase and Oliver Williamson and sought to reorganize public services as a series of principal-agent problems between ministers (as principals) and senior public servants (as agents). Although many other jurisdictions implemented aspects of New Public Management and variations of similar themes, New Zealand is widely regarded as having gone further and faster than any other government has.[6]

The New Public Management's intent was to embed the theory of the marketplace and business-like culture in public organizations.[7] Permanent secretaries, as the heads of departments, were replaced with fixed-term chief executives. These executives were given extensive autonomy to manage their organizations to deliver outputs. Central agencies became relatively weak, and the vertical relationship between individual ministers and their agencies was made paramount.

New Zealand took accountability extremely seriously—perhaps too seriously.[8] The separation of outputs and outcomes was intended to strengthen the attribution of accountability for outputs to chief executives, whereas ministers would be held accountable for the ultimate outcomes.[9] Outcomes—the desired result of public services in terms of consequences for the community—were considered to be outside the direct control of chief executives. Conversely, performance of agencies could be measured in terms of outputs (products and services) and managed by contract-like accountability documents.[10] This explicit decoupling of outcomes and outputs has been the subject of considerable debate and criticism, as other countries did not draw the distinction between outputs and outcomes quite so sharply.[11] The separation trend was rooted in New Zealand's New Public Management reforms and sometimes very specific conceptions of accountability in public management. A more clear-sighted perspective on the issue would be that "both outputs and outcomes provide useful and important definitions of public value, and overemphasis on either can produce dysfunctional results."[12]

The New Public Management reforms resulted in an abundance of largely single-objective agencies and semiautonomous organizations, with policy design deliberately separated from implementation in many areas of government. This separation was intended to generate efficiency gains through specialization, facilitating contestability, and clearer accountability for both policy and operational tasks.[13] The linear approach to accountability adopted by New Zealand exacerbated the focus on achieving single objectives rather than broader outcomes that require agencies to work collaboratively. It also tended to emphasize the achievement of short-term outputs over longer-term outcomes and could be punitive rather than constructive. Iain Rennie, New Zealand's State Services commissioner[14] from 2008 to 2016, described it this way:

> Individual ministers answer in Parliament for the resources under their direct control, and for the issues and agencies for which they have direct responsibility. Accountability mechanisms are strong in scrutinising

short-term performance, especially when failure in the near term is apparent. Department performance is reviewed by select committees with a focus on the year past. The adversarial nature of partisan political debate and robust media scrutiny encourages a focus on poor performance, a blunt approach to accountability (e.g. "heads must roll"), and the specifics of particular cases as opposed to learnings of a broader application. In contrast, much less emphasis is placed on rewarding and learning from good performance or adopting a proportionate and fair approach to assessing performance.[15]

The reforms of the late 1980s solved the problems of the time to a considerable extent by increasing accountability, increasing transparency of resource allocation, and lessening the inertia generated by large departments that were input-dominated. But the reforms also created new problems. The separate agencies were enterprising about their own resources but were not incentivized to connect with others.[16]

By the late 1990s, the state services exhibited worrying signs of underperformance in several areas, including the following:

- Duplication;

- Numerous variably specified priorities across government;

- Issues that no one was responsible for;

- Priority and resourcing decisions not made from a whole-of-government perspective; and

- Interagency working too often exclusively dependent on the personal commitment of chief executives (and sometimes ministers).[17]

The following years saw successive attempts at breaking down the agency silos that had been producing this underperformance.

Past Attempts at Breaking Down Silos (Managing for Outcomes)

The decoupling of outputs and outcomes resulted in agencies becoming efficient at delivering things of questionable value. If the government couldn't hold agencies accountable for the outcomes they achieved, at least they could require them to describe, through intervention logic, how their outputs contributed to outcomes.

In response, the New Zealand government introduced the "Managing for Outcomes" initiative, which sought to encourage agencies to focus on the underlying value of their outputs through the use of intervention logic. Because outcomes (unlike outputs) are typically influenced by more than one agency, the government introduced "Managing for Shared Outcomes" to encourage management horizontally across agencies. [18]

Managing for Outcomes struggled to sustain momentum for several reasons. No obvious link existed between the actions agreed in the Managing for Outcomes meetings and any observed change in the outcomes desired. Long delays in achieving any impact meant that decisions could not be improved based on feedback and that participants could not see the fruits of their labor. Furthermore, there were problems with accountability, and chief executives were effectively held accountable for the actions of other agencies in interagency work, even if they had no control over these actions. Program reports were delivered to Parliament and audited as part of a chief accountability mechanism. Auditors searched for evidence of cause and effect—proven attribution of outputs to outcomes—which was often difficult to establish. Unsurprisingly, these factors drove managers to be conservative and defensive in their ambitions for interagency outcomes.

Managing for Outcomes was never officially canceled, but it was referenced less frequently over time and seemed to have disappeared entirely by 2005. Although the program had stalled, some of the public servants involved in the Managing for Outcomes groups found their meetings useful. Some groups continued to meet, evolving into what became known as the "sectoral approach." Agencies grouped themselves into clusters or "sectors" responsible for overlapping outcomes—the natural resources sector, the justice sector, and so on. The central agencies never mandated or even strongly encouraged sectors; rather, they emerged organically and by necessity. As the Managing for Outcomes initiative waned, agency leaders could see that they still required structures whereby to deliver on outcomes that crossed organizational boundaries. In some cases, these were the same groups of agencies as for Managing for Outcomes, and in others, new sector groups formed in which overlapping interests were identified. The self-organized nature of the sectoral approach led to sectors that didn't perfectly group the agencies, and membership of different groups overlapped (for example, the agency responsible for mining was in both the natural resources sector and the economic development sector). Some agencies with particularly broad responsibilities found themselves part of multiple sectors.

The sectors created their own governance groups, supporting secretariats, aspirational statements, dedicated websites, and branded products. To the extent that the performance of sectors was judged at all, it was done so on the basis of process measures. Ministers chided agencies for not joining up when they should, and agencies responded by providing evidence that they were indeed working together. When the sectors were discussed in performance meetings between the State Services Commission and the leaders of agencies, agencies were praised for demonstrating process successes, such as a joint strategy or a new governance arrangement. The sectors seen as high performing were those with the most active governance groups, a proliferation of subcommittees, and the greatest number of joint statements.

Process success is one type of policy success Alan McConnell identifies, generally associated with following best practice.[19] Process measures address the shortcomings of end-outcome measures. They can be achieved quickly and therefore provide rapid feedback on which changes to make. They also provide opportunities for celebration (and the potential to generate momentum) as they are ticked off. They are often within the direct control of the participants to deliver and therefore don't suffer from the attribution problems of end-outcome measures. There is only one significant disadvantage to the use of process measures—they have no intrinsic value to society. In some cases, the sectors became more focused on working together than on solving policy problems. It should be noted that collaboration is a means to an end, not an end in and of itself. A focus simply on improving collaboration can be counterproductive in terms of improving outcomes. As put by Hon. Bill English,[20] the minister leading the Results program in New Zealand:

> How do we collaborate? Well, collaboration is a word I've banned from my office. What we want is impact. What did you do that made a difference because every week you take to fix that problem out in that community adds to the cost of failure, and to misery in that community?[21]

Some of the sectors achieved some success, for example, the natural resource sector colocated policy analysts to develop a joint policy statement on freshwater, and the justice sector started to work more collaboratively to join up the pieces of the criminal justice pipeline. However, ministers were frustrated that the sectors lacked a sense of purpose and therefore struggled to make a difference for New Zealanders. A national-led government elected in 2009 tried structural change—merging several departments so they could more effectively work together. Structural change was proving a slow and expensive way to achieve limited gains in joined-up government. In the third year of its first term, the government turned to central agencies to find a more enduring public management solution.

New Zealand in 2011

Just like the changes of the 1980s, the drive in 2011 for a new solution was in part driven by crisis. The global financial crisis (GFC) of 2008 affected jurisdictions around the world, and New Zealand was no exception. The government took urgent action to reduce spending in the immediate aftermath but still faced a long-term outlook that was less favorable than it had been before the crash. Other countries responded with austerity—slashing public service budgets and reducing the quantity and quality of service provision. Though we understand the New Zealand government discussed this, the ultimate decision was slightly different. This may have been because New Zealand public services in 2011 were not in bad shape; unlike when targets were introduced in the United Kingdom, New Zealand public services were not seen as "failing."

Although New Zealand avoided the worst of the austerity policies pursued elsewhere, there were significant constraints on government expenditure. Governments in the past had sought to solve their most pressing policy problems by throwing resources at the problems in the hope that this would improve them. However, the aftereffects of the GFC meant that agencies were operating under flat nominal baselines—that is, budgets that were declining in real terms due to inflation. The government's efforts to solve these problems were constrained by the same fiscal context that made their success so necessary. This is an important factor to note because it negates any arguments that the successes of the program were due to the provision of additional resources. Leaders were expected to make better use of the money that was already applied to the policy problems; more money cannot explain the improvement of the Result measures, because no additional money was provided.

Various agencies had invested in actuarial valuations to understand their future liabilities, and each reported a similar story, namely that a relatively small number of New Zealanders were disproportionately responsible for government costs. The best way to reduce government expenditure, the New Zealand government reasoned, was to reduce the demand for services. And the best way to reduce the demand for services was to improve outcomes in some of the most seemingly intractable problems that the government still faced (despite significant prior attention and action). The Finance Minister Bill English remarked, "What works for the community, works for the government's books."[22]

When the government examined these problems, it concluded that the most important problems, and the ones that had historically been most difficult to solve, were those that spanned agency boundaries. Ministers requested advice on improving the collective impact of the public sector. To provide this advice, leaders from public, private, and not-for-profit organizations formed the Better Public Services Advisory Group. The group found that although government was generally effective at managing problems that fell within the responsibility of one agency, it was less effective at addressing problems that crossed agency boundaries. The sectoral approach was viewed as useful for getting agencies to talk to each other but was also seen as limiting in its focus on process above outcomes:

> Running individual agencies well is important, but should not get in the
> way of progress on the complex, long-term social and economic issues

. . . The most challenging social and economic issues facing New Zealand need action across agency boundaries, and currently this action
takes too long. [23]

Some of these cross-cutting problems had existed for a long time. Most
of the problems eventually chosen in the Results program had been on the
agendas of successive governments since at least the 1990s. This meant that
improvements would not be a simple consequence of labeling them as important and providing them increased attention. The government knew that
these problems could not be solved by more of the same: "The status quo is
not viable."[24]

If these problems could have been solved simply through trying harder
(using the old management styles), then they wouldn't have still been problems
in 2012. Each of the long-standing problems was complex, and public servants
did not know what would work. They couldn't rely on a detailed, comprehensive long-term plan. Instead they needed something that would allow them to
both collaborate across agencies and to have the courage to experiment, get
feedback, and adapt. Furthermore, these problems had to be solved using existing (or declining) resources. Fortunately, some factors existed that would work
in New Zealand's favor, building toward the success of the Results program.

The first such factor is strong institutions. When targets are associated with
rewards and sanctions, public servants have powerful incentives to manipulate
the measures to achieve the target. This is known as "gaming" or "cheating."
Andrew Gray and Christopher Hood suggest that gaming and cheating are at
least in part determined by the organization's culture.[25] Gaming and cheating
have no fixed definitions in the performance target literature, suggesting the
difference between them is a somewhat flexible construct. For the purpose of
this book, we distinguish between the two with respect to accuracy of information. We define gaming as when the measurement is accurate but misleading,
for example, when UK hospitals left patients waiting in ambulances to reduce
the recorded time waiting in emergency rooms. They had "gamed" the measure—it was accurate to say that patients were spending less time in emergency
rooms, but those patients were not being seen any sooner. This has been described as "hitting the target but missing the point."[26]

Conversely, we define cheating as when the measurement itself is intentionally falsified.[27] For example, in the United Kingdom, when a target was set to
reduce ambulance response times to less than eight minutes, there was a spike
in the recording of wait times of seven minutes and fifty-nine seconds, presum-
ably as a result of manual recording of inaccurate information (see figure 1-1).
(As discussed later, there may also be differences between output measures and
outcome measures in terms of susceptibility to gaming.) There is a significant

body of literature demonstrating that cheating or gaming almost always accompanies high-powered performance incentives.[28]

Fortunately, the prevailing culture of the New Zealand public service was (and continues to be) of high integrity and low corruption. For example, New Zealand has consistently ranked first, equal first, or second as the least corrupt country in the world in Transparency International's Corruption Perceptions Index.[29]

New Zealand had a strong, statutorily independent official statistics system to verify the data validity, which limited the potential for cheating. The government statistician has several legal and procedural protections in the production of official statistics. Many measurements used in the New Zealand program were "Tier 1" statistics, the highest level of independence and highest standards of accuracy and verification. An independent Ministerial Advisory Committee on Official Statistics oversees production of Tier 1 statistics.[30]

A second relevant condition was the culture of accountability. As mentioned earlier, New Zealand takes accountability extremely seriously. A competing set of checks and balances holds departments (and their chief executive as representative) accountable for their achievements to Parliament, ministers, their employer (the State Services commissioner), and the public. These mechanisms

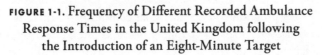

FIGURE 1-1. Frequency of Different Recorded Ambulance
Response Times in the United Kingdom following
the Introduction of an Eight-Minute Target

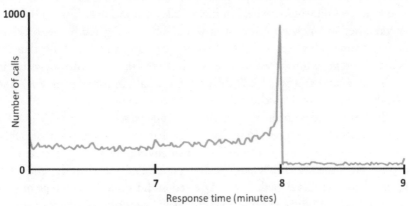

Source: the Commission for Health Improvement produced the data for this figure in its 2003 report titled "What CHI Has Found in: Ambulance Organisations," published by the Government Stationary Office. A similar analysis appeared in an article by Gwyn Bevan and Richard Hamblin (2009), "Hitting and Missing Targets by Ambulance Services for Emergency Calls: Effects of Different Systems of Performance Measurement within the UK." *Journal of the Royal Statistical Society: Series A (Statistics in Society), 172*(1), 161–190.

are discussed further in chapters 6 and 13 as they apply to the Results program. This meant that mechanisms were already in place for making public servants answerable for what they had achieved and that the new mechanisms the target program had introduced were not entirely foreign.

The third relevant condition was a government that was willing to think about savings in the long term. Though other governments around the world slashed government budgets under the guise of austerity, the New Zealand government did not respond to the global financial crisis of 2008 with deep cuts. Instead, the government operated under the assumption that the greatest cost savings in the long term would come from reducing demand for government services. By investing in solving long-standing problems, such as improving educational achievement and reducing the crime rate (among other items), government would reduce subsequent demand for public services, such as unemployment benefits, policing, courts, and prisons.

Various calculations by the New Zealand Treasury had concluded that a relatively small number of citizens, primarily with complex needs that cross multiple departments, were responsible for a disproportionate amount of government spending. The Treasury concluded that by addressing these hard cases, government could save much more money in the long term than by making cuts to service provision in the short term.

A fourth condition was a result of good luck more than of good planning. For the Results program to engender goal commitment, there needed to be a stable period over which the public servants could be held responsible for what they had achieved. The program was set to run from 2012 to 2017, but a general election would be held in the middle of it, in 2014. If the 2014 election resulted in a new government, it would not be obligated by the previous one's promises. However, opinion polls provided an early indication that the National-led government would likely be reelected in 2014. This suggested to public servants that it was likely the program would continue until 2017 and that they would remain accountable for their achievements.

This contrasted with the second round of targets, set in the middle of 2017 with another election looming in September that year. This meant that public servants were operating in a more uncertain environment that generated less urgency than the immediate post-election period in 2012 when the first set of Results had been developed. The 2017 election did result in a change of government, one with different priorities. The new Labour Party–led government discontinued the targets of the previous government and replaced them with higher-level outcome targets in different policy areas.

The preceding political calculations provide some basic prerequisite conditions for publicly setting and using targets. Although the factors that led to the New Zealand government choosing to govern by interagency performance targets were specific and unique, some general contextual characteristics might provide transferable lessons.[31] There are likely to be certain types of problems in which an interagency performance target regime is indicated. From the New Zealand case, the following characteristics appear the most generalizable, namely, challenges with interagency problems, resistance to previous attempts to solve, unknown solutions, and resource constraints. The following enabling conditions that increase the likelihood of success may also be generalizable, including strong institutions with authoritative information, a tradition and culture of accountability, willingness to think about savings over the long term, and the stability to credibly implement a multiyear program. Perhaps most important of all, New Zealand benefited from a government willing to risk the embarrassment of failing to achieve its own targets in exchange for the chance to make real improvements in long-standing and previously intractable problems.

2

The Holy Grail of Public Administration

Around the world, the practice of dividing governments into smaller administrative units (departments, ministries, commissions, etc.) is thought to be more efficient than trying to manage government as a whole is. We collectively refer to them as agencies, and each one has a narrower focus and can specialize in certain competencies. This section addresses what happens when problems do not fit neatly into the responsibility of a single agency.

The field of public administration has, since its beginning, been preoccupied with how to divide government. The first wave, "traditional" or "old" public administration, was dominated by the concept of hierarchy.[1] Agencies were simply a reflection of the dominion of agency leaders. Just as a president or prime minister might be responsible for the performance of government as a whole, other leaders (cabinet members, ministers, secretaries, agency heads) might each be responsible for one aspect of government's performance. Each leader had resources afforded to them to achieve their goals, including a collection of public servants arranged hierarchically underneath them within their respective agencies.

Since the 1980s, a second wave of public administration changes were retrospectively named New Public Management.[2] The dominant construct of New Public Management was the market. Under New Public Management, agencies were conceived of as separate performance entities that could enter into a market-like or contract-like performance agreement on what they would deliver. In New Zealand, each agency had a "purchase agreement" that described what goods and services the government was purchasing from the agency.

Both models assumed that government could be neatly divided into different functions. Either those functions were discrete, or any interdependencies could reasonably be foreseen and planned for. Yet the experience of public servants in solving cross-cutting problems, and that of the public in engaging with public services, was different. Problems that fell to a single agency proved easiest to solve, and performance in these areas tended to improve. Those that fell across multiple agencies were the most difficult to solve and tended to persist. This was at least in part because interdependencies cannot be perfectly foreseen, and these cross-cutting problems tend to have the characteristic that each "solution" reveals more about the problem and changes our understanding of it (so-called wicked problems).

Periodically, governments reorganize their administrative boundaries to place politically salient problems together to make them easier to solve. However, any reorganization merely creates new boundaries elsewhere. Regardless of how and where these administrative boundaries are placed, responsibility for some problems inevitably falls between these boundaries or, more commonly, across multiple agencies. Such problems cannot be managed within traditional hierarchies, nor can they be managed through traditional performance management systems that assume responsibility can be divided and that accountability can always be singular. Many problems that span agency boundaries can only be solved by agencies working together.

Interagency Working

In the field of public administration, "coordination" refers to having the work of the different agencies fit seamlessly together and contribute to a greater whole. "Collaboration," on the other hand, usually refers to different agencies working together to create something new. Or sometimes it refers to different agencies having shared responsibility for an outcome. Sometimes coordination and collaboration are used interchangeably, or collaboration is used to refer to all kinds of interagency working. Sometimes coordination and collaboration are put on a continuum (usually with cooperation as a third category and sometimes with a fourth or fifth category as well). Many authors who write about these topics have strong opinions on which are which, but the respective definitions are far from settled.[3]

Other terms for similar or related practice include "interagency collaboration"[4] and "joined-up government."[5] The more general alternative term "joined-up government" was popularized by the UK's Blair government. It sometimes seems to refer to coordination or collaboration (or that collaboration is the means to achieve a more coordinated service).[6] "Horizontal management" is another term for working across agencies boundaries, described in contrast to "vertical" hierarchical management. But many aspects of interagency working are vertical—for example, an interagency governance group consisting of leaders from different agencies making decisions and then passing them down through their respective hierarchies. Horizontal management is sometimes equated to leading through influence rather than authority, but some of the following solutions New Zealand employs relied on formal governance arrangements and highly specified decisionmaking authority.

In this book, we use the rather bland and inclusive term "interagency working" to describe different approaches and arrangements by which various agencies work together, whether they be cooperating, coordinating, collaborating, joining up, or managing horizontally. We refer specifically to the challenge of addressing cross-cutting problems as "managing horizontally" following the work of B. Guy Peters.[7]

Managing horizontally has challenged public servants and those who study them for at least forty years. In 1978, Kenneth Hanf and Fritz Scharpf noted that getting agencies to develop a shared policy perspective remained an important but elusive goal.[8] By 1984, Jeffrey Pressman and Aaron Wiklawsky claimed that a lack of coordination between agencies was the most frequent complaint made about bureaucracies.[9] By 1994, Edward Jennings and Dale Krane were claiming that solving the coordination problem was "the philosopher's stone"[10] of public administration, whereas Peters described it as the "Holy Grail" of the field.[11]

Since then, many important contributions have been made to the field—studies that claim to tell us how agencies can work more effectively together. In 1998, two decades after Hanf and Scharpf identified horizontal management as one of the most important problems in government, two seminal works appeared, namely, *Getting Agencies to Work Together*, a book by Eugene Bardach, and "Managing Horizontal Government," an article in the journal *Public Administration* by B. Guy Peters.[12] Both described cases wherein coordination had been effective and attempted to distil some general principles about how horizontal management works. Even the leading works over the last ten years continue in this vein, developing generalizable principles for "collaborative governance."[13]

This book makes a claim that is far less grand. We claim instead that the following lessons can be drawn from the New Zealand experience and that these are most applicable for solving particular kinds of problems in a specific context. Simply copying the Results program is unlikely to recreate its success. The following chapters explore the conditions whereby a similar approach is likely to be successful, drawing out the principles that underlie that success. In this way, the text is intended to present generalizable but contingent lessons for using a target approach for horizontal management.

In this way we hope to echo in horizontal management a progression seen in the study of vertical management over the last sixty years. Many readers will be familiar with the ideas of "scientific management" (otherwise known as "Taylorism" after the works of F. W. Taylor).[14] Scientific management proposed that there were a general set of management practices that should be applied across all situations. A series of experiments in the 1950s began to suggest that instead of general practices, it may be that certain practices are more useful in distinct contexts.[15] This was later described as "contingency theory," in that the right solution was contingent on the nature of the problem. William Scott (no relation to the author) put it succinctly: *The best way to organize depends on the nature of the environment to which the organization must relate.*[16]

We see no reason to think that horizontal management is not also contingent.

Why Is Interagency Working So Hard?

To anyone outside of government, it can be frustrating to see government acting as a collection of separate agencies rather than as an integrated and coordinated whole. Yet the persistence of fragmentation, and difficulty in addressing cross-cutting problems, is not because of a lack of effort. Coordination is the Holy Grail and philosophers' stone, not just because it is important, but also because it is so elusive.

Collaboration—the act of working together—has been described as "an unnatural act between non-consenting adults,"[17] but why? At the most basic level, working in a hierarchy is easier to control; a superior can instruct a subordinate in what to do, but two or more parties working side-by-side must negotiate with each other. When there is a single decisionmaker, decisions can be made more quickly, and it is easier to subsequently attribute responsibility for that decision. Working in this way tends to be familiar for public servants, who have been socialized in their roles to expect strong vertical hierarchies for delivering goods and services, as well as vertical accountability mechanisms for properly using public funds and authority. For most public servants, working across agency boundaries is a deviation from hierarchical arrangements in which they are most comfortable.

Furthermore, working across agency boundaries often involves aiming for outcomes that don't neatly align to individual agency responsibility. This is an example of "the problem of many hands," whereby attributing responsibility for achieving the desired outcomes is complicated.[18] Multiple agencies are required to act together to achieve the outcome, so responsibility should be shared, and praise or blame likewise needs to be carefully distributed. This results in high transaction costs—the inefficiencies of coordinating multiple parties[19]—and the diminished would thus feel responsibility of each individual party (as well as their subsequent "goal commitment"[20]). We can think of these respective considerations as the hurdles (transaction costs) that collaborators face and the heights they are willing to jump or scale to succeed (goal commitment).

Horizontal management remains a costly and fraught endeavor, and success is very difficult.[21] Nonetheless, governments persist in attempting to solve

BOX 2-1. Soviet Union Target Regime

Any discussion of targets must address the most notorious examples—output targets used in the USSR from the 1930s until the 1980s. Introduced by Joseph Stalin, production output targets were intended to drive rapid industrialisation and growth of the USSR's economy and went through several iterations with varying degrees of success, distortions, and collateral damage.

Bevan and Hood, prominent scholars in the use of targets as a public management tool, often reference the Soviet Union target regime to illustrate their arguments about targets in the UK. They note that the Soviet targets were associated with substantial improvements to production in the 1930s, followed by recognition of the problems with gaming and cheating from the 1950s onward.[1]

They imply that the consequences for managerial failure to meet the Soviet output targets were loss of "life or liberty"[2] and "gulags and death squads."[3] At other points, they acknowledge that any such terror was at its worst under Stalin and that "state-owned enterprise managers seemed to become relatively secure in their jobs" after his death.[4]

Indeed, following Stalin's death, it appears that distribution of bonuses for achieving output targets was the "principal managerial incentive in Soviet industry."[5] Across multiple industries, there were "large premiums (bonuses)

---

1. Bevan, G. and Hood, C. (2006). "Have Targets Improved Performance in the English NHS?" *The BMJ*, 332: 419–422.

2. Ibid.

3. Hood, C. (2006). "Gaming in Targetworld: The Targets Approach to Managing British Public Services." *Public Administration Review*, 66(4), 515–521.

4. Ibid.

5. Richman, B. M. and Farmer, R. N. (1963). "The Red Profit Motive: Soviet Industry in Transition." *Business Horizons*, 6(2), 21–28.

for fulfilling and overfulfilling quarterly aggregate output, cost of production (that is, cost performance below plan), and labour productivity targets."[6]

Unsurprisingly, these strong incentives (first negative and then positive) were associated with the prevalence of gaming and cheating practices under the Soviet system.[7] Braguinsky and Yavlinsky note "unsuccessful Soviet attempts to prevent ratchet effects in the target system during the 1970s and 1980s."[8] Likewise, the oft-cited Nove (1986) points out that "a large book can easily be filled with quotations from the works of Soviet economists which show how hard it is to devise efficiency criteria and how the plan targets give rise to undesired and frequently perverse results."[9] While gaming and cheating must be managed in any target regime, the Soviet regime provided a perfect storm of incentives and rampant corruption.

The Soviet regime provides an interesting historical record, frequently referred to and yet with some aspects shrouded in secrecy. By most accounts, there were real performance improvements, gaming and cheating, corruption, and (in the Stalin years) terrible reprisals. The Soviet experience is frequently invoked in the case against using performance targets, to claim that all target regimes are inevitably undone by distortionary effects. We note the Soviet example because it is impossible to ignore it in a book on targets but caution that there are limits to the analogy and that New Zealand is not the USSR.

---

6. Ibid.

7. Hood, C. (2006). "Gaming in Targetworld: The Targets Approach to Managing British Public Services." *Public Administration Review*, 66(4), 515–521.

8. Braguinsky, S. V., and G. Yavlinsky. (2000). *Incentives and Institutions: The Transition to a Market Economy in Russia*. Princeton University Press.

9. Nove, A. (1986). *Socialism, Economics and Development*. Allen & Unwin

boundary-spanning problems, as they must. As simple problems are improved, many of the remaining persistent social harms are the kinds that span multiple agencies. Hence interagency working must become the "new normal" for public servants—a reality they must learn to navigate, even as reports of failure are far more readily available than reports of success.[22]

Challenges with Targets

The Results program constituted an unlikely marriage between two fraught practices. Although it's interagency working that causes the most significant barriers in public administration, there are also cautions to be given about the use of target regimes. Governments have historically been reluctant to publicly commit to specific, measurable priorities with deadlines, preferring instead to keep their goals vague and undefined. Bob Behn recounts one U.S. governor instructing his staff to "Never put a number and a date in the same sentence."[23]

This is with good reason. Christopher Hood and Ruth Dixon studied the effects of performance targets in the United Kingdom and found no direct electoral benefit to setting and achieving targets.[24] Other studies have shown negative consequences from setting targets and then failing to achieve them.[25] Governments may be better off politically by keeping their options open. After all, given the myriad ways to measure success, a government can be confident that at least one such measure will improve over any given period—much better, then, to "paint bull's-eyes around bullet holes" and claim that the achieved state was the desired one.[26]

Conversely, a target regime specifies the measures on which the government wants to be judged and what levels constitute success. The most effective targets for improving performance are set at a level that carries the risk of failure. Those in New Zealand were selected to be "at the edge of possible."[27] In an interview for this book, one U.S. public servant (who has used targets at federal and local levels) suggested targets should be set using a rule-of-thumb of 70 to 80 percent chance of being successfully achieved. Any greater, and the targets didn't create as much urgency and focus as they could have. Any less, and the targets were seen as impossible, leading to incredulity, apathy, and despair. To use targets effectively, a government has to be willing to publicly declare what it intends to achieve, with the knowledge that it will fail some of the time.

This would be a compelling argument against targets if all a government cares about is taking credit for successes (and avoiding blame for failures). But Hood and Dixon identified direct electoral benefits as only the first of three political considerations in setting targets. The second consideration is symbolic—setting targets can contribute to a narrative that the government is rational, scientific, and business-like. Certain constituencies react favorably to rhetoric about "cracking the whip"[28] and driving complacent or lazy bureaucrats to work harder. These benefits are realized "up front" at the time the target regime is implemented—the punishment for failing to achieve them is not felt until much later.

The third consideration is more practical. *Targets work.* That is, when used appropriately, they improve the performance of the item in question. They reduce long-term unemployment. They increase rates of infant immunization. They reduce the crime rate. And for some governments, that is important, even if achieving these things doesn't directly translate into votes.

But even as targets work to improve performance, they come with significant downsides. Targets can encourage gaming and cheating, create perverse incentives (often discouraging collaboration), and tend to be unpopular and unsustainable. At their worst, they introduce such distortions that they undermine the integrity of public institutions and decrease overall performance (see box 2-1).

3

Something New Does Work

The New Zealand government isn't alone in having concluded that targets were a useful way to improve performance and one worth the political risk of failure. Similarly, other jurisdictions experimented with various prioritization schemes. As part of its work in preparing recommendations for the government, the Better Public Services Advisory Group studied these jurisdictions around the world that had claimed success in improving the performance of public services. This was despite the sentiment Tony Bovaird best captured: *Nothing new works, and if it works somewhere else, it must be because they're weird.*[1]

Bovaird is referring to the tendency in public administration to view all situations as unique and the corresponding assumption that the context faced by any jurisdiction is so heavily influenced by local factors as to make the transfer of lessons meaningless. This view purports that any variation in performance—like a jurisdiction experiencing programmatic success—can be discounted due to extrinsic factors.

However, the advisory group was influenced by several programs from other jurisdictions, which are explored further in the paragraphs that follow:

- "-Stat" data-enabled leadership strategies (NYPD, the City of Baltimore, the State of Washington, and many others);[2]

- prioritization as implemented in various jurisdictions using names like "Performs" (both the Commonwealth of Virginia and the nation of Scotland following devolution from the UK civil service), "Thrives" (the State of Oregon), or "Growing Victoria Together" (the State of Victoria, Australia); and

- the UK prime minister's Delivery Unit and its "deliverology" approach to performance targets.

In this text, we repeatedly return to these two of the highest profile performance management systems in the English-speaking world in recent years: the UK Delivery Unit and the various -Stat performance management systems in the United States. In 2017, we were fortunate to receive an author stipend from the IBM Business of Government series to write a short report on the Results program. We put this stipend to use in exploring practices in the United Kingdom and the United States through observations, interviews, and debate in 2017 and 2018, with the intention of testing our own findings from the Results program against other cases that had used similar methodologies.

NYPD CompStat

NYPD Police Commissioner William Bratton committed to reducing the city's crime rate by 10 percent in the first year, 25 percent over two years, and 40 percent over three years. To achieve this, in 1994, he employed a leadership strategy developed with his deputy, Jack Maple, which became known as "CompStat."[3] CompStat was based on four principles:

1. Accurate and timely intelligence;

2. Rapid deployment;

3. Effective tactics;

4. Relentless follow-up and assessment.

In formal structured meetings, the police commissioner (or deputy commissioner) would question precinct commanders about crime statistics in their precincts and what tactics they were employing to improve performance.

Baltimore CitiStat

NYPD's great success in reducing crime in the 1990s attracted significant attention. Police departments around the world implemented systems based on Maple's four principles. Eventually, police departments weren't the only agencies to implement CompStat, and it was used by a range of social, economic, and municipal services agencies. In 1999, Martin O'Malley asked NYPD Deputy Commissioner Jack Maple to help him create a CitiStat for Baltimore. As mayor of Baltimore, and later as governor of Maryland, O'Malley demonstrated that the principles of CompStat could be applied across an entire jurisdiction.

In his definitive book on the subject, Robert Behn describes -Stat systems (like CompStat and CitiStat):

> In an effort to achieve specific **public purposes**, its leadership team **persists** in holding an ongoing system of **regular, frequent, integrated meetings** during which the chief executive and/or principal members of the chief executive's leadership team plus the director (and the top managers) of different subunits use **current data** to **analyse** specific, previously defined aspects of each unit's recent **performance**; to provide **feedback** on recent progress compared with **targets**; to **follow up** on previous decisions and commitments to produce **results**; to examine and **learn** from each unit's efforts to improve **performance**; to identify and solve **performance-deficit** problems; and to set and achieve the next **performance targets**.[4] [bold in original]

New Zealand drew inspiration from several of the -Stat systems, particularly the focus on leadership, persistence, and regular social processes for discussing performance data.

Growing Victoria Together

One of the pioneers of whole-of-government priorities was the State of Victoria in Australia.[5] In 2000, following a change of government, Steve Bracks was sworn in as the new premier of the state. Shortly after being sworn in, Premier Bracks organized a gathering of 100 senior public servants to identify the chief priorities for Victoria for the following ten years. The resulting framework, "Growing Victoria Together," was published in 2001, containing five areas and ten goals (shown in table 3-1).[6]

The Growing Victoria Together framework was refreshed in 2005 and survived until the 2010 election. One senior official described the framework as the start of a "shift from thinking about outputs of government agencies, to thinking about the outcomes that government is seeking to achieve."[7] The framework was an organizing principle for the budget process and reporting to Parliament.[8]

Growing Victoria Together involved thirty-six measures but no targets. Victorian agencies were required to "explain how their work fits in with the Growing Victoria Objectives,"[9] but not to take responsibility for achieving them. Nonetheless, the government saw the Victorian model as a success, and it was continued for nine years, long enough for it to serve as the inspiration for other jurisdictions. The lesson that New Zealand took from the Victorian

TABLE 3-1. Growing Victoria Together (2001)

AREA	GOAL
Thriving economy	1. More quality jobs and thriving, innovative industries across Victoria
	2. Growing and linking all over Victoria
Quality health and education	3. High-quality, accessible health and community services
	4. High-quality education and training for lifelong learning
Healthy environment	5. Protecting the environment for future generations
	6. Efficient use of natural resources
Caring communities	7. Building friendly, confident, and safe communities
	8. A fairer society that reduces disadvantage and respects diversity
Vibrant democracy	9. Greater public participation and more accountable government
	10. Sound financial management

Source: This framework is available at: www.parliament.vic.gov.au/archive/council/SCFPA/Pt Phillip/Submissions/SCFPA_PtP_Sub_34_Part_A.pdf.

experience was that the act of describing a small number of priorities (specifically the selection of ten cross-cutting goals arranged into areas), and talking about the outcomes that government is seeking to achieve, can change the way public servants go about their work.

Virginia Performs

New Zealand and Australia both operate under a system of "responsible government," in which the executive branch of government consists of ministers who are also part of the legislative branch (Parliament). This makes it possible for a government to both set and achieve priorities. In contrast, the US model separates executive and legislative branches more clearly.

In 2004, the Commonwealth of Virginia implemented a program like Growing Victoria Together, involving the setting of long-term goals.[10] To overcome the separation of legislative and executive branches, the process to select these goals was handed to the Council on Virginia's Future. The Council on Virginia's Future included the executive and legislators from both houses along with community and business leaders.

The Council on Virginia's Future set seven long-term goals (see table 3-2) and forty-six indicators. Virginia reported on performance against these indicators with a simple "Virginia Performs Scorecard" that indicated (with an arrow) whether performance was improving, staying the same, or getting worse.

TABLE 3-2. Virginia Performs

LONG-TERM GOALS

1. Be a national leader in the preservation and enhancement of our economy.
2. Elevate the levels of educational preparedness and attainment of our citizens.
3. Inspire and support Virginians toward healthy lives and strong and resilient families.
4. Protect, conserve, and wisely develop our natural, cultural, and historic resources.
5. Protect the people's safety and security, ensure a fair and effective system of justice, and provide a prepared response to emergencies and disasters of all kinds.
6. Ensure Virginia has a transportation system that is safe, allows the easy movement of people and goods, enhances the economy, and improves our quality of life.
7. Be recognized as the best-managed state in the nation.

Like Victoria, Virginia reported that having long-term goals changed the dialogue from "being about inputs to being about outcomes."

Source: Jane Kusiak, executive director of the Council on Virginia's Future, as cited in Kohli, J. (2010). "Golden Goals for Government Performance: Five Case Studies on How to Establish Goals to Achieve Results." Center for American Progress, 13.

Scotland Performs

While Virginia's experience seemed to draw some inspiration from Victoria, the lineage of Scotland Performs was more explicit.[11] In 2007, the Scottish National Party campaigned on the promise of adopting Virginia's approach to prioritization. Scotland chose one overall purpose and then five strategic objectives (see table 3-3) and forty-five indicators.

Scotland Performs added one crucial innovation that distinguished it from Virginia Performs: making officials responsible. Senior public servants were each assigned responsibility for achieving one of the five strategic objectives.

In an illustration of how ideas are cross-fertilized internationally, an official in the Scottish government who had worked on the Scotland Performs program joined the Better Public Services team in New Zealand for several months and contributed to the design of the BPS Results program.

GMAP Washington

In 2002, Governor Gary Locke launched "Priorities of Government" for the State of Washington, with similarities to Growing Victoria Together, Virginia Performs, and Scotland Performs. As in Victoria, the budget process was used to align agency activities around achieving a small number of goals (see table 3-4).

TABLE 3-3. Scotland Performs

OVERALL PURPOSE

To focus the government and public services on creating a more successful country, with opportunities for all of Scotland to flourish, through increasing sustainable economic growth.

STRATEGIC OBJECTIVES

1. *Wealthier and fairer:* Enable businesses and people to increase their wealth and more people to share fairly in that wealth.
2. *Smarter:* Expand opportunities for Scots to succeed from birth through to lifelong learning, ensuring higher and more widely shared achievements.
3. *Healthier:* Help people sustain and improve their health, especially in disadvantaged communities, ensuring better local and faster access to healthcare.
4. *Safer and stronger:* Help local communities flourish, becoming stronger, safer places to live and offering improved opportunities and a better quality of life.
5. *Greener:* Improve Scotland's natural and built environment and the sustainable use and enjoyment of it.

Source: Scottish Government consolidated accounts 2016 to 2017 (2017). Government of Scotland. www.gov.scot/publications/scottish-government-consolidated-accounts-year-ended-31-march-2017/.

TABLE 3-4. Washington Priorities of Government (2002)

HIGH-LEVEL OUTCOMES

1. Improve student achievement in elementary, middle, and high schools
2. Improve the value of post-secondary learning
3. Improve the health of Washingtonians
4. Improve the security of Washington's vulnerable children and adults
5. Improve the economic vitality of business and individuals
6. Improve statewide mobility of people, goods, and services
7. Improve the safety of people and property
8. Improve the quality of Washington's natural resources
9. Strengthen government's ability to achieve results efficiently and effectively

In 2005, Governor Locke was replaced by Governor Christine Gregoire. Governor Gregoire saw that it was not enough to set priorities; it was also necessary to put in place the social processes to drive performance improvement aligned with those priorities. In one of her first executive orders, Governor

Gregoire created a new program called "Government Management Account-ability and Performance" (or GMAP) that changed reporting requirements for agencies.[12]

But GMAP was more than a reporting requirement—it was also a lead-ership strategy through which Governor Gregoire could use public meetings to hold agency leaders responsible for achieving results. GMAP was explic-itly modeled on CompStat and CitiStat,[13] and agency leaders were required to demonstrate how they were making decisions based on accurate, up-to-date information, correcting course where necessary, and taking responsibility for improvement. By 2008, *Governing* magazine reported, "No state in the nation is better at developing and sharing information than Washington."[14]

The Prime Minister's Delivery Unit (England)

Victoria, Virginia, Scotland, and Washington were each setting and reporting on a smaller number of priorities through specific results, targets, and mea-sures. They all reported improvements from lifting the focus of public servants from inputs and outputs onto the outcomes they were achieving. In contrast, the UK government was trying something very different.

Tony Blair's Labour party swept into power in the 1997 UK general elec-tion and discovered public services they perceived to be in a sorry state. Blair's solution was to replace a blind trust in agencies doing their best with a system of measurable targets and accountability for performance. In 1998, the gov-ernment set 350 targets to be achieved over a three-year time frame, and these were periodically updated until 2007. These targets were considered successful in improving public services from "awful to adequate."[15] (It should be noted here that the target regime primarily applied to public services in England. In 1998, the British Parliament passed the Scotland Act and the Government of Wales Act, which devolved considerable powers to the Scottish Parliament and National Assembly for Wales, respectively. Many public services that had previously been delivered in accordance with London-based policies were now designed locally in Scotland and Wales.)

Blair created a "Prime Minister's Delivery Unit" to manage the target regime. The unit's practices have been described elsewhere as consisting of two tactics: "targets and terror" and "naming and shaming." Targets and terror de-scribed the practice of holding leaders personally accountable for achieving tar-gets. Beyond earning the ire of the prime minister, the worst performers were fired. This was an effective way of eliminating leaders who would not or could not achieve even a basic level of performance. What remained was a cadre of basically competent managers, who Blair believed needed to be pushed (or "flogged") to approach improvement with more urgency.[16] The Delivery Unit began to publish tables illustrating relative performance at (for example) different schools and different hospitals. It found that the shame of being at the bottom of the table was enough to motivate those organizations to improve. However, shaming was ineffective at motivating performance above average.[17]

Furthermore, while some targets were focused at an outcome level, such as reducing certain types of crime, others focused on activities or outputs, such as reducing ambulance waiting times. These output measures risked misplaced effort at best, and gaming and cheating at worst, as discussed later in this book. The first set of targets were described by their author, Sir Suma Chakrabarti, as "a little rough and ready,"[18] and over time, outcome targets became preferable.[19]

What New Zealand Took from the Experience of Other Jurisdictions

The attraction of these experiments for the team working on the Better Public Services reform was not the use of targets per se but rather the use of data to drive action. Data could show the extent of the problem, demonstrate the progress being made, and stimulate conversations about action required (similar to CitiStat). Publishing priority outcomes on one page was also attractive, particularly when combined with graphs and rating scales showing the extent of the problem and progress made over time (as in Virginia Performs).

These ideas were combined to provide the basis for the Results program—a few Results that were important for New Zealanders, expressed in a compelling way, with the nature of the problem illustrated by what some started to call "killer facts" and progress reported in a way that would capture the interest of the public as well as ministers.[20] Targets were added in the late stages of the program design as ministers decided that they wanted to express the level of the government's ambition and to generate urgent action by public servants. The following sections reveal more of the detailed aspects of the Results program that drew on the experiences of these other jurisdictions.

PART II

DELIVERING RESULTS

In this part, we outline the program the New Zealand government developed to overcome the difficulties of interagency working and to therefore improve outcomes for New Zealanders in specific cross-cutting social problems. Throughout the chapter on development (chapter 4), we discuss some of the considerations of goal setting, including prioritization (selecting problems to improve) and targets (defining the level of improvement required). Chapter 5 outlines the program itself, specifying each of the target measures, and describing some of the features and events of each Result, including the agencies that were required to work together to address each of them. This chapter is intended to provide context for the analysis and discussions later in the book. The implementation chapter (chapter 6) gives more detail about how the program operated in practice, discussing governance and reporting in particular. This part of the book concludes with the refresh and renewal of the Results program looking forward another five years, before a new government elect discontinued the program at the start of 2018 (chapter 7).

4

Development

In response to the Better Public Services Advisory Group report, the New Zealand government created a new program in which groups of agencies would be held collectively responsible for achieving Results. Ministers, supported by the Department of the Prime Minister and Cabinet, selected ten problems that were important both to the public and to public servants (listed in table 5 in chapter 4). Each problem spanned the responsibility of several agencies and thus required those agencies to work together if their efforts were to be successful. Work to address these ten problems became collectively known as the Better Public Services Results program (sometimes shortened to the "Results program").

Grouping and Selecting

Governments have countless problems to solve. From the very small, such as individual potholes in a country lane, to very large, like climate change. Governments try various methods for organizing how they aim their efforts. These can generally be described as "grouping" or "selecting" (see figure 4-1). Grouping involves organizing all the similar problems into categories. Selecting involves picking a few problems out of many. Both solve the problem that it is impossible to focus on many things at once—governments must reduce the number of problems they are working on to something more manageable.

Before the Results program, New Zealand used a "grouping approach." For example, the Labour-led government in 2006 grouped all the government's activities together into three broad goals: "economic development," "families young and old," and "national identity." Broad inclusive groups make it easier

FIGURE 4-1. Grouping versus Selecting

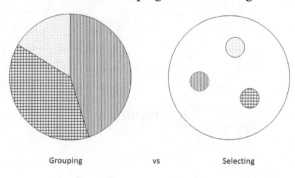

Grouping   vs   Selecting

Source: Authors' rendering.

to make sense of the breadth of what government does, but they don't provide a sense of what is important or where to start. That is not to say that broad grouping doesn't have its place. As noted later in this book, Australia's Social Inclusion Agenda provided a broad orientation for public servants to align their activities with. And the United Nation's Millennium Development Goals have helped different nations coordinate their foreign aid efforts.

A more selective approach is to pick a few narrower problems and accept that this means not selecting other equally important problems. For example, the Results program selected rheumatic fever as a health problem and did not choose obesity, asthma, cancer, or any of the other important health problems New Zealanders face. One way to rationalize selecting some problems over others is sequencing, which argues that it is better to fix one problem first and then move on to another than it is to distribute effort more evenly across many problems and never solve any of them. This was a valid approach used as part of the Results program, whereby some problems were solved to the point that they were no longer high priorities, and effort could be moved to the new priority. For example, enrollment rates in early childhood education rose so high that effort could be shifted to bolster the quality of the education received.

The problems ultimately selected for the program were from different policy areas but had several features in common. First, they were all priorities for the government of the day and had been for many years due to the inadequacy of previous attempts at solving them. The solutions were unknown, and all the previous policy interventions of even the cleverest public servants had been unsuccessful. If the problems could have been solved by analysis and planning, they would no longer have been government priorities.

Second, the problems all involved the intersection of multiple domains. (For example, the crime rate is influenced by conditions as diverse as economic opportunity, education, family unity, social identity, inequality, mental health, and addiction.) This meant that multiple actors from across several agencies would need to be involved to solve the problems. In the absence of a single hierarchical leader, and without known solutions, those agencies would be required to work together (often in ways that could not be fully anticipated at the time) if their efforts were to be successful.

These features indicate that the problems selected for the Better Public Services Results program were each what Cynthia Kurtz and Dave Snowden would describe as "complex."[1] In complex problems, cause and effect can only be deduced in retrospect. They tend to be resistant to deliberate planning. Leaders must conduct experiments that are safe to fail and learn from the results in an approach Kurtz and Snowden call "probe-sense-respond."[2]

Wording the Targets

New Zealand distinguishes between a "result" (the intended change), a "target" (the level of aspiration or challenge) and a "measure" (how progress toward that change will be assessed). In other target or priority regimes, these may be conflated, but New Zealand found benefit in keeping them separate because each one accomplishes something different. As discussed further below, a result should be simple and emotive, a target should create both urgency and hope, and a measure should clarify the detail.

To provide the greatest motivation for public servants and be the most meaningful for the public, the Results needed to be simple, easily understood, and remembered. For example, "Reduce the crime rate" does not provide any technical detail about how the crime rate is measured. In some cases, this might be considered a negative feature, restricting the usefulness of the Result to the experts involved in achieving it. However, in the case of the Results program, it was more important that the Result was directly related to improving the lives of New Zealanders. The emotive power behind such simple Results meant that the public cared about them. Every six months, when progress was reported, all the major media outlets discussed it. This attention provided a motivational boost that may have been more valuable than any specificity that could have been gained by a lengthier jargon-filled goal.

The public is a core source of felt accountability for public servants and politicians, so Results that mattered to the public would also tap into the intrinsic motivation of public servants to do things that helped their community. This would also mean framing Results to be consistent with the professional values of the public servants delivering them.

Result 1 was originally framed as "reducing long-term welfare dependency." Public servants working with unemployed people typically do not see their job as getting people off welfare. Instead, they see their job as getting people back on their feet, or back into employment. This Result might have been more motivational had it been framed in these terms. By contrast, other Results spoke directly to the professional values of those working on them. Results like "reducing incidence of rheumatic fever" or "reducing assaults on children" were simple, emotive goals that connected public servants to some of the reasons they joined the public service in the first place.

The targets simply added a number and a date to the Result, for example: "Reduce the incidence of rheumatic fever by two-thirds by 2017." These were usually very simple as well (a few exceptions are discussed in chapters 5 and 7). They described how much things were going to get better. They needed to be set at a level that created a sense of urgency and bias for action. The importance of "laying the challenge" is described in a section below.

Unlike the Results and targets, the measures were often quite technical, for example, a seasonally adjusted rate for first-time hospital admissions for rheumatic fever per a 100,000-person population. The seasonal adjustment allowed for better month-to-month comparisons, given that rheumatic fever is more common in winter. The focus on first-time hospital admissions excluded repeat bouts, which would otherwise focus effort more on treatment than on prevention. Setting the rate relative to population size excluded any effects from migration or population growth. These are the kind of detailed considerations that make measurement precise, meaningful, transparent, and comparable. Separating clear and emotive Results from ambitious targets and detailed, technical measures allowed the Results program to communicate different information to different audiences.

Managing Performance

The original program to put in place a set of ten BPS Results was agreed by the Cabinet with no hint of introducing a target regime. Initially, the plan was to implement something like Virginia Performs: a few clear priorities, with clear measures, around which groups of agencies would organize. As work got under way, the group of ministers leading the reform decided to up the ante by adding a target based on the lead indicator for each Result—the degree of change to be achieved over five years, from 2012 to 2017. The rule of thumb was one target for each Result, but more than one target was set when it made sense to do so (for example, infant immunization and rheumatic fever were discrete components of a single Result, and a target was set for each).

Anyone working with targets can find it tempting to start with measurement—what are the problem areas for which data are available? New Zealand decided on the Results first. Its assumption was that it was more important to pick the right problems to work on, and then to find the data to understand them, rather than the reverse. But having selected the problems to be solved (priorities), the government needed to determine how to manage performance against those problems.

Governments have few choices for managing the performance of their various administrative units. Perhaps the most common is some variant of moral suasion and hope, wherein governments don't specify how performance will be measured and then hope that public servants do their best. Sir Julian LeGrand and others have described this method as "trust and altruism."[3] The second option is to introduce some sort of quasi-market mechanisms (otherwise known as "choice and competition") to encourage the flow of resources toward the most successful organizations.[4] Despite their theoretical appeal, quasi-market mechanisms have repeatedly failed to deliver the promised benefits in the social sector due to problems of both supply and demand.[5] New Zealand has traditionally been an advocate of market-based reforms, but even in New Zealand, the experience of applying quasi-markets to education and health services (in particular) is described as a "cautionary tale."[6]

In education, quasi-markets tend to be regressive, with better services going to children of wealthier and better educated families. The theory of quasi-markets in education is that "successful" schools will grow and that "unsuccessful" schools will close, meaning that over time, more students receive high-quality education at successful schools. In practice, schools become more popular by declaring themselves "full."[7] This means that successful schools don't grow; rather, they are able to be more selective about the students (and parents) they pick. Those students/parents not picked by the school must still go somewhere, so the unsuccessful schools retain student numbers and do not close. Choice and competition in school systems tends to result in schools picking students/parents rather than in the intended outcome of students/parents picking schools.[8]

Furthermore, middle-class families tend to be more able to arrange transport to distant schools and are more likely to act on performance information than are working-class or poor families. This means that over time, the rich get better quality education, even in a publicly funded school system. In numerous studies, school choice has been shown to increase socioeconomic segregation without improvements in performance.[9]

Quasi-markets have not fared much better in health care. Across multiple countries, effective markets have failed to develop[10] because most patients do not make decisions on which hospital to visit on the basis of hospital performance data.[11] Instead, patients go either to the closest facility or the one that they have been referred to by another health professional (for example, a referral from a family doctor to a specialist).[12]

For many of the problems discussed in this book, the challenge has been in reaching those New Zealand individuals and families who are hardest to reach rather than providing more choice for those actively seeking services.

Difficulty in reaching citizens can be due to a lack of knowledge, trust, or willingness to engage. But in a sparsely populated country like New Zealand, "hardest-to-reach" can have a literal and geographic component as well. It's often not practical to provide choice between services in rural and small-town New Zealand. Patients find little value in knowing that the local hospital is poorly rated when the nearest alternative is several hours away.

The third option for managing performance is to describe how performance will be measured (quantitatively) and to apportion rewards and sanctions based on the achievement of targets. The challenges of targets are many. Targets assume that it is possible to specify in advance what "good" performance looks like and ignore the many extrinsic and unanticipated factors that will make performance easier and harder. They introduce distortionary effects—through things like effort substitution, wherein only "what is measured gets managed,"[13] and gaming, wherein agencies "hit the target but miss the point."[14]

Targets tend to experience cyclical periods of popularity in government jurisdictions around the world. Their ongoing popularity is because they work—they tend to be associated with performance improvement in the things measured. Their short lifespan can be explained by their side effects—they survive until these unintended consequences become untenable. Targets are effective when they spark increased effort due to fear of punishment, but such fears tend to decrease public servant morale over time. They are also effective because they focus public servants on the task at hand, but this can be at the expense of other valuable activities and can discourage working cooperatively to help other public servants be more effective. Despite these challenges, performance targets remain in use because of the lack of viable alternatives; they are frequently the "least worst" system of governance available.[15]

Ministers must have been aware of the downside of using targets—they can be gamed, and they can be used by the opposition as weapons, particularly if not achieved. Targets were introduced to drive the public service to do better for New Zealanders. When this is the intent, the targets need to stretch the public service and incentivize it to try different things. If management of political risk becomes the dominant motivation, the government will tend to set targets that are easily met. The degree of risk appetite varies among ministers, and senior ministers often set the tone.

Targets are political tools, conveying to the public service and the public generally the level of government's ambition. Targets had been used by New Zealand governments in the past, with mixed effect. An early attempt to set targets in tertiary education failed because there were too many targets and they were so unrealistic that they quickly became irrelevant. More recently, health sector targets were set and publicly reported against. These were much more realistic and successful in driving action, although mostly in more measurable, transactional areas (in tertiary health rather than public health) and arguably not driving the most critical health outcomes.

Laying the Challenge

The targets for the Results program were set in discussion between officials, who knew the data well, and ministers, who knew the level of the government's ambition. The following story began to circulate around the education sector about one of these target-setting discussions with a minister. Officials appraised the minister of the risk of setting a target that was too difficult, but he was more concerned with driving change than with managing political risk:

> *Officials:* We recommend setting the target in the range of 50 to 53 percent.
> *Minister:* I want a target of 55 percent.
> *Officials:* But Minister, all our data tells us that on current trends, with the programs we have in place, we won't achieve that target.
> *Minister:* My point exactly. You will have to do something different. We need to do better for New Zealanders.[16]

In the end, Cabinet agreed on a Result (the desired outcome) and a target (how that change would be measured) for each problem. The full list of Results and targets is set out in table 4-1.

The required timeliness of measures varies across different programs based on their complexity and overall duration. The need for rapid feedback, the "sense" in Kurtz and Snowden's "probe-sense-respond," drove the selection of measures for the Results program that was closer to outputs than to outcomes. The Results program was set to last five years, and performance information would be needed much more frequently than that to learn from what was working and to adapt if needed. The Results used a limit of six months as a rough guide—the measures needed to provide feedback on whether interventions were working within six months of when those interventions took place. Progress on each of these measures would be reported to Cabinet and released to the public every six months. Statistics New Zealand, the government's official statistician, provided advice on the measures for assessing progress, many of which were "Tier 1" official statistics (New Zealand's highest level of statistical integrity).

The Cabinet paper that set out the targets had this to say about them:

> The targets proposed in this paper are not easy. They will be difficult to achieve in full, which is consistent with our high expectations and desire to lift public service performance. Both individually and collectively, the

TABLE 4-1. Better Public Services Result Areas, Results, and Targets

RESULT AREA/ PRIORITY	RESULT		TARGET
Reducing welfare dependence	1	Reduce long-term welfare dependence	Reduce the number of people continuously receiving Jobseeker Support benefits for more than 12 months by 30 percent, from 78,000 to 55,000 by 2017.
	2	Increase participation in early childhood education	By 2017, 98 percent of children starting school will have participated in quality early childhood education (up from 94.7 percent in 2012).
Vulnerable children	3	Increase infant immunization and reduce rheumatic fever	Increase infant immunization rates to achieve and maintain 95 percent coverage of eight-month-olds fully immunized with the scheduled vaccinations by 2017, up from 83 percent in 2012. Reduce the incidence of rheumatic fever by two-thirds to 1.4 cases per 100,000 people by June 2017, down from 4.3 cases per 100,000 people in 2012.
	4	Reduce assaults on children	By 2017, 85 percent of 18-year-olds will have achieved the National Certificate of Educational Achievement (NCEA) Level 2 or an equivalent qualification, up from 74 percent in 2011.

RESULT AREA/ PRIORITY	RESULT		TARGET
Boosting skills & employment	5	Increase proportion of 18-year-olds with NCEA L2	85 percent of 18-year-olds will have achieved NCEA level 2 or an equivalent qualification in 2017.
	6	Increase proportion of 25- to 34-year-olds with NZQF L4 or above	By 2017, 55 percent of 25- to 34-year-olds will have a qualification at level 4 or above, up from 52 percent in 2011.
Reducing crime	7	Reduce the rates of total crime, violent crime and youth crime	Reduce the crime rate by 15 percent (and the violent crime rate by 20 percent and the youth crime rate by 5 percent) by 2017.
	8	Reduce reoffending	Reduce the criminal reoffending rate by 25 percent by 2017.
Improving interaction with government	9	NZ businesses have a one-stop online shop for all government advice & support	Businesses' costs of dealing with the government will decrease by 25 percent by 2017, through a year-on-year reduction in effort required to work with agencies.
	10	New Zealanders can complete their transactions with government easily in a digital environment	By 2017, an average of 70 percent of New Zealanders' most common transactions with government will be completed in a digital environment, up from 24 percent in 2011.

Source: Cabinet paper: "Better Public Services Results: Targets and Public Communication," June 25, 2012.

BPS targets challenge Departments and contributing agencies to deliver substantial progress by refocusing and reshaping public services.

In addition, we want to establish the BPS results high in the public consciousness so that New Zealanders can grasp our ambitious vision for better public services and hold us to account for performance achieved.[17]

The Better Public Services Advisory Group described the targets as bringing about change and spreading innovation across government:

The stretch targets are about more than numbers; [they are] about change. People can achieve great things within a set target and a challenge is leveraging off successes across the system.[18]

In announcing the targets in June 2012, Prime Minister Sir John Key challenged the public service to take action on difficult problems. He said, "These targets are not a wish-list—they are a to-do list." The prime minister went on to set out the level of the challenge:

Some of these targets are very aspirational—in fact, some of them will be extremely difficult to achieve. But I make absolutely no apology for having high expectations and wanting New Zealanders to get the most out of their public services.[19]

From these statements, it is clear there were two drivers for the BPS Results program: it was established to improve outcomes for New Zealanders in key problem areas that had proven resistant to interventions in the past, but equally, it was part of a state sector reform movement that set out to address some long-standing issues in New Zealand's public management system. In particular, service delivery was fragmented because the strongest incentives were for agencies to deliver the outputs they were funded to deliver, rather than to manage horizontally to achieve cross-cutting outcomes. As Hon. Bill English, deputy prime minister explained when announcing the targets in June 2012:

We want to change the way the public sector works so it is more focused and organised around delivering results, rather than just outputs. We're making public sector leaders accountable for achieving things that make a real difference to the lives of New Zealanders, not just managing a department or agency.

5

The Results Program

This chapter outlines each of the Results and discusses some of their more notable features.

Result 1: Reduce Long-Term Welfare Dependence

ORIGINAL TARGET: Reduce the number of people continuously receiving working-age jobseeker support benefits for more than 12 months, by 30 percent, from 78,000 in April 2012 to 55,000 by 2017.

UPDATED TARGET: By June 2018, reduce the number of people receiving main benefits by 25 percent and reduce the long-term cost of benefit dependence (as measured by an estimated accumulated actuarial release) by $13 billion.

The New Zealand government provides an extensive social safety net of financial support for those in need, intended to catch people who might otherwise become homeless, malnourished, or ill. But to have people dependent on benefit payments is not a good outcome, for those people or for the country. Benefit dependence increasingly became a problem for New Zealand even beyond the simple fiscal impact of benefit payments. The longer-term costs to the economy in terms of lost productivity were paired with extensive social costs. Benefit dependence can be intergenerational, with benefit receipt spanning generations and affecting whole communities and reentry to the labor market becoming more difficult after longer absences. Being out of paid work increases the risk of poverty, whereas being in paid work has proven positive impacts on health and well-being, both in terms of self-esteem and connection to the community.

In 2011, New Zealand was grappling with the impacts of the global financial crisis. Prudent financial management in preceding years meant that the government had headroom to increase debt, but it needed to constrain expenditure. With 12 percent of New Zealand's working age population on a benefit, the annual cost of working-age benefit payments was more than $8 billion and the lifetime costs much higher. Reducing the number of people who were long-term recipients of job seeker support payments and getting them employed instead was a way to cut government costs.

Reducing welfare dependence ticked several of the boxes to be a candidate for the Better Public Services Results program—it was a priority for the government and important for improving the lives of New Zealanders. But even more significantly, it was a problem that required a different approach, which made it perfect for inclusion in a program that set out to disrupt the status quo and that required the public service to be innovative.

The minister of finance characterized the shift required as being from "servicing misery" to "improving lives." The task for agencies became one of creating pathways into paid employment rather than simply ensuring that those entitled to financial support received it.

As the agency responsible for administering benefit payments, the Ministry of Social Development put in place incentives and support to shift beneficiaries into productive work wherever possible. However, many of long-term benefit recipients faced real barriers to getting back into paid employment, often due to physical or mental health problems or a lack of relevant skills or training. To help these clients, the Ministry of Social Development would need to work with the Ministry of Health (to address health-related barriers to employment) and the Ministry of Education (to address education-related barriers).

The first step to making a reduction in welfare dependence was to recategorize several existing benefit classes into a new benefit class called Jobseeker Support, intended to support individuals in a crisis and get them back into work. The government then set a target to reduce the number of people continuously receiving Jobseeker Support benefits for more than 12 months, targeting those who were increasingly at risk of becoming welfare dependent.

As of April 2012, some 135,416 people were receiving Jobseeker Support benefits. Of this number, 78,074 had been receiving a benefit for more than 12 months. The target was set to reduce this number by 30 percent, from 78,074 down to 55,000, by 2017. This would be a 30 percent reduction over five years. This was considerably beyond forecast reductions of long-term benefit numbers expected to occur from improved economic conditions and current policy settings and was at the top end of what international evidence suggested was possible. Officials considered it to be a real stretch, and this is exactly what ministers wanted.

In addition to being an ambitious target that would force the Ministry of Social Development to develop more effective approaches, the target was effective in several other ways. A reduction in long-term job seekers clearly contributed to a reduction in welfare dependence, providing strong synecdoche; the target would drive specific action; success or failure of that action would be evident within six months (short lag period), allowing for regular publishing of progress; and the target was motivational—public servants could see the returns on their efforts reflected in the data.

Result 2: Increase Participation in Early Childhood Education

ORIGINAL TARGET: In 2016, 98 percent of children starting school will have participated in quality early childhood education.

Participation in high-quality early childhood education is a good predictor of lifetime educational achievement. Despite considerable effort by agencies over decades, many New Zealand children were never enrolled in early childhood education and did not participate. Most of those missing out on early childhood education were children who would benefit the most from early learning. Based on trends between 2000 and 2012, participation was expected to rise from 94.7 percent in 2012 to 95.8 percent by 2017. To achieve the target of 98 percent would require progress three times as rapid as what had been achieved in the previous decade. Progress was expected to be become more difficult as the rate of early childhood education enrollment rose, as those who remained unenrolled would likely represent the most challenging cases.

New Zealand is a multicultural society with significant Māori and Pacific Island (Pasifika) populations. These two ethnic groups were underrepresented in early childhood education. In 2011, 98.2 percent of children of European descent attended an early childhood education service before attending school, compared with 90.0 percent for Māori and 85.9 percent for Pasifika children.[1] This disparity in achievement had long been known. A program was already in place to increase participation in early learning before the introduction of the Results program through which the Ministry of Education contracted existing community groups to find families that were not participating and to encourage them to enroll their children. But the focus on the participation data in a high-profile program such as the BPS Results prompted a complete rethink about the effectiveness of the existing program. It more actively drove discussions about why this situation had developed, and although it was challenging and somewhat uncomfortable for the Ministry of Education at first, it was necessary to spark action and improvement. Reaching these populations would require close relationships and intimate knowledge of cultural differences. Two smaller agencies, Te Puni Kōkiri and the Ministry for Pacific Peoples, were able to help the Ministry of Education connect with these groups.

Despite the inclusion of two other targets for improving education outcomes (at secondary and tertiary levels) in the Results program, the early childhood education target was not grouped with them and was instead included in the Result area for "Vulnerable children." Along with one health and one social development Result, all focused on improving outcomes for young children. This reflected the government's emphasis on improving social outcomes for a cohort of the population rather than economic outcomes across the board (which was the focus of the other two education Results). The State Services Commission's website cited evidence from the OECD PISA 2009 study that showed that at-risk students have less access to early childhood education in almost every country. The effort to increase participation in early childhood education was orientated to particularly at-risk communities:

> Regular participation in high-quality early childhood education (ECE) significantly increases a child's likelihood of future educational success, particularly for children from vulnerable families. Time spent in early childhood education enhances future learning.[2]

Inclusion of the Result in the vulnerable children Result area was intended to enable early learning to contribute to improved social outcomes through better connection to the work of other social policy agencies. This intention was evident in the governance and accountability arrangements: the minister of social development and the chief executive of the Ministry for Social Development were held responsible for achieving the target, and governance was managed through the Social Sector Board. Despite this, the target was operationally considered to be an education target that would require education interventions, and there was little visible impact of cross-cutting work in the first few years of the program. This changed as it became clear that achieving the target would require drawing some especially "hard-to-reach" families into the government's network of services, meeting financial, housing, health, and welfare needs and accessing the benefits of early learning. By the end of the program, multi-agency initiatives were being put in place, with case workers coordinating the response of several agencies.

Result 3: Increase Infant Immunization Rates and Reduce the Incidence of Rheumatic Fever

IMMUNIZATION TARGET: Increase infant immunization rates so that 95 percent of eight-month-olds are fully immunized by December 2014 and maintain this until June 2017.

RHEUMATIC FEVER TARGET: Reduce the incidence of rheumatic fever by two-thirds to 1.4 cases per 100,000 people by 2017.

This was the only Result split into two targets of equal importance, with progress toward the targets assessed separately. Among public servants, there has been some debate about whether it is more appropriate to describe the program as consisting of eleven Results, with "Result 3i" relating to infant immunization and "Result 3r" relating to rheumatic fever. Officials were able to propose several explanations as to why the two targets were packaged as one, but the strongest driver seemed to be that ten was a more appealing overall number of targets for ministers and would therefore "retail" better.

Childhood vaccinations provide important protection against a range of often serious communicable diseases. Immunization was the only BPS Result with an existing target before the program had begun. The existing target applied to two-year-old children, and the immunization rate for that age was sitting at 92 percent when the Better Public Services program began. However, the evidence indicated that children between three and eighteen months are the most vulnerable to infections such as whooping cough. Therefore, the new target for the Results program was set for the younger age group of eight-month-old babies for an immunization rate of 95 percent by December 2014, to be maintained until June 2017. This was difficult because there were no good existing data for the new age group. However, New Zealand's overall immunization rate of 83 percent compared well to most other developed nations, and data were available for six-month-olds indicating an immunization rate of 59 percent.

Conflicting opinions from experienced health professionals were (at one end of the spectrum) that the 95 percent target was unrealistic, especially given the fact that immunization rates had not changed significantly from 2005 to 2012 despite substantial effort and (at the other end) that similar gains to the 92 percent immunization rate of two-year-olds could be made to meet the target within the first three years. Officials and the minister believed that the five-year target would be achieved halfway through the period; the ongoing challenge would be to maintain it for successive cohorts. Using the rate of immunization within a population cohort as a measure made it necessary for this to be the only BPS Result with an interim target.

Rheumatic fever is an acute respiratory disease most commonly occurring in childhood, but it is also associated with long-term damage to the heart in some cases (particularly following multiple attacks). Compared with other developed nations, New Zealand had a high rate of rheumatic fever, which had been steadily rising since 1995. The incidence of rheumatic fever was projected to rise from 4.3 cases per 100,000 people in 2012, to 5.0 cases per 100,000 people by 2017. The BPS target was set to instead reduce the incidence of rheumatic fever to 1.4 cases per 100,000 by 2017—a two-thirds reduction on the 2012 baseline, or almost three-quarters less than the projected trend. The level of ambition for this target is best conveyed when the target is framed in terms of the two-thirds reduction rather than in terms of "1.4 cases per 100,000." Hospital admissions for acute rheumatic fever would determine the incidence measure for acute rheumatic fever.

There was a rheumatic fever program in place before the Results program, but it was dominated by clinicians looking for solutions to the more serious condition—rheumatic heart disease. This was the internationally accepted approach but was not particularly successful in preventing the condition from occurring, as the target required. The rheumatic fever target was unique in that it targeted a tiny proportion of the population and demanded a very large improvement in percentage terms. For different reasons, it was widely considered by officials to be the worst target. Many thought it was too ambitious and would never be achieved; others considered it to be too narrow to drive significant improvement to service delivery. It had been known for some time that the risk of rheumatic fever was increased in certain housing conditions, particularly overcrowding. However, health and housing services were delivered separately, and the administrative data for housing and health were unconnected. Additionally, poor awareness of how to prevent or else detect rheumatic fever contributed to its high incidence. Progress would depend on agencies responsible for health, housing, and education working together.

Result 4: Reduce Assaults on Children

ORIGINAL TARGET: Halt the ten-year rise in incidence of assaults on children and reduce it by 5 percent in 2017.

It is difficult to compare rates of assaults against children across countries due to variations in reporting and therefore to know how New Zealand compared. All data rely to some extent on reported incidence of assaults, which is likely to be less than the actual incidence. The government chose to focus on physical abuse that has been reported to the authorities and verified by a social worker. Although this represented a smaller set of cases than other possible measures, it was thought to represent the best and most reliable source of data and least affected by surges in reporting following public awareness campaigns. Nonetheless, it was anticipated that increased efforts to address assaults against children would increase awareness of the need to report assaults and would thus see the measure rise further.

The number of children who were the subject of a substantiated finding of physical abuse had grown significantly between 2007 and 2011, rising at a rate of about 5 percent a year. In 2011, this number was 3,086, and was expected to rise to 4,019 by 2017. Just to halt the rising trend was expected to be extremely ambitious—public servants thought it would be a herculean effort. Ministers felt that halting an increase did not have the same psychological effect, both for public servants and the public, compared to the effect of setting a more inspirational target to reduce the number of assaults on children. In the end, ministers chose a target of reducing the incidence of assaults on children by 5 percent, which was more ambitious than the target public servants suggested. The target number of incidents was 2,936 by 2017, 1,083 fewer than the projected figure.

The Result to "reduce assaults against children" was the closest in the program to an end outcome. Assaults against children reflect not only the acute and immediate setting in which abuse occurs but also societal attitudes and intergenerational family dysfunction than can take many years to change. The fact that this target sought only a 5 percent proportional change signaled awareness that this was not a problem for which government could put in a short burst of activity and then declare the problem solved and move on to something else.

The Ministry of Social Development historically holds lead responsibility for protecting vulnerable children from physical assaults. The Ministry of Social Development conducts investigations into suspected abuse and has the power to place children in statutory care to remove them from dangerous situations. However, by the time an investigation has been opened by the Ministry of Social Development, it is likely that significant harm has already taken place. Frontline public servants from the Ministry of Justice, Ministry of Education, and Ministry of Health (among others) are likely to be in contact with these families, can spread positive parenting messages, and are often the first to notice possible signs of abuse.

Children suffering from physical abuse are frequently found in families with other problems, and providing a safe and positive environment for these children often involves a holistic approach to improving family well-being. For example, physical abuse often occurs alongside substance abuse problems, which are recognized and treated by the justice and health agencies.

Result 5: Increase Proportion of 18-Year-Olds with NCEA Level 2

TARGET: Increase the Proportion of 18-Year-Olds with NCEA Level 2 to 85 Percent by 2017.

New Zealand employs particularly complicated institutional arrangements for delivering public education:

- the Ministry of Education sets education policy;

- the New Zealand Qualifications Authority checks the quality of assessment tools and materials used in secondary schools, including achievement standards and unit standards;

- the Education Review Office checks the quality of education and student support in secondary schools, primary schools, and early childhood education centers;

- secondary schooling is delivered by a combination of state, state-integrated, and private schools; and

- NCEA-level 2 equivalent training programs (toward trade qualifications) are administered by a range of public and private education providers.

Improving the achievement rate of students would require all parts of the education system to work together.

NCEA Level 2 is an education qualification approximately equivalent to a high school diploma in other countries. It is considered the baseline qualification for many jobs and for entry into many tertiary education programs. This meant that this Result was pitched as an important building block for the future health, wealth, and happiness of individuals. It was considered important for individuals so they could achieve their potential, but this was framed as a contribution to economic growth from which individual benefits would flow. This was noted in the rationale provided at the start of the program for the secondary school qualification target:

> Success in education is an essential contribution to the Government's goals of: economic growth that delivers greater prosperity, security and opportunity for New Zealanders; and developing the skills to enable citizens to reach their potential and contribute to the economy and society . . . [the] qualification gives people better opportunity in terms of further education, employment, health outcomes, and in terms of a better quality of life generally.[3]

As would be expected when considering NCEA-Level 2 achievement as part of an education life course, data and solutions for this target had many similarities with the early childhood education target. New Zealand's high school graduation rate of 67 percent was similar to that of other developed nations but, as was also the case for participation in early childhood education, graduation was lower among Māori and Pasifika students (50 percent and 57 percent, respectively).

Although the ethnic disparity had long been known, it was unacceptable to many in the education sector, and the focus on data as part of the Results program was drawing more attention to how and why the situation had developed. The lead indicator for all the education Results was broken down into population groups when reporting the Results to illustrate the ongoing disparity that needed to be addressed. It quickly became apparent that the education Results were unlikely to be achieved without targeting those groups that were pulling down the achievement of the cohort. The catch cry was "we cannot achieve the target unless we raise the levels of participation and achievement for Māori and Pasifika kids."

The Ministry of Education senior manager responsible for coordinating the education Results noted that the program changed the conversations within the ministry to increasingly focus on data.[4] The strategic policy team, the data and analytics team, and specialist action teams became involved in joint problem solving to an extent that had not happened in the past. Graphs were drawn showing the current and projected trend, which anticipated an increase from 68 percent in 2011 to 73 percent by 2017, the target date. Superimposed on these data was a steep line showing what the trend had to be to reach the 85 percent target—the publicly stated ambition that ministers had signed up to achieve. Analysis of areas of non-achievement and non-participation raised questions about what it would take to make a difference in these areas. The data showed that it would be necessary to address both low achievement and non-enrollment/high absenteeism. Programs to get students engaged in learning, such as Count Me In and Achievement, Retention, Transition (ART) became crucial to achieving the secondary school target.

The data conversation spread to schools because meeting the target would mean achieving success for individual young people by meeting their unique needs. Previously, many schools had been focused on successful students who worked hard, were capable students, and left school for further learning having achieved a sound academic foundation. However, the data on achievement and retention for different population groups shifted focus to the points of failure in the school system, enabling schools to work with the individual students ("you know their names"). The data showed greater disparity of achievement within a school than between schools, which was something schools could, and should, do something about. The mantra "Numbers, Names, Needs" was adopted to reinforce the new way of working.

The new data conversations were also significant due to the highly devolved nature of the New Zealand school system, in which groups of parents provide the governance of individual schools. This meant that schools were initially suspicious of targets set by people who were well outside their community. Allowing schools to access data on student achievement so they could see how comparable schools were improving student achievement encouraged them to set their own school-specific achievement targets.

Result 6: Increase Proportion of 25- to 34-year-olds with NZQF Level 4 or Above

ORIGINAL TARGET: Increase the proportion of 25- to 34-year-olds with NZQF Level 4 or above to 55 percent by 2017.

UPDATED TARGET: Increase the proportion of 25- to 34-year-olds with NZQF Level 4 or above to 60 percent by 2018.

The education sector was considered particularly insular, with many in the sector believing that its core business was to improve education outcomes so that individuals were enabled to achieve their potential. In this paradigm, education is seen as primarily for the benefit of individuals, to meet individual needs and improve their lives. While individual benefit is a central outcome of public education, there are many demonstrated spillovers in the form of wider public benefits from more engaged and healthy citizens and a skilled and productive workforce.

The view that advanced qualifications are important for building a highly skilled workforce to contribute to New Zealand's economy was adopted by the government, which wanted to harness education to support its Business Growth Agenda. This political framing led to inclusion of the secondary and tertiary education Results in the Result area called Boosting Skills and Employment. Individual benefits from tertiary education were couched in increased contribution to the society and the economy:

> We need to increase the level of skills in our workforce to support New Zealand's economic growth. A higher skilled workforce supports better innovation and productivity.
>
> Individuals with higher qualifications tend to have better economic and social outcomes than those with low qualifications. People who gain higher level qualifications, especially at degree level and above, are more likely to be employed, have higher earnings, and less likely to be receiving a benefit.[5]

The minister of education and the chief executive of the Ministry of Education were responsible for Result achievement, but governance was through a group of economic ministers and agencies known as the Skilled and Safe Workplace (SSW) group. The motions for these structural and governance arrangements had begun before the announcement of the Results program in 2012, when the government combined several of the economic agencies into a single organization—the Ministry of Business, Innovation and Employment (this new agency combined the existing agencies for economic development, labor, building and housing, and science and innovation). The responsible minister for the new department was also the minister for tertiary education. He held the view that tertiary education was insufficiently focused on aligning qualifications with business needs. Having governance oversight provided by an economic ministers group ensured that both secondary and tertiary education qualification Results focused on supporting economic outcomes.

The secondary-tertiary education interface was significant for the life course conversation about this target. The average level of qualifications in the workforce tends to change very slowly—usually over generations, as one generation leaves and is replaced by another. Programs to transition students from school to vocational learning in the tertiary sector and to increase educational achievement had been in place for several years. However, the rate of advanced qualifications had peaked at 53 percent in 2007 and stayed relatively stable ever since. In looking back at the historic trend for improving workplace qualifications, public servants thought that the most qualifications could improve over five years was 3 percent.

While ministers accepted the difficulties presented by the slow rate of change in qualification, they still challenged public servants to decide on a number that the public would see as ambitious. In the end, ministers insisted on a 5 percent increase. The target was therefore set to increase the proportion of 25- to 34-year-olds with NZQF Level 4 or above to 55 percent by 2017. This proportional increase was smaller than for many other Results because the measure covered a large age range, and interventions aimed at a specific age take a long time to permeate the group.

The Result saw the initiation of additional school-based programs that motivated students to achieve the school leaver qualification by highlighting how it would contribute to their vocational goals. The Youth Guarantee scheme placed regional advisers in schools to work with teachers to ensure that vocational programs were based on the curriculum and could support the achievement of qualifications. Trades academies were established to retain students by providing clear pathways from school education to trade qualifications.

New Zealand has a high rate of inward and outward migration, which affects the makeup of the domestic workforce. Changing the proportion of 25- to 34-year-olds with advanced qualifications would therefore require actions by the education system to improve educational attainment along with immigration policies (by the Ministry of Business, Innovation and Employment) to attract and admit highly skilled immigrants and to encourage New Zealanders with advanced qualifications to stay in New Zealand.

Result 7: Reduce the Rates of Total Crime, Violent Crime, and Youth Crime

ORIGINAL TARGET: By June 2017, reduce the violent crime rate by 20 percent, the youth crime rate by 5 percent and the total crime rate by 15 percent.

UPDATED TARGET: By 2018, reduce the total crime rate by 20 percent and the youth crime rate by 25 percent.

While New Zealand has a generally low crime rate, the social and economic costs of crime are still significant. The total crime rate had been slowly declining in New Zealand and many other countries by about 1 percent per year. A reduction of 15 percent therefore marked a tripling of projected progress (5 percent) over five years. Violent crime, though infrequent, is of particular concern to citizens and so was included as a "supporting" target. When young people commit crimes, they tend to be associated with poor social outcomes over their entire lifetimes, so another target was added to focus effort on reducing youth crime. In contrast with the total crime rate, youth crime had remained stable or increased, and so the target was set at a more modest 5 percent reduction.

The justice sector was well-established, with clearly specified interdependencies and some of the most advanced governance arrangements of any Result area. Various agencies that work in the area of crime prevention have long recognized the contribution of their respective actions to the flow of the criminal justice "pipeline." This made a difference in their preparedness to work together to identify a few critical Results and develop targets at the commencement of the program. When asked during the formative stage of program design for the critical Results and measures for the sector, the justice sector group came up with Results and measures very similar to those that appeared in the final program.

The program allowed the sector to strengthen the way it already operated to improve collaborative effort. Police arrest offenders and therefore have the most obvious and direct relationship to the crime rate, but other agencies contribute to the conditions under which crime occurs and can take preventative action. Crime is considered a "social disease" and is therefore an example of the "problem of many hands," wherein no one party can be held responsible for reducing crime. However, New Zealand took the approach of assigning responsibility to a small range of agencies, balancing the opportunity to leverage resources from different agencies with the need for leadership and accountability. This approach is interesting to compare with the NYPD's CompStat program in New York City. It took the approach of police assuming responsibility for reducing the crime rate, even though they were only one of many agencies that had an influence, because it was preferable for one agency to have complete responsibility than for no agency to have responsibility.

In New Zealand, the justice sector had been collaborating by way of regular meetings of officials to discuss work programs and opportunities for strengthening interagency work. These were large meetings involving representatives from the youth justice parts of the Ministry of Social Development, the parts of the Ministry of Health running drug and alcohol rehabilitation programs, ministries focused on improving outcomes for Māori and Pacific people (who are overrepresented in the criminal justice system), and the core justice sector agencies (justice, corrections, and police).

Under the BPS Results program, a Justice Sector Leadership Board was formally established to replace the large group meetings. Responsibility was assigned to chief executives of the Ministry of Justice (which sets criminal justice policy and administers the courts system), the Department of Corrections (which administers correctional facilities), and the New Zealand Police. The terms of reference for the leadership board laid out an agreement to be collectively responsible for the overall performance of the sector, with specification of when decisions would be made collectively and when they would be made separately. The board would not cut across the line accountabilities of the board members to their ministers or make decisions that would override their authority over their respective agencies. The purpose of the board was to set a joint direction for the justice sector, make collective decisions, assign accountability for delivering initiatives to achieve targets the board sets, share information, and build interagency working relationships to model and promote throughout the sector.

Result 8: Reduce the Reoffending Rate

TARGET: Reduce the reoffending rate by 25 percent by 2017.

A significant portion of crime is committed by repeat offenders; more than one-third of offenders commit additional crimes within twelve months of completing their original sentence. These people are known to the agencies that work with them, providing an opportunity to break the pattern and create lasting change in the lives of the offenders and their families. Breaking the cycle of repeat offending helps reduce the financial and social cost of crime in our society.

In setting the target for this Result, public servants looked around the world for examples of reducing criminal repeat offending. While there were international cases of substantial reductions from a very high baseline, there was nothing to suggest that New Zealand could drastically reduce the reoffending rate. After much debate, ministers eventually decided to set a target of reducing criminal reoffending by 25 percent—a number many policy experts thought was unrealistic.

Reducing repeat offending involves many agencies in the justice and social sectors. The Department of Corrections, Ministry of Justice (through the courts), and the New Zealand Police play the most direct role in working with those who have committed crimes, but other agencies also contribute. The Ministry of Health has a role to play in the treatment of health problems that contribute to crime, particularly mental health issues and substance abuse, and the Ministry of Social Development and the Ministry of Education help released offenders enter into meaningful work or study.

One of the principal drivers for change in this Result area was an effective campaign to mobilize the front line of public servants that would contribute to progress toward the target. The chief executives from the Justice Sector Leadership Board pushed messages of thinking about the justice sector as a whole rather than in terms of its individual agencies. The targets themselves were an important part of the campaign, developing "bumper-sticker" status in some regions, with big posters in police stations and prison offices prominently displaying slogans like "RR25" (referring to the target to reduce reoffending by 25 percent). The RR25 slogan took on a life of its own, becoming the subject of workplace graffiti across the justice sector and reminding public servants why they come to work every day—to improve the lives of convicted criminals so they did not offend again. Copies of the Result Action Plan (RAP) were readily available to explain to anyone who did not know how the target would be achieved.

Deputy Prime Minister English had also coined a slogan to describe the focus on Results, picking up the term collective impact from the literature and applying it to what was happening in the program. The justice sector turned the slogan into action, setting up a collective impact toolbox for use at the front line. The toolbox contained a motivational letter from the chief executives, case studies of frontline action, project management templates (how to set out a meeting agenda, a project scoping tools, planners and the like), and guidance on issues perceived to be barriers to collaboration such as privacy legislation (which affected local data sharing).

The poster child for the mobilization of the front line was the Hutt Valley Innovation Project. A working group comprising operational managers from the three core justice sector organizations and the Ministry of Social Development used strong local knowledge through workshops to identify small operational changes they believed would reduce crime. They identified ten changes, including introducing audio-visual link facilities at the Hutt Valley court, end-to-end case management from arrest to administering sentences, a review of the Family Violence Court; and a community outreach mobile office van. The project was so successful that in 2013, the workshop approach was expanded nationally.

Result 9: New Zealand Businesses Have a One-Stop Online Shop for All Government Advice and Support

MAIN TARGET: Reduce business costs of dealing with government by 25 percent by 2017, through a year-on-year reduction in effort required to work with agencies.

SUPPLEMENTARY TARGET: Government services to business will have similar key performance ratings as leading private sector firms do by July 2017, and businesses will be able to contribute to this through an online feedback system from July 2013.

Businesses told the New Zealand government that they found government services complex and fragmented and that dealing with government took more cost and effort than it should. One of their main frustrations was providing the same information to multiple agencies. The aim of the Result was to ensure that the services government provides to business are more cost-effective and easier to use. David Smol, the chief executive of the lead agency for the Result, explained the importance of achieving this aim:

> The public sector represents around a quarter of New Zealand's real economy, so has a big influence on how our economy performs. The Government delivers significant services to business and the quality and speed of these services makes a difference to businesses' ability to perform, grow and export. Result 9 agencies need to find new and different ways to deliver greater value and better results for New Zealand businesses and through that, the New Zealand economy.[6]

From the outset, both Results 9 and 10 were different from the other BPS Results. They were areas with limited history of collaborative operation across government but were intended to achieve whole-of-government outcomes and would therefore need to influence all agencies across the public service rather than a few agencies in a sector. Both targets were also based on new measures that had no history and that were not very well aligned with their Results.

These Results were also different from the others because they had not been selected to solve a significant social problem. They were focused on improving customer experience rather than social outcomes. Although New Zealand was already ranked number one in the world by the OECD for ease of setting up a business, the government saw a great deal of opportunity for improving the delivery of services, particularly with rapid advances in enabling technology. This was also intended to deliver better government that was connected to the public and valued customer feedback, and it constantly strove to improve service delivery across the board.

Result 9 presented an administrative challenge in terms of how it was framed. Ministers had been struggling with the outcome, particularly in contrast with the other Results agreed to by Cabinet in 2012. For example:

Result 7: reduce the rates of total crime, violent crime and youth crime

Result 8: reduce reoffending

Result 9: tell us once, get it at once—I can transact with government on compliance and get help for business growth from one place.[7]

The statement for Result 9 is a clear outlier compared with the crime Results. Although it is relatively descriptive, it is neither catchy nor memorable. In the next Cabinet paper, the minister adopted a metaphor for the Result statement—that businesses have a one-stop online shop. But this was not well aligned with the target—that costs were reduced by 25 percent—and did not effectively communicate what the program was trying to achieve.

In the first instance, officials tried to work out what a one-stop online shop looked like. They concluded (correctly, as it turned out) that their task was not to establish a single online portal through which businesses could have all their questions about government answered but rather to use a variety of means, including (but not limited to) IT integration, to make it easier for businesses to interact with government. Ministers shared their interpretation, but the Result descriptor continued to be expressed as a metaphor. In the end, it was more useful in terms of understanding the government's goals to focus on the two targets.

Focusing on the targets led agencies to create a survey instrument to measure the cost to businesses of interacting with government. Unfortunately, measurability turned out to be a significant issue to address. It was difficult to determine whether it was the cost or the effort of dealing with government that should be measured. After exploring the possibility of putting a dollar figure on the cost of transactions with government, it was determined to be too difficult. Furthermore, gathering cost data would have been counterproductive, as it would have added to compliance costs for businesses. To compound the situation, the proposed targets were not adequately discussed with the agency responsible for target achievement and were announced before the measurement approach for the targets was determined. The upshot was that Result 9 had limited measurement of progress toward Result achievement until almost two years after the targets had been first announced.

Eventually, effort was introduced as a proxy measure for cost. A survey of a cross-section of more than 1,500 businesses was administered every six months, asking about the experience of dealing with government, assessing whether it had become easier or more difficult and to what extent. Businesses were also asked to compare government agencies with "best-of-breed" private sector firms to see whether the government was improving against this external benchmark.

While many agencies interacted with businesses, some did so more frequently than others. Public servants identified eight agencies that imposed the greatest administrative burden on businesses: Ministry for Business Innovation and Employment (which led the Result), Accident Compensation Corporation, Callaghan Innovation, Inland Revenue Department, New Zealand Customs Service, New Zealand Trade and Enterprise, New Zealand Transport Agency, Ministry for Primary Industries, Statistics New Zealand, and WorkSafe.

Result 10: New Zealanders Can Complete Their Transactions with Government Easily in a Digital Environment

ORIGINAL TARGET: An average of 70 percent of New Zealanders' most common transactions with government will be completed in a digital environment by 2017—up from the 29.9 percent baseline.

Many public services still required paper forms, and where digital services existed, these were often difficult to use. The New Zealand public had an expectation that accessing public services should be as easy as accessing services in the private sector. People were increasingly getting and sharing information online using search engines and social media, routinely doing business such as banking and shopping using sophisticated online tools or apps on their mobile phones. They expected transactions with government to be as easy and efficient.

One reason digital services were difficult to access was that each agency required different information to verify a customer's identity. A second problem was that (as with Result 9 above) New Zealanders were frustrated that they had to provide the same information to multiple agencies regarding a single event. The outcome statement for Result 10 that New Zealanders would be able to complete their transactions with government easily in a digital environment was clear from the start. The target was also clear, and the measure was quickly developed.

However, Result 10 suffered from similar difficulties as Result 9 had in terms of synecdoche between the measure and the desired outcome. Officials were not convinced that increasing the number of online transactions would actually increase the ease of interacting with government, especially given that poorly designed online services could actually make it harder to interact with government. The underlying disquiet among officials was due to the knowledge that the real game-changer for improving interaction with government was online service integration so that citizens would not have to visit the websites of several different agencies to carry out transactions that could be done in one visit to one website. Unfortunately, the measure did not drive behaviors toward this outcome. Instead, agencies were driven to simply provide more of their transactions online, regardless of whether that meant integrated service delivery for customers.

Regardless of the mismatch between Result and target, clarity of vision among the senior leaders for the target meant that progress was made; the Result was simply a means to an end, and that end was different from and more meaningful than the end that the target indicated. Similar to the approach used in Result 9, eight agencies that provided New Zealanders with the highest volume of transactional services were selected by the Result lead agency (the Department of Internal Affairs): Department of Internal Affairs, New Zealand Customs Service, Department of Conservation, Ministry of Business Innovation & Employment, Inland Revenue Department, Ministry of Social Development, New Zealand Police, and the New Zealand Transport Agency. These agencies sought to increase the number of online transactions with New Zealanders in their flagship programs—for example, completing a tax return online, issuing electronic passports online, implementing electronic identity recognition at the border (SmartGate), and having social welfare clients use secure self-service kiosks. The target measure was simply the aggregation of the online uptake for this basket of programs.

The basis for many of the improved online services was secure identification of users. The Department of Internal Affairs and New Zealand Post developed and tested an online tool for secure online identification over several years. The tool, known as RealMe, was given new purpose as a platform for service transformation with the introduction of Result 10. RealMe lets New Zealanders easily and securely prove their identity online and provides access to several online services with a single username and password; these include applying for superannuation, opening a bank account (with participating banks), registering to vote, renewing an adult passport, transferring foreign currency, or applying for a student loan or allowance. It can also be used to file company returns and conduct some business with local government.

The nature of many innovations for the program (such as the development of unique business identifiers for businesses under the New Zealand Business Number scheme and for citizens using RealMe) required long-term investment in a new, expensive ICT system that did not need to reestablish users' identity each time they dealt with a different government agency. This brought a host of new issues to light in terms of funding initiatives that would provide a complex distribution of benefits across agencies. This was heightened by the fact that the agencies involved in the "improving interaction with government" Result area were participating in programs with no historic basis outside the Results program and therefore had no existing funding mechanisms, unlike the justice sector, for example.

6

Implementation

Of course, setting Results, targets and measures is only part of the story. Public servants still needed to deliver new services that improved the lives of New Zealanders. This chapter considers how the Results were implemented: through mechanisms for collective governance and through regular reporting.

Setting stretch targets for outcomes that required collective action by groups of ministers and chief executives meant that the first challenge for designated Result leaders was to organize themselves differently. The leaders had to determine which other agencies controlled resources that needed to be combined to succeed in meeting the target. Then they needed to put together interagency and cross-ministerial-portfolio governance groups to make decisions about a program they were collectively responsible for designing and delivering.

The second challenge for those responsible for achieving the target was not only to do things differently (in the way they operated with others), but also to do different things, meaning innovation in policy and service delivery design. Ministers were adamant that agencies doing the same things, albeit more collaboratively, would not achieve ambitious targets. As the prime minister put it, "These targets are central to the government's plans to create a public service that is more innovative, enterprising, driven, and focused on results." He went on to explain how agencies would need to focus more on delivering services in ways that met individual needs, saying, "It's about delivering what New Zealanders really want and expect from their public services."

The third challenge arose from the tight fiscal environment in which the Results program was to operate. In short, there was limited or no new money for new initiatives. Deputy Prime Minister English referred to delivering better public services to New Zealanders within tight financial constraints. In announcing the program, he said:

> This is a fundamental shift that requires different thinking. We are not a government that thinks spending more money on something is an end in itself. We are a government that thinks getting results is what's really important.

Faced with these challenges, lead ministers and chief executives needed to set new priorities within existing agency baselines and/or mobilize resources that lay outside government. They were challenged to partner with nongovernmental organizations and community groups so that solutions were designed with people closest to the action and resources were combined.

Collective Responsibility

The Results were grouped into five Result areas, and the Cabinet appointed a lead minister for each Result area. This is a common arrangement in many other jurisdictions but was relatively novel in New Zealand, where ministers tend to only have responsibilities related to resources under their direct control. Nevertheless, there was also an understanding among ministers that all were expected to support and contribute to achieving the targets.

Cabinet met every six months to discuss progress in each of the ten Results. The focus was not on berating or punishing those public servants responsible for Results that were not going as well but instead to understand what was happening, what the barriers were, and whether there was anything that responsible ministers needed to do to help overcome those barriers and let public servants do their jobs better. Much like Bob Behn's descriptions of -Stat systems across the United States (and those observed in person by the authors), no one got in trouble for the measure going up or down.[1] Good performance, in these meetings, entailed demonstrating a felt sense of responsibility for the measure and for improving it, showing you had a relentless drive to understand the problem and improve it, and providing a plan for what you would try next.

Public servants reported that ministers were interested in learning rather than assigning blame or delivering sanctions. And perhaps as a result, throughout the whole five years there was very little cynicism or resentment evident. Ministers were clearly very interested, and paying attention, so public servants were interested as well. But this wasn't seen as an excuse to whip the public service and may be why the program was viewed positively by public servants—in contrast to the UK Delivery Unit, which was deeply unpopular with professionals.[2]

Ministers also met more frequently to discuss each Result separately. For example, the three agencies with the greatest responsibility for reducing the crime rate were the New Zealand Police, the Ministry of Justice, and the Department of Corrections. Their corresponding ministers were the minister of police, the minister of justice, and the minister of corrections. These three ministers met informally every month to consider the collective advice of their agencies.

The Results program was primarily driven by the executive branch of government, the prime minister and ministers of the governing coalition. However, the legislative branch (Parliament) also played an important role. Each year, all the departments must present information to Parliament: what they achieved last year, what they intend to achieve this year, and what they will achieve over the next four years. These are scrutinized by subgroups called Parliamentary Select Committees and are also reviewed by the Treasury and the Office of the Auditor General. Previous attempts at managing horizontally had been stymied by a parliamentary reporting system that always defaulted to individual agencies acting separately to achieve separate things. In the Results program, each agency that contributed to one or more of the ten Results incorporated this into the planning documents; agencies' "four-year plans" included not only what they would do to achieve separate goals but also how they would contribute to shared goals. The Office of the Auditor General was an important ally in shifting agencies' thinking to reference their contributions to larger initiatives.

The same system of separate agency reporting originally limited the commitments that individual chief executives could make to each other, as they typically each prepared separate advice for their respective responsible ministers and engaged in bilateral discussions. They might agree to one (joint) action only to have that agreement overruled by an individual minister with their own priorities. The informal ministerial groups provided an alternative to this. Instead of separate advice to separate ministers, the agencies agreed to work together to provide a single consolidated view to their respective ministers on issues that had implications for their shared goals. Ministers responded by considering this consolidated advice together. If an individual minister wanted to advance separate interests, they had to make this explicit to their colleagues. The precise nature of these groups might be peculiar to the New Zealand system of government, but the need for some mechanism for resolving political trade-offs may apply to other jurisdictions.

In New Zealand, public servants are appointed independent of political consideration and are expected to be politically neutral in their advice and actions. The State Services commissioner appoints the chief executives of departments, who in turn appoint the staff within those departments.[3] The State Services commissioner then manages the performance of those chief executives on behalf of the government. The State Services commissioner tried different systems for managing the performance of chief executives on contributing to shared goals like the Results, such as individual responsibility for performance, individual responsibility for behaviors, and collective responsibility for performance.

Initially, in addition to the Cabinet-appointed lead minister for each Result area, the State Services commissioner appointed a chief executive to lead each Result area. Neither Cabinet nor central agencies specified how these chief executives should organize themselves to achieve targets, and practices varied widely across each of the ten Results. Initially, these chief executives were effectively "first amongst equals," with responsibility for influencing their peers to achieve the targets. Some public servants involved in the program believe that this was an important step in breaking tradition and signaling a change in the responsibilities of chief executives. However, the limitation of this approach was that too much emphasis was put on the nominal "lead," which resulted in the other chief executives feeling less committed.

The organization of the chief executives gradually changed such that in 2014, all contributing chief executives were judged based on their perceived contribution to the collaborative effort. The intention was that subsequent performance appraisals could be used to hold individual chief executives responsible for the success or failure of the group of agencies responsible for meeting the targets. Due to the asymmetry of information between the State Services Commission and the agencies, the State Services Commission was forced to rely on the assessment of behaviors that were seen to support collaboration. However, judgment based on behaviors was unpopular with chief executives, who felt that their full contributions were not appreciated.

By 2016, another shift had occurred, one toward greater collective responsibility (see also the "Signaling Equal Responsibility" section of chapter 13). Chief executives were either rewarded or sanctioned based on the collective performance of the interagency group in addressing the nominated problem. Performance bonuses for chief executives were awarded based on collective (group) achievement. In this model, contributing chief executives are held jointly and equally responsible for what happens, regardless of individual contribution. This system is undoubtedly unfair—freeloaders may be rewarded for the efforts of others and overachievers punished because of their peers' failures. Yet it seems to produce the best outcomes. It is likely that there is no ideal or perfect model for managing performance toward shared goals, but collective performance appeared to be the most effective, especially when the number of responsible chief executives could be kept small (as discussed in the "Managing Group Size" section of chapter 13).

The final aspect of responsibility in the program is the sense of obligation that public servants feel to the public. The New Zealand government has many internal targets: "output plans" describing what goods and services each department will produce, performance specifications for every contract, and "key performance indicators" for every individual and every unit. A principal difference for the Results program was that it never failed to generate interest across the popular media. In contrast, the media almost never reports on output plans or key performance indicators unless something has gone terribly wrong.

Many of the reasons the program captured public and media interest were to do with the nature of the Results and targets themselves, as described in the preceding chapters. There were only ten, which meant each was considered very important and the volume of data released was not so overwhelming that it couldn't be captured in a short media story. The Results were framed as intermediate outcomes, with intrinsic value, rather than activities or outputs. They were phrased simply so that everyone could understand them. They were issues that the public (and not just policy wonks) cared about.

The way in which progress was reported affected how the public and the public servants viewed the Results, and the way the public viewed the Results affected the extent to which public servants felt responsible to the public for their actions. This was especially true for reporting of successes or failures.

Funding

Funding government-wide improvement as part of the Results program more generally presented many of the familiar issues with interagency working (see chapter 2). Funding the implementation of large and complex projects is always difficult. In New Zealand, agencies administer individual budgets (called appropriations) for specific purposes. When projects related to only one agency, that agency was called on to own the business case and to fund it from reprioritization of existing appropriations or win new funding in the government's annual budget round. But because of the government-wide nature of many of the initiatives in the Results program, it was difficult to fund new ideas that spanned multiple agencies. One agency would often end up providing funds that benefited other agencies, sometimes disproportionately. The balance of costs and benefits was unequal across agencies. There was a novelty to "taking one for the team" that would work for a while, but an external "program health check" of Result 10 pointed out:

> Human nature studies would indicate that the goodwill won't last long
> unless budgetary and performance management systems quickly change
> to provide support for this cross-government benefit realisation.[4]

Some Results teams engaged consultancy firms to produce these program health checks, and funding was identified as a central and recurrent challenge.

Findings included that interagency work involves innovation and that risk and benefits are unclear, it is difficult to get early commitments, and commitments to fund were often short-term and uncertain. Interagency funding is also technically difficult, with complex transactions requiring multiple levels of agreement, different agency processes, and unclear lines of cost attribution. The impact was that it took a long time to get decisions, funding was often insecure, and outcomes were driven more by negotiation than by value. Despite no new funding being available (and in the context of flat nominal budgets), the Results program used various funding innovations for redistributing existing funds to facilitate interagency work. A "sector fund," such as the one used in Results 7 and 8, was a way to pool funding together to heighten the stakes of governance. A "club fund," like that used in Results 9 and 10, was used to fund mature interagency projects based on known distributions of costs and benefits. And a "seed fund," available to all, was a mechanism by which to develop new initiatives where the distribution of benefits was not yet clear. Each proved useful for solving specific problems, but funding remained an ongoing point of contention.

A sector fund proved to be the final piece of the governance jigsaw for driving innovation in Results 7 and 8. The Justice Sector Leadership Board agreed to put aside a portion of its respective budgets and pool this into a Justice Sector Fund (rising to approximately NZ$100 million in 2016). The Justice Sector Fund was used as start-up or seed funding to test the effectiveness of new solutions that contributed to the shared crime targets. Particularly earlier in the program, having a pool of funding to administer provided the "glue" for the sector; it kept people coming to the governance meetings. As Aphra Green, general manager, justice sector group, put it, "If you're not at the table every fortnight, you're going to miss a trick, an opportunity for your organization."[5] As the sector matured, the allocation from the fund became more based on joint interagency activities than on investment in individual agency programs.

The Treasury continues to point to the Justice Sector Fund as an effective solution that could operate in other sectors. The Treasury is also clear that successful operation of joint funding mechanisms depends on effective governance with clear decision rights. Because the justice sector operates as a pipeline, its interdependencies are stronger and therefore so are its incentives to work collaboratively. This is the main reason given that the justice sector arrangements are not simply adopted by other sectors. The justice sector is seen within New Zealand as an example of more formalized horizontal management, perhaps representing the procedural culture of the agencies involved. The justice sector governance arrangements are discussed in more detail in relation to managing group size and signaling equal responsibility in chapter 13.

Result 9 and 10 program agencies faced many of the same funding difficulties. Unlike the other BPS Result areas, Results 9 and 10 involved agencies that in many cases had no prior history of working together. There were no "pipe-lines" or existing governance arrangements to leverage. There were a few multi-agency projects that had been started before the Results program and that were subsequently incorporated into the Results program (like the New Zealand Business Number and RealMe), but these had not yet delivered benefits.

Both lead agencies for these Results initially set up a program office by redeploying some of their own agency funding and then sought contributions to the operation of the program, either in cash or in kind, from agencies ben-efiting from it. This funding mechanism became known as "club funding." Club funding contributions had to be negotiated with each member of the "club." The question immediately raised, particularly for Result 9, was, what is the benefit to my agency? This was less of an issue for Result 10, whereby the value proposition was accepted early on the back of a well-articulated vision for the future. The agencies involved in Result 9 eventually agreed on a con-tribution for a year but balked at multiyear agreements, so the contributions had to be renegotiated every financial year. (Result 10 didn't have this prob-lem because agency contributions became part of baseline funding.) The zero budgets during the GFC years meant that the contributed funding often had to be reprioritized from existing baselines for each agency. Every year the ne-gotiations became more difficult and were often delayed, causing uncertainty about the ongoing viability of the program. The fallback position was for the lead agency to provide the funding for the program office, which the Result lead chief executive was reluctant to do, arguing that all the agencies concerned should have "skin in the game."

Because of the nature of the problems they were trying to solve—namely, to better integrate service delivery—the lead agencies involved in Results 9 and 10 had to make business cases for funding from the budget to build the necessary systems. The development of business cases was critical to greasing the wheels of progress by establishing the value of the proposed investment and identifying which agencies would benefit. But business case development is expensive. The initial attempt to address this was to use the club funding from participating agencies, on the basis that the program would provide benefits to each individual agency that was participating as well as to all of government. However, agencies were reluctant to contribute funds from their own oper-ating budgets before they knew more precisely where benefits would fall and therefore what proportional contribution they should make—information that could only be provided once the business case had been developed. This catch-22 was a significant barrier to progress.

The solution, provided by a determined Treasury official, was a "seed fund." Typically, each agency is allowed to spend up to its allocated budget but no more; in practice, this means that agencies tend to undershoot their allocation, resulting in "underspends." These underspends are usually returned to a centralized pool. In this case, the Treasury official was able to gain government agreement to establish the Better Public Services Seed Fund from the under-spends, adding up to several million dollars every year.

The Better Public Services Seed Fund was similar in practice to the Justice Sector Fund, but it was administered by central agencies rather than a sector board and was accessed by agencies through a submission process. While al-locations were made for several different projects (including the development of an innovation lab in Auckland), the majority of the funding was for Results 9 and 10 to develop business cases. The Result 9 program team became very good at applying for seed funding, clearly expressing the nature of innovation and the beneficial outcomes that would be achieved. The biggest problem con-tinued to be the uncertain, short-term nature of the funding.

In retrospect, funding challenges provided a catalyst for change to New Zealand's public finance system. Setting ambitious outcome targets surfaced problems and tension in the way horizontal initiatives were planned, managed, and funded. The Results made it necessary to set priorities across different portfolios and to allocate funding for activities done by one agency on behalf of another or by multiple agencies acting together. This need sparked innovations in the way New Zealand thinks about managing cross-cutting problems. These emergent approaches to shared funding in New Zealand were more "radical incrementalism" than "grand design,"[6] taking place over several years. This approach to reform can be messy and painful, and it never really ends. The ex-perimental approach involved taking bold actions, upsetting the current equi-librium and introducing tension, sparking response and solutions, and then learning from and embedding what worked.[7] Sector funds, club funds, and seed funds have remained part of the ongoing legacy of the Results program. Minor amendments to the Public Finance Act 1989 were passed in July 2020 to make it procedurally easier to implement some of the funding approaches described above.[8]

Reporting

Reporting on progress was a central aspect of implementation of the program that was common across all Result areas. This section describes the Results reporting and explores some of the features that contributed to its success, including periodicity, perspective, and recognition. Public reporting has been a feature of several target regimes, with "league tables" and "star ratings" in the United Kingdom and performance data presented in various graphic forms in several of the -Stat variants in the United States.

In New Zealand, there were two drivers for publication of performance in the BPS Results. One was public accountability—the government invited the public to hold it to account for public sector performance. The other was open government—a desire to provide information to the public in ways that allowed it to know what was going on and also to allow data use and reuse by individuals, researchers, and lobby groups. To this end, agencies were required to make available the indicator data that targets were based on through publication on www.data.govt.nz—an open data website. However, a third driver emerged incidentally as the program got underway. The reporting served to motivate the public service further in its work. The relationship between reporting and motivation is explored in more depth in chapter 14 as part of the discussion on valence.

Many governments are working to share more and more data with their constituencies through open data portals. In discussions with several administrators of these initiatives around the United States, the push seemed to be to update the data as often as possible, but not for the reason you might think. Continually released data removed the *event* of releasing data. Periodically released data attract a round of new attention because the data provide information that is new. Continually released data rarely attract attention because the data vary gradually and there is rarely an obvious, sudden, or dramatic story to be told. City, county, and state officials reported that the more often their data were updated, the *less* they were accessed (as recorded on website traffic) and the less media attention the data received.

The timing of the release of information was an important consideration for the reporting artifacts used in the Results program. In all, there were four separate mechanisms for reporting on progress of the Results program, each reporting every six months. Six months seemed about right for a five-year program—it created eleven rounds of news interest. And the public reporting of progress every six months did coincide with a flurry of media attention, particularly in the major news organizations. Some commentators and charitable organizations (such as the Salvation Army) carried out their own analysis of the publicly released data and published their findings, thus intensifying the public debate about progress. If the reporting had been too frequent, it might have lost its impact. But if it had been too infrequent, public servants would have missed the burst of motivation that came with public attention, and the government would not have had the same level of public accountability. The "right" reporting period is likely to be influenced by the length of the program, with shorter programs perhaps able to support more frequent releases.

The first of the mechanisms was a report prepared for the Cabinet, mostly text and running to ten to fifteen pages. This was a management document—it helped ministers understand what was going on, to know how and where to challenge public servants to do better, and to understand what they could do to help. While the early Cabinet papers simply described what agencies were doing to make progress toward their targets, as the program matured, the papers increasingly addressed public management issues and explored emerging themes. This reflects the interest of ministers—the program was established as part of public management reform, and ministers wanted to learn from the "experiment" with a view to applying what was learned more widely. Some Result lead ministers asked their agencies to apply "the Results approach" to cross-cutting issues in other portfolios, for example, for an accident prevention strategy.

The State Services Commission nominally wrote the Cabinet report, but in doing so, it relied on input from the "Results Network," approximately one hundred people across the public service with central roles in delivering or enabling the ten Results. Sniffing out the management challenges, the unrealized opportunities, and the barriers that only ministers could remove was an intelligence gathering exercise that relied on triangulation of information from a variety of sources. Those involved considered it one of the hardest documents to prepare—the culmination of six months of chasing down leads and corroborating different perspectives.

The Cabinet reports became better over time. Reporting on horizontal management is not a deterministic science. It is a craft that involves extensive relationships, trusted sources, and a generous helping of judgment. Public servants eventually realized that they had as much to gain from making ministers aware of the barriers that they faced, such that greater political force could be brought to remove these barriers, as they had to lose from increased scrutiny. Consequently, managers became freer with the stories they were willing to share.

The reports were the subject of lively discussion around the Cabinet table and frequently resulted in follow-up actions. When Cabinet reports are released in New Zealand, they tend to be delayed for several weeks after Cabinet deliberations. So although the reports were released publicly, they had a very small readership outside of the public service. Despite containing the greatest potential for scandal, they received very little attention, possibly because the main stories had died down by the time they were published. Perhaps they were considered yesterday's news.

At the other extreme was a simple one-page snapshot of the data for all the Results (see appendix 3). This included simple line graphs of progress toward the ten targets along with a color-coded rating of progress for each (see appendix 2). This was a public communications tool, published online to support the public announcement of progress in the Results program.

The third reporting mechanism was the "dashboard," a three-page report with one column per Result, which accompanied the Cabinet paper and drew the most attention from ministers. A typical column is illustrated in figure 6-1.

At the top of each column is the title of the Result and the target. Beneath this is a color-coded progress assessment. Progress was rated on a four-point scale: green for "on track," yellow for "on track but changes not yet embedded," amber for "progress, but issues to resolve," and red for "urgent attention

FIGURE 6-1. Excerpt from the 2015 End-Year Dashboard

5. Increase proportion of 18-year-olds with NCEA L2.

Target: 85 percent of 18-year-olds will have achieved NCEA Level 2 or an equivalent qualification by 2017.

Progress toward target: (Yellow)

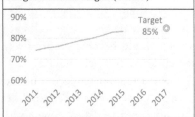

What the data tells us

The final end-of-year data for 2015 show that 83.3 percent achieved NCEA Level 2 or equivalent in 2015. This is lower than the indicative estimates from earlier in the year (84.4 percent) but represents an increase of 9 percent since 2011. We are on track to achieve the 85 percent target for all learners by 2017.

While achieving the national target is the primary objective, equitable achievement for Māori and Pasifika young people remains a clear goal.

Percentages of 18-year-olds with NCEA L2 2011–2015

	2011 (%)	2015 (%)	Change (%)
All	74.3	83.3	9.0
Māori	57.1	71.1	14.0
Pasifika	65.5	77.6	12.1

What has happened for NZers

"Count me in" finds and supports Māori and Pasifika 16- to 18-year-olds who are outside the education system, to reengage in learning (primarily through fees-free tertiary pathways).

"Youth Guarantee" supports the development of pathways from education to employment through 61 projects involving 45 secondary-tertiary-industry partnerships.

Notes: Edited for brevity and clarity to explain New Zealand–specific language, stylized for printing.

required" (see appendix 2). The color assessments were proposed by a group of agency chief executives and confirmed (or amended) by ministers.

The color assessments were necessary because different Results were expected to take a different path toward the target. The measure for Result 4 was expected to rise before it fell because the target was to reverse an upward trend in assaults against children. The measure for Result 2 was expected to improve most in the first two years because enrolling each additional child in early childhood education would become progressively more difficult as the enrollment rate moved closer to 100 percent. Result 3 was expected to show a seasonal pattern, as rheumatic fever tended to be more common in winter months. In other cases, a delay occurred between an intervention and when the effects of the intervention were expected to show up in the data. In Result 9, changes to the tax system were expected to make it much easier for businesses to comply with their tax filing obligations, but this wouldn't be reflected in the survey data for another six months.

The color assessments allowed senior public servants and ministers to interpret the data and apply a qualitative filter to what they saw. The colors signaled which of the Results required their attention and action. The color ratings had high stakes for agencies and ministers, though sometimes for different purposes. Some argued for higher ratings, to manage their reputations. Others wanted lower ratings, to bring greater attention and effort to the problems they faced. Because of these high stakes, criteria were developed and agreed upon by ministers. However, the subjective nature of the assessments made them less trusted and meaningful to the public. Subjective assessments can therefore complement but cannot replace the reporting of more objective and quantitative data.

Below the color assessment, the quantitative data were reported in the form of a line graph. The line graph illustrated how the measure changed over time and how much further change would be required to achieve the target. The line graphs illustrated performance before the Results program (for context and historic trends), performance during the program, and the target level of performance.

Below the line graph was the first of two text boxes titled "What the data tell us." This section told the story from the perspective of government. It included interpretations of the main measure and other data sources, explanations of new government programs, and grand plans for what was ahead. For Result 5, there was a breakdown of high school graduation rates by different ethnicities and a description of specific interventions design to help Māori and Pacific Islander children. For Result 7, the box included an explanation that violent crime had been reduced in public places, but family violence and violence in dwellings had remained at nearly the same levels as they had been at the beginning of the program. At the very bottom of each column was the final component of the dashboard, a section titled "What has happened for New Zealanders?" Like the box above, this also told the story of the Result but from the opposite perspective. Rather than describing what the government had done, this section was intended to explain how changes had been experienced by individuals, families, and communities. This provided a context in which to discuss the targets that would also affect their emotional pull and provide another chance for the government to prove the meaningfulness of the targets to the public.

As an example, in June 2014, the report for Result 2 included the following story about a local innovation:

> The Early Learning Taskforce ran a Tamariki Zone at the annual Ratana celebrations, providing early learning activities for tamariki and information for parents. Whānau engaged in learning activities alongside their children in a setting where they naturally come together. The space attracted hundreds of whānau and their tamariki and received positive feedback.[9]

A year later, in June 2015, the report featured a description of the use of tradition Māori stories to give confidence to parents as teachers, in the small community of Seaview:

> Naku Enei Tamariki (NET) delivers Poipoia te Mokopuna in Wellington's Seaview region and has developed a programme using atua and iwi pūrākau (traditional stories based around different concepts). The organisation has seen parents' confidence as first teachers grow through acknowledging their strengths, and drawing on familial and community connections: "everything we do is about modelling and about us constructing a relationship with whānau."[10]

Then, eighteen months after that in December 2016, the report described how services were being delivered to small and remote communities that could not support a dedicated learning center of their own:

> Plunket NZ established a Pop Up and Play Mobile Playgroup that operates four days a week in Noehari and Raumanga (Te Tai Tokerau). This playgroup has a group of eight children attending regularly with more children attending when the weather improves. These children have had no prior early learning experiences.[11]

This section was intended to describe the world from the perspective of those who use the service. It was picked up by the media, and then public servants themselves started submitting case vignettes to describe how what they were doing was helping people. The point of reference had shifted. The communication wasn't about what public servants were doing; it was about why this mattered to citizens. It was interesting to observe how difficult it was for some public servants to describe their contributions in this way (the Result 2 excerpts above were some of the better examples). Nonetheless it was these human-centered stories that proved popular, whether from the dashboard or the vignettes described below. The line graphs were useful for demonstrating that change had occurred, but it was the stories that made these changes seem real.

At the beginning of the program, these were the only three forms of reporting. Following the interest in the stories shared in "What has happened for New Zealanders," the State Services Commission started to publish slightly longer case vignettes (200–600 words) on its website. The story of Sam, a teenager who had committed a crime, and Fati, the caseworker from the Ministry of Social Development, is included as an example below.

> Youth Service is a new way of supporting disengaged 16- and 17-year-olds as well as 16- to 18-year-old parents back into school, alternative education, training, or work. The teenagers get one-on-one mentoring and support from specialist workers, such as Fati, who work for Work and Income or contracted community youth organisations.
>
> They work intensively with the young people, helping them make plans and get whatever help and services they need to make more of their lives. In one case, where it seemed certain that a client was facing a jail sentence, it was through Fati's support that the judge decided to give Sam a chance. Instead of jail, Sam was sentenced to community work.
>
> Fati found community work linked with a youth programme, hoping to get Sam thinking about a positive future.
>
> "It made me stop and think big time," says Sam. "My brother got stabbed up in jail, just about died. I don't want to follow in his footsteps."
>
> Fati says that Youth Service focuses on young people at a pivotal time in their lives, when almost every decision has the potential to be life-changing.
>
> "You have to tackle them in that period where they are experimenting, when they are easily swayed by negative influences. The important thing is to get your foot in the door, start listening to the young person and working out what their barriers are," says Fati.
>
> "Once we start sorting through the issues together and making a plan, it's great to see that spark of hope in a young person's eyes. That's what it is all about."

Tracey Burge, a counsellor for Catholic Social Services in Wellington, has been surprised at the range and flexibility of support Fati can co-ordinate through Youth Service.

"When (Fati) said he could help me with literacy courses for a client, I thought he had misunderstood. Young people who weren't on a benefit didn't used to be able to get support like that from Work and Income," says Tracey.

"It opens the support network wider for the young person, rather than just relying on one provider. (Fati) can get all the relevant people on board when they are needed. It feels cohesive."[12]

This story allowed public servants to tell the story of a new program (Youth Service) and to celebrate the importance of an individual (the case worker, Fati). However, the focus of the story is Sam—a teenager whose life has changed as a result of Fati's help.

First there was one case vignette. But it proved so popular that soon all ten Results teams were submitting their own stories to show how they were helping New Zealanders. The stories were regularly updated with new information to show how people's lives were changed for the better. Then one of the teams sent in a short video, which was quickly followed by many of the other nine Result teams submitting videos of their own. Initiatives such as the community outreach van from Result 8 featured in videos not only on the justice sector agencies' websites but also on the State Services Commission's website, alongside the other examples of innovative practice. There are now eighty-nine written case studies and twelve short videos. Sharing stories about helping people became a friendly, but keenly contested, source of pride and motivation. Most agencies also published the stories on their own websites, and some even used them to submit their work for awards.

Result Action Plans

Because the program was designed to make progress on previously intractable issues, many of which crossed agency boundaries, the design of the program had to facilitate agencies working together to address these interconnected problems. One design feature was a requirement for Result teams to develop Result Action Plans. The primary purpose of the Result Action Plans was to determine the actions needed to achieve Results, how lead and contributing agencies needed to interact on interventions, what governance arrangements would be established to oversee the achievement of the Result, what the success indicators would be, and, within this, who was responsible for doing what. The plans imposed a disciplined way of thinking at the start of the program, requiring agencies to answer questions like what are we doing, with whom do we need to work, what actions will we take (separately and together), and what data will we use to tell us about progress?

In short, the action plan was designed to focus agencies on delivering results that are important to citizens and businesses; ensure alignment of resources around results that cross agency boundaries; and stimulate innovation and new approaches to achieve results in difficult areas, based on evidence of what works in practice. Completing a Result Action Plan was the first action agencies involved in the BPS Results program were required to take.

At the core of the planning process was the development of an intervention logic map. These maps were familiar to those in public management reform in New Zealand, as they were also the core tool for the Managing for Outcomes reform a decade earlier. Unfortunately, the Managing for Outcomes reform had been ineffectively implemented, and intervention logic mapping had proven to be a bad experience for most. Public servants had struggled to produce the sort of detailed, evidence-based logic map that central agencies were asking for, against which they would be held to account through an audit process.

Furthermore, no one in the New Zealand public service had developed an action plan like the Result Action Plans before. They were asked to develop an intervention logic that identified the critical actions needed to achieve the Result, including interventions across the BPS Results program. Then, based on the intervention logic, they were to determine the key agencies they should collaborate with to achieve the Result. This information was then used to determine the governance arrangements to be established for coordination of the work. These requirements were explained in guidelines that agencies were provided (see appendix 1).

Having learned from earlier failures in the Managing for Outcomes program, the Results program team didn't issue a best-practice example for an action plan for agencies to follow. Instead, the team looked to agencies to develop something that worked for them—the lead agencies and lead ministers needed to own the plan if it was to drive action.

The program coordinator (the second author) established a network of Result leaders from each agency and invited these leaders to form a community of practice. They met from time to time in workshops to share with practitioners what they were doing, with the intent of learning from each other. They were encouraged to share early drafts, exposing new ideas as they were being formulated. It was a high trust model that most rewarded those people willing to contribute the most. (The community of practice is outlined in more detail in appendix 5.) The first action plans shared in this permissive environment were long, detailed, dense planning documents destined to live their lives gathering dust on a shelf somewhere rather than becoming living plans that drove action.

Like the plans themselves, intervention logic maps can be incredibly detailed and complicated, or they can be breathtakingly simple. In despair at having received the former, the program coordinator looked for an agency Result leader who was willing to think differently and take some risks. The person he worked with had recently joined the justice sector in a second-tier leadership position. They set about developing a new brief—an attractive, diagrammatic booklet of no more than twenty pages that would work for ministers and for the public. The action plans were not only designed as strategic policy instruments but also needed to communicate, to government officials and the public, why the Result was a priority and what actions would be taken to improve outcomes for New Zealanders.

The criminal justice pipeline (see figure 6-2) was provided on the second page of the plan and became the basis for explaining the nature of connections that was needed between agencies to achieve ambitious targets.

The criminal justice pipeline provided a good start for answering many of the questions required for the action plan, but more was needed. This came in the form of its more comprehensive intervention logic diagram (see figure 6-3).

The justice sector chief executives took their draft Result Action Plan to the justice sector ministers' group, where it hit the mark. The justice minister was so pleased that he provided it to his colleagues at a subsequent Cabinet committee. Ministers not only endorsed the document but also demanded the same of their agencies—down to the same design approach. This was not exactly what was anticipated in the open design brief the program coordinator had originally given agencies, but ministers had moved way ahead of him. They wanted a plan of action, yes—but they also wanted a public communication tool that told their constituents what they were doing about important problems. When the justice sector plan was shared in the community of practice, there were many "light bulb moments" as participants saw what could be done with effective design, few words, and compelling actions.

FIGURE 6-2. The Criminal Justice Pipeline

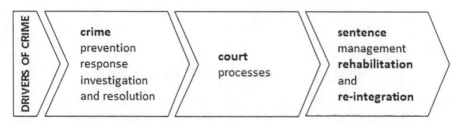

Source: Ministry of Justice. (2012). "Result 7 Action Plan, 2." New Zealand Government. (Converted to simple line drawing for publication).

FIGURE 6-3. Justice Sector Intervention Logic
Map from the Result Action Plan

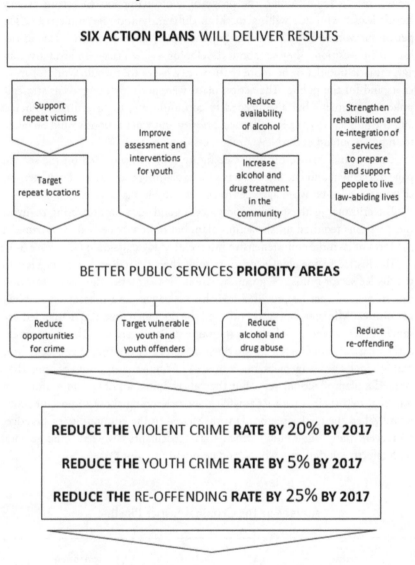

Source: Ministry of Justice. (2012). "Result 7 Action Plan, 3." New Zealand Government. (Converted to simple line drawing for publication).

Action plans were important at the beginning of the program, but they tended to atrophy over time. They should have been refreshed from time to time to keep them as living documents. Instead they became artifacts, replaced by other mainstream, internal planning mechanisms. In retrospect, this may not have been a bad thing. The Results program needed to become embedded into the "way we do things around here" if it were to have a lasting impact. The actions needed to become central to business as usual, fully integrated with associated actions, to be most effective.

7

Changing Course

After some of the interventions that would contribute to progress in the Result areas had been implemented, monitoring and reporting on progress was beginning to yield some insights about the program. Of significant interest was progress in three Results—1, 6, and 7—in which it became apparent that the targets would be met. In Result 1, the target was to reduce the number of people continuously receiving Jobseeker Support benefits by 30 percent over five years, but the number was tumbling by almost 10 percent per year. In Result 7, the target was to reduce the rate of youth crime by a total of 5 percent over five years, but instead this fell by 6 percent per year. And in Result 6, where no one thought it was possible to increase the proportion of 25- to 39-year-olds with advanced trade qualifications, diplomas, and degrees by 5 percent over five years, the target was achieved in just three years. In each case, achieving the original target was no longer in question.

Armed with this knowledge, the New Zealand government then faced a choice. It could leave these targets as they were and report success in at least three of its goals. Alternatively, it could set new, more difficult targets to keep pushing public servants to improve. Ultimately, ministers were concerned that easy targets would no longer motivate public servants to act with urgency, so they decided on the latter option.

In 2014, they set revised targets for each of the three Results that had proven too easy to achieve. In Result 1, a revised target was set to reduce the total welfare liability (using actuarial forecasts) by $18 billion. In Result 6, the target was raised from 55 percent to 60 percent. And in Result 7, the target for reducing youth crime was increased from 5 percent to 25 percent. The government set each of the new targets to be achieved by June of 2018 (rather than

June 2017, as with the original targets set in 2012). Ministers then asked that reference to the original targets be removed from subsequent reports to make sure that the new, harder targets were the focus.

The choice to revise the targets in which improvement had been so rapid, and especially to remove reference to these original targets from subsequent reporting, indicates the intention behind the program. It would be naïve to suggest there were no political considerations in how a high-profile government program would be administered. However, if the Results program had been primarily intended as a means to win public approval, the government would surely have taken the opportunity to declare victory in Results 1, 6, and 7, which were on track to be achieved early. It could then have focused effort on ensuring the targets were also achieved in the other seven Results. Revising the targets to make them more difficult to achieve meant that public servants remained under pressure to perform. This suggests the ministers were more interested in using interagency performance targets to drive goal commitment than in taking political credit.

There was further risk in revising the targets, both in 2014 and in 2017 (as discussed in the second half of this chapter). In public administration theory about targets, targets are susceptible to a type of gaming that Gwyn Bevan and Christopher Hood refer to as "ratchet effects."[1] This refers to the tendency to set future targets based on previous performance, which can incentivize managers not to overachieve targets even if they are able to do so. As noted by Alec Nove regarding ratchet effects in the Soviet economy: "A wise director fulfills the plan 105 percent but never 125 percent."[2]

Those public servants responsible for Results 1, 6, and 7, faced this exact situation; they overachieved and were "rewarded" with revised targets that were more difficult. This decision was not expected and therefore was unlikely to have affected behaviors from 2012 to 2014. It is possible that the experience of revising the targets in 2014 might have discouraged public servants from overachieving in the future, but the program was ultimately canceled in 2017 after the general election, which was too soon for any behavioral consequences to be observed or indeed for progress on the revised targets to be assessed. Ratchet effects remain a potential consequence of revising targets based on past performance that governments should consider.

Renewing the Program for Another Five Years

Most of the targets were set to be achieved by 2017, with the targets revised in 2014 set to be achieved by 2018. By the start of 2016, discussions were well under way about what to do next with the Results program. In the end, some Results were extended with new (higher) targets, while others were replaced by new Results with different measures. For example, the government had achieved what it had set out to achieve for immunization and early childhood participation and was ready to move on to the next big problem. The purpose of the targets was neither to celebrate achievement nor to assign blame for failure, but rather to drive public servants to be better. Therefore, the government focused on launching the new set of Results rather than reflecting on the old ones. No final report was issued regarding which of the original ten Results were achieved, but at the time of the 2017 renewal, one target had been clearly achieved (Result 5), two would not be achieved (the revised Result 1 target and Result 8), and seven were still in question. Internal and operational considerations for the Results refresh were trumped by the complicating factor of the 2017 general election. Without a final report, even the program coordinator is not sure exactly how many targets were met. In his view, making progress was a more important indicator of success than reaching targets. A prominent newspaper reported that "about two-thirds of the targets were met, while others fell short."[3]

By the beginning of discussion about the renewed (or "refreshed") program, the Results program was already considered a success, not only in terms of improved outcomes in difficult areas but also in terms of a more innovative and connected public service, more focused on delivering services to meet New Zealanders' needs. Many public policy leaders were keen to apply the approach to new areas, to embed it as a public management tool. The reaction of ministers to this idea showed that, at least to some extent, the program had become a victim of its own success.

Having publicly facing targets, together with regular publication of progress, meant the program became strongly associated with the success or otherwise of the government's change agenda. Ministers had staked their reputations on achievement of the targets, and while this had created significant momentum for change, it had also bound them to stay the course. Ministers became increasingly reluctant to change a target until it had been achieved, and this became one of the principles of the Results refresh. This political perspective was at odds with the prevailing policy perspective, which held that there were diminishing returns on efforts to achieve the last few percentage point gains for several of the targets and that the effort would be better spent on new, more pressing problems. In fact, progress had stalled for some of the Results, as the most difficult, resistant and hard to reach families were engaged in an effort to reach the target.

A situation emerged in which the government wanted to move onto new priorities but equally wanted to keep existing targets until they had been met. For ministers, ten had become a magic number not to be exceeded in policy design because it aided in both focusing effort and selling the program to the public. If there were to be no more than ten Results, then new priorities could only be introduced as existing targets were achieved. Unfortunately, only one target was likely to be fully met by 2017. Something had to give. In the end, ministers decided that it was better to manage the political risk of "retiring" a Result before the target was reached than to either increase the total number of Results or curtail the number of new priorities introduced.

Success also meant that public servants increasingly valued being part of the Results program, and they were reluctant to leave the program. This was due in part to the recognition the program gave to their efforts and in part because the publicly facing targets drove progress they felt would fall away once the program was removed from the spotlight. Some argued to stay in the program and set higher (or different) targets once existing targets had been met. One of the issues addressed in the refresh was how to transition existing Results back into mainstream public management processes without losing the momentum the program had generated. In some cases, progress for Results that had been retired from the program continued to be reported alongside the new Results, at least for the first year of the new program.

The process to refresh the BPS Results was different in many respects from the process to develop the first set of Results. Of course, much had been learned from both success and failure that could be applied to the design of the program the second time around. But the single biggest difference was the increased trust that government had in the capability of the public service to design and deliver on the government's agenda. During several years of stable government, the public service had demonstrated that it could be agile, be innovative, and deliver improved services, all of which contributed to the government's success.

On the back of this increased confidence in the public service, officials were much more closely involved in the design of the refreshed Results program and in setting targets. The first set of Results was developed by ministers (facilitated by the Department of the Prime Minister and Cabinet) deciding their priority Results, and the sort of measures they wanted, and testing them with selected officials in a tightly held process. A very different process was used for the refresh of the Results: Ministers asked officials to design the new program and to bring it to them for discussion and decision.

Officials first considered the scope of the program. The original Results concentrated on solving difficult cross-cutting issues in the social sector, the exceptions being Results 9 and 10, which set out to improve interaction with government. Other sectors required more effort to organize around a Result, for example, to improve people's experience at the border and improve both environmental and economic outcomes in the natural resources sector. The government was now prepared to branch out into areas in which it had less control over the outcome, for example, supply of housing (which depends more on the effectiveness of local authorities and the private sector than on government efforts). Ministers were also interested in alternative framing of high-level outcomes, for example, having a Result area for child poverty (which would replace the Vulnerable Children Result area).

Officials also worked on the design of the Results package, building on what had been learned from the first set of Results. Of particular interest was the way Results contributed to each other and were interdependent, described earlier as a pipeline effect. This concept was applied to different stages of life and termed a "life course approach."

Officials applied a life course approach to refreshing the Results in the social sector, selecting a set of Results that contributed to each other; identifying interventions at early life stages would reduce the need for more expensive and less effective interventions later in life. Taking a life course approach meant that agencies were jointly responsible for addressing crucial issues facing individual New Zealanders at each life stage. The Results were seen as a series of coordinated interventions along a life course rather than separate interventions taken by multiple agencies.

The social investment approach used in the Reducing Welfare Dependence Result described in chapter 5 was also influential in the design of the new set of Results. The approach uses information and technology to identify where additional early investment will improve long-term outcomes—put simply, identifying what point of intervention will make the most difference. It identifies those people most at risk of poor outcomes later in life, uses data to better understand their needs and what works for them, and then adjusts services accordingly. For example, the justice sector considered the impact of crime on the victims and set out to frame a Result based on reducing victimization (as opposed to reducing the crime rate), leading to a focus on reducing serious crime and family violence.

The central design elements for the BPS Results refresh were included in the Cabinet paper that established the new program:

- **Build on what works.** In particular build on what had been learned from Social Investment and from the effectiveness of existing BPS Result targets.

- **Retain existing Results and targets until targets are met or almost met.** Achieved targets will continue to be monitored by responsible agencies as performance measures to prevent regression but will be replaced with new Results and targets to address current challenges.

- **Do not aim to be comprehensive.** Instead, have a small number of critical Results that will have the most influence on long-term outcomes for New Zealanders, based on evidence of impact.

- **Targets and measures should be meaningful and important to, and easily understood by, the public.** In addition to headline measures on which targets are based, supporting measures will be drawn from both "upstream" and "downstream" events where possible, based on the intervention logic for the Result. Supporting measures will also be used to show progress by vulnerable or high-risk groups.

- **Understand how Results are linked.** Report on and describe the interrelationship between health, education, social, and justice outcomes. Linking Results will require more complex multi-agency work to improve long-term outcomes and reduce cost to government.

- **The Results clearly communicate key government priorities and level of ambition.** The refreshed Results will be designed to build on the existing Results and orient the program so it supports the direction of government policy over the next five years.[4]

Several meetings took place between senior ministers and officials to determine the new set of Results. The early meetings worked through which Results should be retained until existing targets had been reached, which should be continued with new targets and/or a different scope, and which should be retired from the program. Ministers also wanted a range of target types, recognizing the unexpectedly effective impact of narrow targets such as reducing the incidence of rheumatic fever but wanting broader targets in the mix as well.

Three of the original Results were retained unchanged. Two of these (Results 1 and 6) had already been refreshed with new targets and target dates set a year or so earlier, and one (Result 9) needed more time to achieve the target. Two of the existing Results were retained with new targets and a wider scope (Results 4 and 10). Only one of the remaining five Results had been fully achieved at the time the program was being reviewed (Result 5), but ministers decided that it was better to introduce new areas to the program rather than to wring the last few percentage points from existing Result areas that had made significant gains over the previous five years. This was not as politically safe as staying the course, but it was the right thing to do in terms of improving outcomes. (As discussed in Chapter 7, ultimately about two-thirds of the targets were achieved, though the exact number is subject to some debate.)

Results in the natural resources sector were considered but not added to the program. Ministers did decide to set targets here but chose a different program to deliver them. The BPS Results program continued to concentrate largely on improving social sector outcomes.

Determining a new set of Results and targets required several more meetings and consideration of different designs and measures officials had developed. Partway through this process, ministers returned to the basics of the Results approach. As they struggled in one meeting to determine which of the new Results were on offer and how many of them the new program should comprise, a breakthrough came from the ministers' reflection on how the first set of Results was determined. What they had done the first time around was to consider the ten most difficult cross-cutting problems that needed to be addressed. Shouldn't they do the same thing again? Housing was the most pressing and politically difficult problem they were facing at the time, but many of the solutions lay outside government, which made including a housing Result risky. But as the minister responsible for social housing put it, how could they make a valid claim to be addressing government priorities if the Results package didn't include housing? The other issue for which ministers returned to basics was how the Results "retailed." By this they meant how they were accepted by the public. The Results in the new set had punchy titles, such as "healthy moms and babies." They also had targets to which people could easily relate. For two of the expanded Results, targets based on sophisticated measures were replaced by targets that were more easily understood (as described in the following two paragraphs).

As described earlier, Result 10 (increasing transactions with government more easily online) had long struggled with a target that measured the volume of online transactions rather than the ease of transacting with government online. For the Result 10 team, the refresh meant the team members could sharpen the outcome description to *People have easy access to public services* and then develop target measures for increased ease of transactions. The target measure the team developed made sense in policy terms, but Ministers couldn't see it retailing. Instead they chose a target that was quite similar to the existing one—"by 2021, 80 percent of the twenty most common transactions will be completed digitally," with the more sophisticated data on ease of doing business used as supporting measures. Significantly, it was very similar to the publicly facing target the Singaporean government in 2018 had implemented as part of its *Smart Nation* push—"Singaporeans will be able to complete between 90 percent and 95 percent of transactions with the government digitally by 2023."[5]

The refreshed Results were announced in April 2017. The program reflected the life course concept with a new Good Start to Life Result area designed to drive investment in vulnerable groups early in their life courses; improve access to social housing, a crucial factor affecting the life outcomes for vulnerable children and families; and create a new Result focused earlier on the education pathway to continue the improvement of educational achievement. There were also new Result areas: "a good start to life" for the two health Results, "strong foundations for work and life" for the two education Results, and "better housing." These were added to the original Result areas of reducing welfare dependence, protecting vulnerable children, reducing crime, and improving interaction with government (see also table 4-1, this volume). The refreshed Results program is set out in table 7-1.

TABLE 7-1. Refreshed Better Public Services Results and Targets

	RESULT	TARGET
1	Reduce long-term welfare dependence	By June 2018, a 25 percent reduction of the number of people receiving main benefits.
2	Healthy moms and babies	By 2021, 90 percent of pregnant women are registering with a Lead Maternity Carer (caregiver) in the first trimester.
3	Keeping kids healthy	By 2021, a 25 percent reduction in the rate of hospitalizations of children for preventable conditions.
4	Safer kids: reduce assaults and abuse of children	By 2021, a 20 percent reduction in the number of children experiencing a substantiated incidence of physical or sexual abuse.
5	Improve mathematics and literacy skills	By 2021, 80 percent of year 8 students are achieving at or above the National Standard in writing, or at Manawa Ora or Manawa Toa in Nga Whanaketanga Rumaki Māori tuhituhi. By 2021, 80 percent of year 8 students are achieving at or above the National Standard in mathematics or at Manawa Ora or Manawa Toa in Nga Whanaketanga Rumaki Māori pāngarau.
6	Upskill the New Zealand workforce	By 2018, 60 percent of 25- to 34-year-olds will have a qualification at Level 4 or above.
7	Reduce serious crime	By 2021, reduce the number of serious crime victimizations by 10,000.
8	Better access to social housing	By 2021, a 20 percent reduction in the median time to house for priority A clients on the social housing register.
9	Easy and seamless services for business	By 2020, business costs from dealing with government will reduce by 25 percent, through a year-on-year reduction in effort required to work with agencies.
10	People have easy access to public services	By 2021, 80 percent of the twenty most common transactions will be completed digitally.

Source: Derived from the Better Public Services Results Cabinet paper (March 2017), www.public service.govt.nz/resources/bps-cab-papers-minutes.

As for the first set of Results, lead agencies were required to develop a Result Action Plan, which was approved by the responsible minister and then published online. Central agencies oversaw the development of the action plans, requiring them to clearly set out the Result to be achieved; success measures (with the target based on the lead measure); how the lead agency would operate in collaboration with others; and key actions. At the core of the plan was an intervention logic diagram that set out the links between actions, outputs, Results, and higher level outcomes. Members of the newly established Social Investment Unit worked with social sector agencies to ensure that social investment principles underpinned the intervention logic. Statistics New Zealand worked with agencies to ensure that the measures and targets used were sustainable, had fidelity, and identified potential perverse incentives.

Ending the Program in 2018

In November 2017, just before the first progress report on the refreshed Results program was to be sent to Cabinet, New Zealand elected a new government to occupy the Treasury benches. The Results program was strongly associated with the previous government and didn't survive the transition and was discontinued in January 2018.

Despite having disbanded the Results program, the new Labour government clearly still saw the value of targets. It grouped its priorities under three broad themes: growing economy, well-being of New Zealanders, and making New Zealand proud, which were remarkably similar to those of the 2006 Labour government discussed in chapter 4.[6] The new program of priorities was driven through Cabinet committees and the annual budget process. In addition, the Labor government enshrined some long-term outcome targets in legislation. These targets, for addressing child poverty and climate change, were intended as a tool for holding itself and future governments to account.

The new government also retained several of the lessons the public service had learned from the experience. The New Zealand public service still uses the governance mechanisms explored in the Results program (and described in chapter 6) to coordinate high-priority and cross-cutting work and has extended these further in recent legislation (making use of the lessons described in chapter 12). It retained and extended cross-agency funding mechanisms pioneered in the Results program (see chapter 6). It sought to harness the spirit of service to the community that public servants bring to their work, discussed later in chapter 14. And it aimed to build on the sense of teamwork from the Results program, with a new focus on creating a more unified public service.

After five years, the government was no longer organized around ten measurable targets, but public servants could not "unlearn" what the experience had taught them. New Zealand public servants had learned different ways of working, and they continued to apply some things they had learned. We return to a fuller account of the lasting impact of the Results program in the conclusion chapter of this book.

PART III

RETROACTIVE SENSEMAKING

Our motivation in writing this book was the contention that the Results program's successes make the program worthy of further study. In this part, we explain what we mean by success and how we went about studying it to determine which lessons should be shared.

The relative success of a program can be contested. We consider whether the program met its goals, its reception in the media and by other political parties, and the extent to which the improvements were real rather than being artifacts of measurement subject to distortionary gaming or outright cheating. We also provide examples of what success looked like—entrepreneurial public servants making innovative changes that improved the lives of New Zealanders.

It's one thing to be able to describe these successes; it's another to understand the factors that contribute to them and how those factors might be transferable to other settings. The state of any complex social problem is due to innumerable factors. The best that we can hope for is to triangulate evidence from a multitude of sources. We bring together formal evaluations, and practitioners' lived experiences, to make claims about how and why the Results program was successful. In this way, the discussion in the remaining chapters of this book constitutes a process of retroactive sensemaking.[1] In explaining why the program was a success, we are trying to understand (or make sense of) what happened in the past.

8

Successes and Failures

We claim that the Results program was a success. The word gets thrown around frequently to describe policies and programs implemented by government. But what exactly does success (or failure) mean in this context? A useful framework is provided by Allan McConell, who suggests the success of public programs can be divided into process, political, and programmatic dimensions.[1]

Process successes are usually associated with the following of good practice. Unfortunately, good practice itself is frequently contested. This book attempts to identify and contribute to our understanding of what good practices might be. We know that many public servants involved in the program experienced it as challenging and frustrating but also as the most important and valuable program to which they contributed in their careers. We contend that entrepreneurialism is an example of process success—public servants challenging the status quo, trying new things, and making a difference. Chapter 10 describes six examples of successful innovations by public entrepreneurs.

Programs can be considered political successes or failures to the extent that they assist or frustrate leaders and governments in the pursuit of their agendas or aspirations. Political success is associated with the way policies and policy makers are evaluated in the political arena.[2] Political success is usually implicit—governments tend to portray public programs as solely in the public interest, as opposed to partisan political interests.[3] Similarly, it is usually hard to attribute the rise or fall of individual leaders to a single program. This makes it difficult to determine whether or not a program has been politically successful. Nevertheless, and as noted in chapter 2, target programs are notorious for their lack of political success—there tends to be no electoral benefit from achieving targets,[4] but negative consequences stem from setting targets and then failing to achieve them.[5] In this case, the minister most closely associated with the Results program between 2012 and 2016 was subsequently appointed prime minister in 2016 by his own party but then lost the next election. The party that introduced the Results program in 2012 (the National Party) won reelection in 2014 but was defeated in 2017.

Programmatic success describes the effectiveness of the program in achieving its goals.[6] This is the type of success that was the rationale for this book. In many programs, it can be hard to determine what the goals were, let alone whether or not they were achieved. This leaves the possibility that governments can claim that when something good happens, this was the intended goal all along. Some of the most influential public administration texts have been criticized as drawing their evidence from selected case studies that involve "painting bull's-eyes around bullet holes." The phrase appears to have first been used in public administration by George Frederickson[7] in critique of David Osborne and Ted Gaebler's best-selling book on government reform, *Reinventing Government*.[8]

In contrast, it is theoretically much easier to evaluate the success of the Results program, as the program was defined by its *a priori* targets and agreed quantitative measures. The New Zealand government painted the bull's-eyes in 2012 and then took aim at them. Programmatic success could be defined as achieving those targets. In this respect, the program was a partial success, as about two-thirds of the targets were achieved, but some were not. Some were achieved and then revised to be more difficult. Others would likely have been achieved soon had they not been replaced in the 2017 program renewal. (See chapter 7 for a fuller discussion on which targets were achieved and why we are left with the rather vague statement "about two-thirds.")

However, we argue that the real purpose of the program was not to reach the somewhat arbitrary targets but instead to improve performance in ten stubborn cross-cutting problems. As Kelman and Friedman note, to determine the programmatic success of a target program, "The appropriate comparison is between an organization's performance level with performance measurement and the dysfunctional responses, and the counterfactual performance level with no measurement."[9] With this interpretation, the program achieved not just partial program success, but full program success in all ten problems. This is because the Results program is unequivocally associated with higher performance than would have been the case without the program.

Although the government did not achieve all the targets, in all cases, it improved the outcomes. Each of the measures demonstrated an increase in performance, above both the 2012 baseline and the historical trend lines where these were available.[10] Having levels of improvement that outperformed historical trends indicates that the program itself was making a difference rather than improvements being the result of some sort of natural progression. (For example, the crime rate has been slowly declining globally and within New Zealand for some time due to factors unrelated to the Results program.)

Had the targets been set at a lower level, they may well all have been achieved. But it is possible that the urgency with which public servants attacked the problems would also have been lower and that the performance improvements would have been less stark. Even among the groups that didn't quite meet their targets, there were still impressive stories to tell. For example, after years of stagnation, immunization rates for one-year-old children rose from 83 percent to 94 percent. While this is slightly short of the 95 percent target, it represents huge progress that will prevent many cases of serious infectious diseases.

Similar stories can be told across all ten Results. More long-term unemployed people were back working, and the projected long-term benefit liability had been reduced. More children were enrolled in early childhood education. More children were vaccinated. Far fewer children suffered from rheumatic fever. Fewer children suffered severe physical abuse. More teenagers graduated from high school. More New Zealanders had advanced qualifications. Fewer crimes were committed, and fewer criminals reoffended. It was easier and less costly for businesses to interact with government, and more services could be easily accessed online.

These were some of the 2012 government's top priorities, and by 2017, substantial progress had been demonstrated in all of them. For each of the ten problems, public agencies began from different levels of readiness to take up the challenge. Some made rapid progress, visible from the first six months, whereas others took two full years to stop downward trends and exceed even their baseline measure. Part of the success of the program was that, while the government continued to push public servants to achieve the targets, they were set at a level for which failure in some was inevitable. They were set by a government willing to fail to achieve a target in order to improve performance.

Media Critiques

But the failures of a government (even in the context of other successes) are rarely allowed to pass unnoticed. Although the Results program garnered significant positive media coverage, it was not totally immune from criticism in the media, among opposition parties, and within academia.

Some critics claimed the targets had unintended consequences like "full prisons and a punitive benefit system" and that they had perverse outcomes because of the close focus of accountability on individuals and departments.[11] The Labour Party particularly criticized the targets for being too narrow, both when the program was implemented and when Labour discontinued it as an incumbent government. Party Leader and later Prime Minister Jacinda Ardern acknowledged the need for accountability but said that overly specific targets distracted from other issues and failed to address underlying causes. She cited the example of a "rheumatic fever crackdown that failed to fix the core issue causing the sickness—poor-quality housing."[12] The Public Service Association (PSA) national secretary, Glenn Barclay, welcomed the implication from Ardern that her government would be taking a more systematic approach.[13]

One of the more notable critiques of the program, from Associate Professor Bill Ryan (at Victoria University School of Government), was that for it to be successful and worthwhile, it would require "extensive, ongoing, independent evaluation of the outcomes" that were actually generated rather than "those desired and hoped for by the Government."[14] Although progress was monitored and reported, monitoring was done internally and released via government press releases. Trust in this monitoring system relies on the extent to which government statistics are seen as credible and reliable, usually regarded as a strength of the New Zealand system.[15]

Other criticisms from Associate Professor Bill Ryan were more political, based on differences of approach and ideology. Although we have positioned the Results program as an alternative to the austerity and cuts that followed the GFC in other jurisdictions, some New Zealand commentators like Ryan did not necessarily see it this way. The flat nominal baselines were viewed with suspicion that the program was "primarily about cost and staffing reductions."[16] This was cohesive with the view of the governing National Party as having an "ideological preference for small government and minimal public expenditure."[17] According to Ryan, equating "better" with smaller, more economical and more productively efficient represents an increasingly discredited economic view.[18] Later on in the program, this leveled off into a simpler observation that no extra resourcing meant that public servants had to meet the targets and keep up business-as-usual,[19] put rather colorfully as "the government is now yelling, 'jump' more loudly, while chopping more furiously."[20]

Other criticism was directed at specific Results, especially the education Results. Some of these points are discussed in the next chapter, acknowledging that they have some legitimacy. This includes, for example, the distortion effect of focusing "disproportionate resources on the small group of students who are most likely to reach the standard with additional support . . . to the detriment of those who have already achieved the standard and those who are less likely to with those same levels of additional support."[21] However, some criticism went so far as to say that this was an "intensification of the very policies we know to be causing harm" and that it "precipitates an overall decline in the achievement of the whole cohort over time."[22] This was leveled especially at NZQA (New Zealand Qualifications Authority) as a public service agency required to work toward the target but also "tasked with maintaining standards for qualifications."[23] The claim was that "in line-call situations about whether, for example, to adjust a marking process when a slightly greater-than-expected proportion of students is attaining credit for a standard, the BPS target might well be in the back of an NZQA official's mind."

Another of the opposition parties for the National government—the Greens—also criticized the education Results for focusing on quantity at the expense of quality. They were particularly concerned that the ECE target was putting children at risk by placing them in unsafe facilities, "pushing participation rates at any cost."[24] They cited evidence from Ministry of Education and the Education Review Office and claimed the National government had "scrapped the requirement for all teachers in the sector to be qualified." It's somewhat unclear whether this criticism was directed at the National government's decision to remove the target to have 100 percent qualified ECE teachers in regulated positions that the Labour government introduced in the sectors' ten-year strategic plan "Pathways to the Future: Ngā Huarahi Arataki" and defer the 80 percent target or whether it was directed at the removal of the funding band for 100 percent certificated teachers in ECE services.[25] While neither action would result in a decrease of teacher qualification levels (instead, removing planned work to increase qualifications), the two taken together do indicate a shift in focus away from continuing to improve teacher qualifications and toward increasing participation.

Results 9 and 10 received criticism for focusing on improving digital service integration and delivery, which did not help New Zealanders without internet connections or devices to access them. In particular, difficulties with accessing digital services disproportionately affect New Zealanders with disabilities, Pasifika, Māori, and senior citizens.[26] More recently, the government has focused on closing the digital divide.[27]

These challenges should each be taken seriously. Priorities should be selected with care not to exacerbate other problems. Reporting regimes are only effective if the reporting is seen as credible. Times of fiscal constraint may increase the strain on public services and public servants. Threshold effects are a real challenge in setting good targets. Improvements are less valuable if an increase in quantity comes at the expense of quality. And whole-of-population data can obscure inequalities and disadvantages particular groups face. These challenges are not inconsistent with those associated with targets elsewhere, as described in chapter 2.

However, what is also notable is the scarcity of these critiques and their narrowness. We were able to find a few media statements by politicians and a couple of opinion pieces in local newspapers. With the exception of the opinion offered by Ryan, these critiques are of the form "yes, but . . .": yes, the Results program reduced incidence of rheumatic fever, but it also should have addressed the supply of good quality housing; yes, the Results program increased the number of children graduating from high school, but it also should have helped children who were already achieving and those who were unlikely to achieve; yes, the Results program increased early childhood education enrollment rates, but it should have also improved teacher quality; yes, the Results program improved digital services, but it should have also improved digital access for those without it. The Results program was criticized not for its lack of success but because it didn't also solve other problems beyond the ten it identified as priorities. Nonetheless, the targets selected were imperfect; the following section provides a more detailed examination about potential distortionary effects of the ten Results.

9

Gaming and Cheating

Any account of the use of targets to improve performance must recognize the challenges of cheating and gaming, which are frequent by-products of target regimes. Cheating refers to instances the data are falsified. In the case of the New Zealand Results program, this was likely to be extremely rare and minor because of the nation's strong institutions, with multiple systems for ensuring independent and impartial reporting. The New Zealand official statistics system produces information generally agreed to be authoritative.

Gaming is a pejorative term used to describe instances where the measurement is accurate but misleading. This can result from perverse incentives set up when otherwise innocuous administrative data are used as the basis for making judgments about success or failure in a high-stakes environment. Input- and output-level indicators, while easier to measure, are more open to manipulation than intermediate outcome indicators are.

Gaming takes a variety of forms, at worst quite blatant, such as reclassification of cases to avoid their being counted. More subtle forms of gaming occur when effort is directed to the easiest cases at the expense of more difficult but also more important cases. The concepts of gaming and cheating were first introduced in chapter 7 of this book, with reference to a type of gaming referred to as "ratchet effects." This chapter covers two remaining types of gaming: threshold effects and output distortion effects.

Case studies from the program are used to explore the possibility that some measures were gamed, or intentionally manipulated, such that the measure improved without an underlying resolution to the problem. We concede that this is possible for some measures, but it would have been difficult or impossible for others. For example, it is difficult to even imagine how one would manipulate (without falsifying data, or "cheating") the incidence of substantiated cases of child abuse. In cases in which gaming may have been possible, the case studies are provided to illustrate the theoretical discussion and explore the likely extent and effects of gaming. However, we have no direct evidence that gaming actually occurred, and we were not able to observe the significant gaming or cheating that has plagued many other target regimes. Further, the narrative of gaming or cheating never really took hold in New Zealand like it did elsewhere—there wasn't a perception within the public service or in the media that the program was undermined by gaming or cheating.

Threshold Effects in Welfare, Immunization, and NCEA Targets (Results 1, 3, and 5)

Threshold effects is a term used to describe the effect of targets on distribution of performance.[1] In a UK example provided in chapter 1, the target to decrease the frequency of ambulances taking longer than eight minutes to respond to emergency calls provided no incentive to quickly respond to a call that had already taken longer than eight minutes. Most of the effort had focused on cases that were closest to meeting the threshold—a miss is as good as a mile. This is a by-product of framing targets as "x percent of a population group meet y condition"—30 percent less people continuously receiving Jobseeker Support benefit for more than twelve months, 95 percent of children are vaccinated by nine months old, 85 percent of eighteen-year-olds graduate from high school. From the perspective of time-bound targets, it is not a case of "better late than never" but rather that late successes do not count at all. This indicates there was certainly potential for threshold effects in the New Zealand Results program, but that potential did not necessarily affect behaviors.

From the perspective of the Result 1 target, no benefit accrues to reducing a person's time on Jobseeker Support from eleven months to nine months—only in making certain that it doesn't reach twelve months. In 2014, the target and measure for Result 1 were changed from reducing the number of people continuously receiving the Jobseeker benefit to reducing the lifetime fiscal liability for benefit recipients. This suggests that the original target was not providing the right incentives to focus effort on helping the right people (however, the revised target was difficult for the public to engage with, as discussed earlier). While this does not provide direct evidence that threshold effects did occur, it does provide indirect evidence that ministers were concerned with the possibility of threshold effects.

The Result 3 immunization target provides no incentive to ensure that children who were not vaccinated by nine months ultimately receive their vaccinations at all. In 2015, those working to improve immunization rates drew encouragement from the fact that they had been able to achieve a 95 percent vaccination rate by twelve months of age. Their logic was that because it was possible to immunize 95 percent of the population, it should be possible to ensure vaccinations were received by a certain age. In this instance, cases that missed the threshold were treated as an encouraging sign, providing anecdotal evidence that threshold effects were not distorting efforts.

The Result 5 target only provides an incentive to ensure that those under the age of eighteen who are at risk of dropping out do not do so; it doesn't encourage efforts to help those who would already graduate to perform better or to help students over the age of eighteen graduate at all. New Zealand does not measure how teachers distribute their time and efforts among students, so there is no quantitative evidence on whether effort was disproportionately directed at those close to the threshold at the expense of other students.

Output Distortion Effects

The final category of gaming—output distortion effects—describes the effects of targets on prioritization of effort across the entire population, particularly in cases where such prioritization leads to outright neglect of some cases. This is a broad category that includes three relevant examples: neglect of quality, effort substitution, and cream skimming. Neglect of quality can occur when a target specifies the number of outputs without specifying their quality, leading to achievement of a greater number of poorer quality outputs. Effort substitution occurs when a target causes a focus on one dimension of performance at the expense of others, following the adage that "what gets measured gets managed."[2] This can result in achieving one dimension of performance at the expense of others. Cream skimming is a type of effort substitution that involves selecting the easiest cases of a problem from within a population. This kind of gaming can be particularly harmful in social policy settings whereby the "easiest" cases are often self-resolving, but the greatest societal change can be achieved from investing effort in the most difficult cases, and these cases wind up receiving little or no attention as a consequence.[3] The following case studies consider whether Results 2 and 5 were susceptible to the neglect of quality, whether Result 3 (rheumatic fever) was susceptible to effort substitution, and whether Results 7 and 8 were susceptible to cream skimming.

Neglect of Quality in Education Targets? (Results 2 and 5)

In 2011, New Zealand children's rate of participation in early childhood education was about 93.5 percent. While on the surface, this seems like a high participation rate, the few children not involved in early childhood education face significant disadvantage throughout their lives. They tend to perform worse at primary and secondary school, are less likely to go on to tertiary education, and find less success in the workforce. The decision to set the Result 2 target at a participation increase to 98 percent was the subject of some debate. In particular, the teachers' union felt that the focus should also be on raising the qualifications of early childhood teachers. This is approaching an accusation of neglect of quality, but the reality is that it is possible to improve performance along a wide variety of dimensions or margins and that it is rarely improved on all or even many at once. Neglect of quality as described in target literature typically refers to cases in which performance in one area comes at the cost of declining quality in another area. In this case, neglect of quality does not apply, because quality was kept constant while quantity was increased.

In the case of Result 5, there is somewhat more evidence for a case of neglect of quality. Although this target's greatest strength was that it translated into actions at the front line that led to success for students who may not otherwise have achieved it, this also became this target's greatest risk—it was susceptible to gaming. The New Zealand qualification system is one of the most flexible in the world. Qualifications are based on achievement of a basket of credits, all set at the same level. Some credits are compulsory. For example, a base level of literacy and numeracy is usually required, particularly at school level. It is a permissive system that encourages everyone to succeed and that sets out to minimize failure.

The real strength of the qualifications system is that it puts academic and vocational learning into the same framework. Achievement of NCEA qualification can be through accumulation of credits from both vocationally based unit standards and academically based achievement standards. Unit standards are assessed using capability-based assessment, mostly using moderated internal assessment, whereas achievement standards are a mix of internal and external assessment, including examinations.

Meeting the learning needs of a range of students in very flexible ways can lead to variation in standards. This translates into not all credits being equal—some are deemed easier to achieve than others, particularly those most suited to nonacademic students. Teachers tend to channel students who are struggling to meet standards into credits these students are more likely to achieve, usually those based on unit standards. This practice is anecdotally known as "credit farming."

Success breeds success, and these students are more likely to stay at school and leave with a qualification that will help their entry into further education and work. However, this was where critics of the use of targets for Result 5 focused their concerns, maintaining that the school qualification target may have amplified this tendency toward credit farming. They thought encouraging students to take "lower quality," easier courses would help schools achieve qualification targets but may not be in the best long-term interests of students (in terms of providing foundations for further learning or work). If this were the case, the target might be achieved, but at the expense of longer term out-comes for less capable students.

A senior education official responsible for coordinating the education Re-sults admitted there were examples of schools that packaged credits that made it easier to gain the qualification but that didn't necessarily provide a good platform for ongoing learning. But there were many more examples of schools catering to students who would otherwise have dropped out. There was an exponential increase in vocational pathways offering credentialed learning in areas "the kids could only dream about previously." There was some noise but scant evidence of the devaluation of qualifications over time and looser as-sessment practices. There was much more evidence of positive than negative outcomes. He concludes, "Far more good than harm came out of this."[4]

It may well have been the case that the target distorted the program choice for a group of students that may have achieved better long-term outcomes if the target had not been in place. But if any gaming did occur, it was likely to be both unintentional and benign rather than a deliberate neglect of quality that constituted harm.

As the ministry official asks, "What is the counterfactual?" What happened in response to the target was a sharper focus on the quality of outcomes for previously low-achieving students. Teachers looked beyond the attainment of the secondary school qualification and guided their students to take complete packages that would have the best learning outcomes, setting students up for further education and training, including work-based training. Would it have been better to return to the pre-target situation in which schools focused most on those students who would succeed in an academic environment? Which is the greater harm—an inadequate base qualification achieved by students at the margin or no high school qualification at all, with the risk of being branded a failure early in life?

In the end, the school qualification target was one of the most successful targets in the program. It ticked the boxes in terms of being easily measur-able and understandable, and it had a clear value proposition that was real and important to individual New Zealanders. But what set this target apart from some of the others was that it was translated into meaningful actions and improvements.

Effort Substitution in Rheumatic Fever Target (Result 3)

In 2015, New Zealand achieved a sudden 40 percent drop in the incidence of rheumatic fever. This was attributed to efforts to integrate health and housing data. As described in chapter 14, the Result 3 team used health data to iden-tity families with children at risk of rheumatic fever and ensured these cases received elevated priority for placement in public housing. While this occurred simultaneously with government efforts to increase the total supply of social housing, any change to elevate the priority of one group means the relative decline in priority for other groups. Effort substitution is the form of gaming in which the group that is measured receives more effort at the expense of other groups, and this seems like a good description for the successful placement of at-risk families in social housing. However, in this case, it is not clear whether effort substitution was to the overall benefit or detriment to the public interest. Due to imperfect information, governments spend billions of dollars providing services in inefficient ways. Services could often be more effective if they were targeted at a different audience. In this case, the reduction in rheumatic fever provides evidence that the services were indeed targeted where they made a difference but does not allow us to assess whether targeting at a different group would have made a greater difference.

Cream Skimming in the Justice Sector Targets (Results 7 and 8)

Results 7 and 8 aimed to reduce the crime rate and the rate of criminal reoffending, respectively. The catchall term crime includes a wide variety of offenses, from relatively minor traffic offenses through to and including violent crimes such as rape and murder. The targets could therefore be achieved by reducing all types of crime equally or by focusing efforts on certain types of crime. The criminal justice sector in New Zealand had traditionally weighted its efforts at preventing the crimes with the greatest social harm—for example, murder rather than traffic offenses.

However, the effort required to prevent these crimes is typically inversely proportional to their harm on society. The efforts required to rehabilitate a murderer so that they can safely reenter society are usually greater than the effort required to prevent a traffic offender from reoffending. There is some evidence that the presence of the targets caused a shift in effort from preventing the most serious offenses to preventing the most minor.

For example, diverting minor offenses away from the criminal justice system (without formal charges) may act to reduce the measured crime rate. Similarly, the criminal recidivism rate can be reduced by focusing resources on preventing reoffending among those who have committed minor offenses (where progress is easier) and away from more serious offenses that are associated with greater social harm. The greatest reduction in reoffending was noted in those sentenced to community service and prison sentences of shorter than one year, with almost no reduction in reoffending by those released from a sentence of five years or longer.

Was this then the "smoking gun" that the justice sector had been caught gaming the system? Public servants in the justice sector were very open about the strategy of focusing on minor offenses. In fact, they reported it to ministers at the time. The logic was simple: being involved in the criminal justice system is a bad thing, and focusing on reducing minor offenses means that fewer people end up being involved. The more that New Zealand can keep people out of being involved in the criminal justice system, away from other offenders, living within society, and hopefully in gainful employment, the less likely these minor offenders are to be turned into more serious, hardened criminals.

This indeed seems to fit the definition of cream skimming, as the justice sector focused on those offenders who would be easiest to rehabilitate. However, the quality of outcomes is difficult to measure, and there are few effective targets based on quality (as opposed to volume). As with the education targets discussed above, this isn't an argument against the use of targets per se, which have proven to drive inertia out of the justice system; it is more a caution about the distortionary impacts of a target regime. Because there was a reduction in reoffending among minor offenders and no increase in reoffending among serious offenders, it seems to be a case of improvement and gaming occurring simultaneously.

One of the officials in the program noted that the downside of the focus on measurement was that it "tended to drive managerialism in a system that is about more than just management." New Zealand's Chief Justice Sian Elias also expressed concerns, pointing out in a speech that some fundamentals might have started to be overshadowed by the focus on the target measure, including institutional values and individual rights (such as the right to a fair trial), which needed to be protected. Speeding up progression through the justice system is a desirable outcome but not if it compromises the quality of the experience and outcomes for individuals. Chief Justice Elias put it this way:

> This is an interconnected system. It is a bit like a cat's cradle. You cannot pull on one thread without causing movement in the whole structure. We have to keep our eye on the system as a whole and not be blinded by immediate pressures and self-interest. Many of the levers are now in the hands of those who are managing for outcomes other than correctness in decision-making and fairness in process.[5]

Far More Good Than Harm

In none of these case studies of distortionary effects did the presence of the target appear to disadvantage groups outside the target area. Governments always have to choose between different priorities based on limited resources, and a program that improves performance in one area cannot be discounted on the basis that it did not improve performance in all areas. As Steven Kelman and John Friedman put it:

Simply to note that a performance measurement regime produces some level of dysfunctional response does not by itself imply that such a regime fails on balance to improve organizational performance.[6]

Evidence of gaming should not automatically condemn targets as ineffective. Yet there's something about reports of cheating and gaming that tend to stick in people's minds. Despite evidence that targets in the United Kingdom did result in real improvements, reports that there was also gaming contributed to the decision of that government to move away from creating and using targets.[7]

Gaming cannot be definitively excluded in other Results in the New Zealand program, but there was no evidence of widespread or systemic gaming of the kind observed in other jurisdictions. It may be that the measures in New Zealand were harder to game because they were intermediate outcomes, with intrinsic value. Output measures, with a less obvious synecdoche to the ultimate intended change in society, may make it easier to "hit the target but miss the point."[8] Another explanation might be that the strong institutions and public service culture acted to limit gaming. Having low levels of corruption may have prevented cheating because cheating requires dishonesty. However, gaming involves honest distortions. Note that in the cases above, the justice sector reports on targeting less serious offenders as a legitimate tactic rather than as a source of shame. The 2017 refresh suggested a focus on reducing "serious crime" because this was the crime category that had the most impact on people's lives.

Ultimately, the real improvements in the underlying conditions associated with each of the ten Results seemed to be beyond what even the most cynical assumptions could attribute to distortionary effects. Each of the problems had a long prior history of failure. Progress was slow (in the case of Results 2, 5, 6, 9, and 10) or nonexistent (in the case of Result 1 and the rheumatic fever part of Result 3). In one case (Result 4: Reducing assaults against children), the problem had been getting worse at an average rate of 5 percent per year. All ten improved from their baselines and ahead of their historic trends. In the comparison to past attempts at solving cross-cutting problems, there can be no doubt that the Results program was effective. As noted in regard to possible neglect of quality in Result 5: "Far more good than harm came out of this."

10

Public Entrepreneurship

It was a core purpose of the program to inspire public servants to explore new ways of working and new solutions for the entrenched problems the program was focused on addressing. It was clear from the outset that success would mean considerable innovation, and a willingness to try and learn from failure. This was indicated by Prime Minister Sir John Key when he launched the program: "We want targets that are going to stretch the ability of the public sector to deliver them, and will force change. This is not an exercise in ticking boxes." This meant that central agencies needed to take a different approach.

The willingness to acknowledge that "'standard operating practice' will not do," combined with the necessity of achieving specific outcomes, is the primary characteristic of what Eppel and colleagues refer to varyingly as policy entrepreneurs, social entrepreneurs, and public entrepreneurs.[1] American political scientist John Kingdon first coined the term policy entrepreneur to describe individuals who take advantage of opportunities to influence policy outcomes to increase their self-interests.[2] Social entrepreneurs are individuals outside of government who resemble for-profit entrepreneurs, except their primary goal is to improve social outcomes; they develop, fund, or implement innovative solutions.[3] Public entrepreneurs are social entrepreneurs who are employed in the public sector, individuals who challenge the status quo and create new solutions.[4] Many of the Result teams in responsible agencies had a public entrepreneur who was willing to change the status quo. Such people have significant "personal and emotional commitment to [their] role," and their pursuit of purpose and efficacy ensures that "they do more than simply say the right things, follow standard operating procedures, and conduct due process."[5] These are people who can work iteratively, experimenting and learning from their actions as a higher priority than following traditional ways of working.

There are several cases in which the BPS Results initiative sparked innovation, new partnership arrangements and design thinking methods like rapid prototyping and co-design of solutions, both through empowering clients to take part and through bringing together a range of relevant agencies. The plan was that these new ways of operating within the public management system, once seen as successful, would "infect" the rest of the public sector. In the words of one such public entrepreneur, Richard Foy: "We introduced a viral infection into the system, the infection took hold, and we got a bit of mutation. Because of the Better Public Services program, we've had some good mutations."

The justice sector ministers and chief executives put the success down to spreading what was learned from innovation in pilot areas to other areas—tapping into the capability and resources of other agencies, both government and nongovernmental, and the energy and knowledge of local bodies and community groups to achieve better results. Eppel similarly identified the characteristics of a public entrepreneur as being important skills for successful interagency collaboration.[6] Many of the public entrepreneurs discussed below and throughout this book put substantial effort into pulling together a team of like-minded people.[7]

Integrated Data Infrastructure for Social Investment (Result 1)

Many of the people we interviewed pointed to new and more powerful ways of using data to drive action as a core success factor for the program. The way the targets refocused agencies on the data relating to the problems they were trying to solve was one of the most central innovations of the program. In Result 1, the focus on data was able to reveal the true interdependency of social problems, resulting in increasingly powerful "data conversations" that drove collaboration across government.

The Results program commenced in 2012. Despite good progress toward meeting the target for Result 1, the government changed the target in 2015. The new target for reduction in welfare dependence signaled a different focus for the government—an intention to encourage "harder-to-reach" people on long-term benefits (such as sickness and sole parent beneficiaries) into the workforce.

By the end of 2015, things were already happening differently. The analytics and insights work had identified population groups that were costing the most (because of benefit dependence) in the longer term, and the social investment approach was changing the way people thought about the harm caused by long-term benefit dependence. The end-year 2015 progress report to Cabinet estimated that $2.4 billion of the $13 billion actuarial release target had been achieved. Almost half of this reduction related to recipients of Sole Parent Support; this program's budget had fallen to levels not seen since the 1980s.

As progress increased, ministers became more interested in the interdependency between Results and asked officials to explore this further. Logic told them that achieving the education Results would ensure more people gained the skills they need early in life to support further skill development and sustainable careers and thus reduce flows onto benefit. They looked to the data for confirmation.

Analysis from the Integrated Data Infrastructure (IDI) supported the interdependency between these Results. Of the cohort of young people born from 1989 to 1990, 21 percent of those with qualifications below NCEA Level 1 were receiving benefits in 2010 compared with 6 percent of those with a NCEA Level 2 qualification (NCEA Level 2 is considered to be the foundation qualification for school leavers in New Zealand). At higher education levels, receiving benefits is the main destination of only 2.7 percent of young graduates with a NZQF Level 4 qualification or above, seven years after completing their qualification (NZQF Level 4 is considered the foundation tertiary qualification in New Zealand).[8]

However, the end-year 2015 Results program progress report to Cabinet observed an even greater level of interdependence, which would require even more agencies to work closely together to improve outcomes:

> The interconnections across the social and economic sectors mean that achieving better outcomes for people through Result 1 [reducing welfare dependence] is at least partly dependent on some agencies performing well against their own BPS Result targets. For example, achieving the Result 5 and 6 [education] qualification targets is associated with lower likelihood of benefit receipt; and work to improve the skills and health of ex-offenders not only contributes to the re-offending target for Result 8, but may also help keep them off benefit, thereby improving progress in Result 1.[9]

Next, the Ministry of Health increasingly took responsibility for addressing the welfare dependence of sickness (disability) beneficiaries and thus for making progress toward the Result 1 target. The progress report to Cabinet described collective action and joint responsibility by social sector agencies to address deep-seated problems. This is precisely what the government intended from resetting the reducing welfare dependence target. The shifts were described in the end-year BPS Results progress report as follows:

> A programme of additional cross-sector work . . . that has a focus on beneficiaries with a health condition, increasing incentives and expecta-

tions for beneficiaries to become self-reliant, ensuring young people are in education and training rather than on a benefit, and other measures focused on reducing the number of people reliant on a benefit over the medium to long term.

The Ministry of Social Development is also now targeting resources to two key cohorts that have been identified as high drivers of future liability. Using Budget 2016 funding, the Ministry will trial new ways of working with ex-offenders and beneficiaries with a health condition or disability.[10]

The justice sector also became involved. The 2014 valuation of the benefit system highlighted ex-offenders as a cohort of clients that merited further analysis. The data showed the following:

- Many of the approximately 7,700 prisoners who leave prison every year have $30,000 higher average benefit system liability than the general population, and 80 percent have benefit periods of more than 12 months after release.

- Prisoners who serve multiple prison spells are more likely to receive a main benefit upon their release. Within twelve months after a first prison stay, up to 58 percent of released prisoners are receiving a main benefit. This increases to 64 percent for second prison terms and up to approximately 70 percent for released prisoners with more than two prison terms.

- Many ex-offenders have low employment-related skills, low levels of education, histories of mental health conditions and substance misuse, and a high likelihood of reoffending.

In response, the Ministry of Social Development, in conjunction with the Department of Corrections, implemented a Supporting Offenders into Employment trial to increase the employment prospects of released prisoners and reduce the likelihood of reoffending.

Using Data and Targets to Drive Innovation in Early Childhood Education (Result 2)

Of the cases for which the Results sparked innovation, what happened in response to the target to increase early childhood education stands out. As for many of the other BPS Results, the early childhood education targets were a powerful driver of action and innovation, challenging the Ministry of Education to identify things that were not working and do something different. As a starting point, the ministry set up an Early Learning Taskforce that Kararaina Calcott-Cribb would lead. She maintains that "having a target based on measurable data was a critical component for success—we could show everyone 'this is what it means.'"[11]

Early in its work with communities, the taskforce team discovered that the problem was not lack of funding but rather better use of existing funding and better connections between government agencies providing support. People from one agency were entering into domestic disputes and making sure children were protected; another agency was getting families out of substandard housing and rehousing them, and yet another agency was addressing health problems. Agencies needed to share information to discover who was getting what for what purpose, what the crossover was among government agencies (which seemed to be all targeting the same people), how effective expenditure was, and how it could be more effective by aligning the efforts of the agencies involved.

The typical way to align the work of government agencies in local areas was to set up interagency committees to share information and assign key workers to families, who then coordinated the interventions of multiple agencies.

But the taskforce team went to the front line to try something different. In the process, it borrowed and adapted a change methodology approach used the local District Health Board used. The model emphasized doing things quickly and results-based accountability. As Calcott-Cribb put it:

> People in the community needed to feel that you were genuine and something was happening. We made small hits, gathered data and used that data to inform how to go about an integrated approach. We tried new things, improved them if necessary and stopped them quickly if they weren't working. We weren't looking for big wins. Our approach was let's trial this, see what the value is, what the result is and see if we can build on that.

As Calcott-Cribb explained, the community didn't accept just anyone: "They accepted people who reached out to them and said, 'we haven't got a plan; we have come to help you, and we have come to listen. This is what the data is telling us. What do you think?'" The model adopted by the Early Learning Taskforce involved developing solutions with families and community groups. The taskforce would typically partner with a local organization and/or another agency, get a program started, and then pull other agencies into it. Where possible, the taskforce provided services where the families naturally congregated, targeted to areas of greatest need. The communities became part of the data conversations and started to feed the taskforce information about participation.

The taskforce team focused on parts of the community, down to specific streets, where participation was low. One person visited all the families in the targeted community—becoming the person they knew—and encouraged the families' participation. The team set up playgroups in targeted streets, went to festivals in the community to provide information on early learning, and went to church groups to explain what was being offered.

Calcott-Cribb described the impact of the taskforce's intervention on one family:

> We set up a playgroup on a suburban street in Huntly. This little boy sat on the steps of his home and watched. We knew this was a gang house. He didn't come anywhere near us until the third week—and then he came and just looked, didn't touch anything. The next week his father came. The family was wary of formal education, having been told, "no, you can't do that" in an earlier encounter. The father felt welcome in this situation and became involved in educational play with his son. A month later the father started to attend a club for families at Huntly school that encouraged healthy eating, growing all produce in their gardens, and giving kids food packages to take home. The family had begun to trust government services and re-engage with them.

Using this model, the taskforce team began to focus on the large Māori and Pasifika communities living in the southern suburbs of Auckland. The team members looked for a government agency that had connections and influence with Pasifika communities and entered into a partnership with the Ministry for Pacific Peoples to co-fund Pacific community projects. Together they identified the local rugby league club as a community group families regularly interacted with. They approached New Zealand Rugby League (the governing body of the rugby league clubs) about how they could help reach these families as part of "Family Violence: It's Not OK" and "Healthy Eating for Kids" campaigns. The original intention was that these groups could be important in promoting early learning to their patrons. The final arrangements exceeded expectations.

The New Zealand Rugby League helped local clubs set up early childhood learning facilities within its clubrooms, which are typically underused on weekday mornings. This was a win-win—the families of rugby league players received an early learning service that met their cultural needs and that was located in their own community of family and friends. New Zealand Rugby League was seen as making the club culture more family friendly and addressing the problem of family violence. The Ministry for Pacific Peoples improved outcomes for its people. The Ministry of Education moved closer to achieving its early learning participation target and strengthening foundation education while simultaneously saving $25,000 per child because it did not have to build childcare facilities. The success of one early childhood playgroup based in a rugby league clubroom led to other clubs adopting the idea. Successful innovation often spreads in this way, and the New Zealand Rugby League is now looking for other opportunities to connect high-needs clients with the services they require.[12]

Once the early learning services were established, other agencies rapidly became involved. The Accident Compensation Commission was eager to reduce injuries, working with the league clubs to reduce abusive behavior on the sidelines and reduce alcohol consumption. The Health Promotion Agency was seeking a safer environment for the game (padded goalposts for example) along with healthier eating options in league clubs. The police saw the opportunity to promote a family-friendly environment in the league clubs that fostered respectful relationships and potentially reduced violent crime. Calcott-Cribb invited them all to "get on the same bus" rather than each to independently strive to achieve its own outcomes. The league club appointed a family liaison person (funded by the government agencies) to be the point of contact for families. The agencies met regularly with the club's liaison person so that everyone knew what was happening.

Interagency work began to infuse everything the taskforce team did. ECE centers took food packs to families at risk of falling out of the system again to keep them connected and engaged. Health services were added to the playgroups where parents were taught to identify and address health issues such as head lice and skin infections. Mothers involved in playgroups started to learn skills needed for workforce participation, such as computer skills, and some went on to become teacher aides or trainee teachers in early childhood education centers.

The taskforce team also contacted established early childhood education providers to help them achieve the target. It approached a large private sector provider, initially to offer spaces for some of the children in families they were working with and then later to establish a center in one of the poorest areas of South Auckland, offering to train the staff in how to work in these communities and how to operate in a low-fees environment. The taskforce offered free pickups and food for targeted local families using the services.

Other local providers contracted to increase ECE participation were also innovative. One example is an initiative in South Auckland that the Fountain of Knowledge Community Trust established. Rather than holding community meetings to extol the benefits of early learning, this community trust sent a SMART Bus into local shopping malls to demonstrate the benefits. The SMART Bus set up a learning environment typical of early learning centers, with colorful posters, play equipment, musical instruments, books, and the like. Children stopped to play, their parents could see them enjoying learning, and the trained educator could describe the learning occurring and encourage the parents to enroll their children in a local early childhood service.

The approach used by the Early Learning Taskforce is illustrative of how the BPS Results program was delivered for many of the Results and included: government agencies combining their efforts, leveraging the resources of non-governmental organizations, and designing services to meet the needs of local families and communities.

Co-design of Rheumatic Fever Interventions (Result 3)

Initial failure to make progress toward the rheumatic fever target caused consternation in the Ministry of Health, and managers started to ask hard questions about the approach the program team had taken. As a result, more emphasis was put on targeting Pasifika families in South Auckland, both through the Healthy Homes initiative and programs to increase awareness in this community. A critical part of raising awareness was defining problems and outcomes from the family's perspective rather than from an institutional or central perspective. As the program coordinator (Dr. Pickin) explained it, "once we buy into the family's view of the world, we focus on what we share rather than where we differ."[13]

Refocusing on the ground-level perspectives of the issues led to an innovation whereby young people were inspired to inform other young people about the risk of rheumatic fever. A local youth theater group worked with the rheumatic fever team to develop a range of storylines to deliver rheumatic fever prevention messages through youth-appropriate language and scenes, in an element of the program that became known as "Dramatic Fever in Schools." These themes and storylines were developed into a play that circulated in secondary schools and local youth centers. The same group of young people involved in the Dramatic Fever in Schools program went on to use music and cultural festivals to promote awareness of the disease. These were talented young people, and the movement went viral—boosted when one of them went on to win the *New Zealand's Got Talent* reality television show.

In addition, students from four secondary schools and two community youth groups were involved with the Rheumatic Fever Film Project. Again, there was a partnership approach—the Ministry of Pacific Peoples led the project in partnership with the Ministry of Health. The project supported schools to design, script, and make films aimed at raising rheumatic fever awareness among 13- to 19-year-old Māori and Pacific youth living in areas with high rates of rheumatic fever. Pauline Winter from the Ministry for Pacific Peoples explained, "We know that kids listen to kids and youth listen to youth, so that's one of the magic ingredients that makes this project such a success. It's really handing over control to young people."[14] The students involved also were able to claim National Certificate of Educational Achievement credits for their films, contributing to the achievement of the Result 5 target.

This work played a role in the achievement of the Result target by raising awareness of rheumatic fever and the link with sore throats among young
people and the communities most at risk of the disease. By working from the
family's perspective rather than from an institutional or central perspective,
the rheumatic fever awareness program shifted from relying on experts and
celebrities in earlier programs to relying more on peers to raise awareness and
stimulate local action.

Accelerating Innovation for Business Interactions with Government (Result 9)

At the start of the program, for Result 9, the hope of finding "new and different ways to deliver better results for businesses" lay in the establishment of the
New Zealand Business Number (NZBN). The NZBN was intended as a single
identifier that would become the only one that businesses need to interact with
a range of government agencies. This was considered a crucial enabler to make
it easier for businesses to interact with government. According to Linda Oliver,
a team leader for Result 9, the chief difference of bringing the NZBN into the
Result 9 program was focus.[15] It provided a single point of accountability with
the agency that took the responsibility for developing and implementing it on
behalf of all contributing agencies and motivated the minister and program
leads to drive it through.

However, the NZBN was also surprisingly difficult to achieve—there had
been at least three attempts to develop a single identifier for businesses before
the introduction of Result 9. Therefore, although a single identifier lay at the
heart of the program, participating agencies recognized that it would take several years for sufficient uptake of the Business Number to realize its full benefit.
In an effort to get quick wins, the Better for Business program, as Result 9
became known, spawned several innovations with more immediate impact.
These included streamlining and simplifying the intellectual property business
processes and moving to a 100 percent online business model (a world first for
an IP office); managing tax affairs online, with digital returns now exceeding
paper based; and a one-stop shop for small business information and advice.[16]
This approach allowed agencies to contribute to the program on an ongoing
basis, mobilizing them and gaining their buy-in.

The innovation that sparked the most widespread interest in Result 9 was
the R9 Accelerator, a facilitated process that enables the private sector to work
with government on challenges that affect business. Oliver describes the R9
Accelerator as "a fantastic story, because it actually changed the way we thought
about things, a lot. It asked the question—'so how do we work with businesses
to make things different?' " The accelerator was itself an innovation that was intended to speed up other innovations in the public sector. Accelerators are used

globally by private sector entrepreneurs to develop an idea from a concept to a solution ready for investment and development. Ideas that are worth pursuing, as well as those that are not, can be identified quickly through the accelerator process. In the New Zealand public sector, a government agency called Creative New Zealand developed the accelerator process.

Earlier in the program, the Result 9 team had surveyed businesses to identify "pain points" in their dealings with government. The accelerator process was brought to bear on these pain points, bringing together teams composed of people from government agencies looking for a solution and private sector entrepreneurs who were capable of providing one. The accelerator creates a hot-house environment where each team "co-designs" a solution for fourteen weeks, after which the entrepreneurs pitch the solutions to potential investors, usually government agencies. Those teams that attract funding interest then test the ideas in a six- to eight-week due diligence phase. If the innovation still stands scrutiny, the final phase is negotiation with the investors to bring the idea into production.

The first round of the R9 Accelerator had promise but didn't work particularly well. As Oliver put it:

> We learned that you just can't take an innovative process that is designed for one thing and just apply it to government. There are new roles, such as networking and brokering, that we need in government to do this well. We put people in the role of "hustlers"—people who could build the community around the outcomes.

With the new roles in place, two further rounds of the accelerator began delivering successful innovation. As the process was repeated, those involved learned more about what worked, and successive rounds had increasing success in finding solutions that could be sold, some as successful exports. Small-scale, highly entrepreneurial businesses began solving problems for government and growing successful innovation to scale while also providing the associated employment benefits. This different approach to identifying and buying innovative solutions through working with third parties began to produce solutions to problems that had proven insoluble using standard government processes.

The successes, and the process, were actively and publicly communicated, with dozens of people (including Cabinet ministers) invited to visit the accelerator workspace, and to listen to the pitches entrepreneurs made. Some innovations produced by the accelerator process that made it easier for businesses to interact with government included making simplified building consent processes available online, with the ability to track progress; using government data to provide location-based information (maps, etc.) to retail and hospitality businesses; and simplifying and improving the process for businesses and employees applying for an essential skills visa.

While the R9 Accelerator is no longer operating, the processes it developed are being applied to other parts of government. For many, the most important legacy of the Result 9 program is the way government agencies think about customers of government. Oliver, now working at the Inland Revenue Department, describes the agency as being "all about the customer." This is a big shift in five years. Other legacies include the language and culture of experimentation, for example, regular use of processes such as "dragon's den." The process has also been picked up by Creative HQ, a nongovernmental organization successfully running an accelerator without government funding.

In Oliver's words:

> It changed the way we worked; more than that, it basically changed the way we think about government. The conversations are different. We are more innovative. We developed new capabilities, and we started believing we can do things across agency, without it being too scary. We came to believe we do things in New Zealand that nobody else does.

Applying Design Methodology to Transactions with Government (Result 10)

The "pain points" research mentioned briefly above was also an example of innovation from early in the Result 10 program, intended to provide an evidence base for doing things differently. This research recognized the need to talk to the customers—to know what they thought and to hear their voices. Public servants are also consumers of public services and can bring some of the customer experience, but Richard Foy (delegated by the chief executive of the Department of Internal Affairs to be responsible for establishing and leading the Result 10 program) saw public servants as "insider traders" in this context.[17] They have a different perspective, tainted by their understanding of how government works. Foy's view was that many customers were victimized by a government that had never heard their voices. He set about collecting their stories, using written, oral, and even visual collection methods.

From interviews with users of public services, researchers developed personas representing customer segments. The personas were used in role play, with public servants taking on a persona in workshop discussions with public service leaders and ministers. The personas were brought to life by these "actors," projected as real people, discussing their experience in accessing and using public services. People at the workshops began to understand the pain of their customers, perhaps for the first time.

Armed with the pain point research, the Result 10 governance group developed the *Result 10 Blueprint* and sent it to the Cabinet for consideration. This document articulated a shared vision for government digital services, where they are designed with the customer at the center and integrated around life events or stages rather than organized around agency boundaries. The shared vision expressed three aspects of the future state:

The customer vision: Digital by Choice

The service vision: Digital by Design

The system vision: Digital by Default[18]

New ways of doing things among Result 10 agencies also involved the Service Innovation Lab. The lab applied a design methodology to service delivery issues across government. Design methodology is an innovative and customer-centered approach to understand a problem and develop multiple solutions. The lab used design professionals from the Department of Internal Affairs and employees loaned from other agencies to seed a range of initiatives, particularly to support integrated services.

Programs began to emerge that demonstrated the benefits of service integration based on sharing data. Online service integration based around a life event, such as the birth of a child (see box 10-1 on SmartStart) or the death of an elderly person became powerful examples of what could be achieved.

Another standout innovation was the online issuing of passports. This service rapidly grew in popularity, largely owing to increasingly rapid turnaround, which was frequently as short as one business day. The new passports were electronic and allowed passport holders to use the "SmartGate" identification service to speed up their passage through immigration. An increasing volume of online transactions with the departments for Inland Revenue, Social Development, and Conservation, driven by customers finding it easier to transact online, was evidence of good progress.

But for all their success, the interagency projects in Result 10 still felt like wading through treacle for those involved. SmartStart took more than two years of hard work to introduce, with most of that time spent in getting agreements between agencies and seeking funding. The difficulty facing service integration was described in the 2014 end-year progress report to Cabinet:

Achieving service integration across government is challenging, and progress is slow. For example, integrating the IRD number application and the immigration visa process would streamline processes for new immigrants. But even with agreement from participating agencies, and for something relatively simple, the work needs to progress through

BOX 10-1. SmartStart

One of the most successful initiatives arising from Result 10 and the ICT Functional Lead programs was SmartStart, an online tool that aims to help babies get off to the best start by having step-by-step information and help all in one place. The digital identity for children are established early to use throughout their lives.

The thinking behind SmartStart is provided in the case study pages of the Better Public Services Results website:

> Life is about events, not agencies. When people interact with government, they do so to have a personal need met.
>
> New Zealanders told us that they wanted to do less running around between government departments and that they find it frustrating to have to provide the same information to many agencies.
>
> We listened.
>
> SmartStart enables new parents to update their benefit with MSD, request an IRD number for their baby, and update their Working for Families application, all from the birth registration process.
>
> This is saving parents time and money so they can concentrate on their new family member.

Source: The SmartStart case study can be found at: www.publicservice.govt.nz/resources /bps-result10-cs3/.

agency governance groups and be integrated into existing agency transformation plans. Consequently, it is expected to take at least five years from business case development to full implementation.[19]

At this rate, introducing customer-centric integrated services clustered around the support for other life events would proceed at a glacial pace. There were increasing calls from ministers and others working on state sector reform to make it easier to integrate government services, especially if the intention was to make citizen-facing integrated service delivery part of the way government operated on a regular basis. When this book went to press, work on improving service integration in New Zealand continued to be a focus for government.

Enabling Public Entrepreneurship

What was it about the Results program that caused these exceptional public servants to flourish as entrepreneurs? While an entrepreneurial spirit is undoubtedly an intrinsic characteristic of some individuals, the boundaries of bureaucracy frequently act to constrain or crush this spirit. Claudine Kearney and colleagues describe the context of public entrepreneurship as the systems and process "that exist within public sector organisations that result in innovative activities."[20] Public entrepreneurship includes "legitimating mechanisms" that provide time and space in contexts that are not otherwise conducive to new ways of working. The Results program was designed to allow for this, with the senior officials and ministers involved acting as guardian angels—sponsors of the work who were able to "navigate the political and organizational hurdles" that would otherwise make innovation an impossibility. These were people who valued innovation, flexibility, and new thinking and who have invaluable awareness of contextual factors.[21]

David Osborne and Ted Gaebler argue that entrepreneurs flourish when autonomy is linked to extrinsic rewards.[22] But the experiences of the entrepreneurs above suggest something a little more complex is occurring. Autonomy is possible when the goals are clear, and the targets undoubtedly provided this clarity. But the effort and persistence of public servants to achieve the Results cannot be explained through extrinsic rewards. Instead, public servants felt a sense of commitment to make a difference; were encouraged to experiment and learn; and felt accountable to government, their peers and, most of all, to New Zealanders for what they achieved. It is perhaps the most important lesson of the Results program that program design should consider how to build and sustain commitment to achieving the goal.

11

Emic and Etic Perspectives

We can say with confidence that the Results program was associated with real performance improvement in each of the ten Results and that these performance improvements clearly exceed any gaming or distortionary effects. The program also provides an example of process success in that it enabled public entrepreneurs to overcome the status quo to try new things that made a difference. However, explaining those improvements is considerably more difficult. The remainder of this book is dedicating to doing so.

As with any complex social problem, the outcomes produced over the course of the program may have been due to innumerable factors. It is certainly difficult, and perhaps impossible, to definitively attribute the improvements to the management approach used. In all social or organizational changes, many influences act at the same time. Any given effect can have multiple possible explanations. The best we can hope for in regard to explaining performance improvements and challenges is to triangulate evidence from a multitude of sources. We are in no way implying that this produces definitive answers. Instead, we draw on a variety of perspectives and methods to provide more clarity for the theoretical underpinning of the program than would be possible any one imperfect method on its own.

More specifically, we use an emic (insider)/etic (outsider) approach to mixed-methods evaluation. Emic/etic is a construct from social science. The emic perspective strives to describe a particular social phenomenon in the terms of those involved, whereas the etic perspective attempts to describe a social phenomenon in a comparative sense, in terms of how it is the same as or different from what has happened elsewhere or in the past.[1] The separate authors each occupy one of these perspectives simply by the nature of our separate experiences, seeking together to provide a complementary understanding of what happened.[2]

The second author, Ross Boyd, provides the emic perspective, having been a central figure in the Results program from its early conception and design through its implementation and refresh in 2017. His contribution is in terms of making sense of his experience, describing the program as it was understood by him and his peers and colleagues. Rodney Scott, the first author, provides the etic perspective—automatically occupying a more critical role as the director of the Public Service Research program, responsible for evaluating public service reforms.

Rodney initially worked with Eugene Bardach, Emeritus Professor of Public Policy at the University of California, Berkeley, to conduct an etic evaluation of the program.[3] This research concluded that the program was successful in achieving performance improvements in the public sector and sought to explain why. The conventional approach to understanding the dynamics of interagency working indicated that successes and failures can best be understood in terms of transaction costs. Therefore, the Results program must have been successful because it reduced transaction costs and its most successful features were those that most reduced transaction costs.

However, the emic perspective provided by Ross and the later evaluations described below were not consistent with this. Those who worked in the Results program reported that progress wasn't easy and that the successes were incredibly hard won. This led us to consider not why the features of the Results program made progress easier but instead how the program was able to be successful despite all those involved claiming that it was difficult.

The initial evaluation proved to be inadequate for explaining the emic perspective, and three further evaluations were subsequently conducted and combined with the original evaluation into a four-part mixed-methods study.[4] In this respect, we are indebted to Professor Jennifer Greene at the University of Illinois. Professor Greene has been one of the leading theorists and practitioners in the use of mixed methods to generate insights from social studies.[5] Through correspondence over several months, Professor Greene helped us design some way of understanding which factors of the Results program contributed to its success.

The first evaluation, the etic study with Professor Eugene Bardach mentioned above, was a comparative study that looked at the differences between each of the ten Results.[6] We assumed that the different design settings, particularly regarding management and governance arrangements, were independent variables and that the progress of each Result over time was a dependent variable. There were twelve significant differences in how public servants organized to achieve each of the ten Results, and five of these were correlated with greater progress. The limitation of this study was that it only detected factors that differ between the ten Results. It could not draw findings on the importance of the many areas in which the ten Results were alike, and it ignored the learning that occurred across the program (as certain practices were disseminated and adopted by others). Furthermore, it relied on source documents authored by public servants involved in the program and therefore reflects their unavoidable selection bias.

The second evaluation assessed the Results program against a published guide for collaborative best practice using process measures. The FSG consulting group had developed a framework based on its observation of horizontal management called "Collective Impact" and subsequently published a guide for developmental, formative, and summative evaluation. Collective Impact was originally designed for use in a cross-sector context, to explore collaboration between government, corporate, and community sectors. We adapted the evaluation framework for use in a governmental interagency setting with help from the original authors.[7] Collective Impact is a normative framework in that it describes what *should* happen; therefore, the validity of this evaluation is contingent on Collective Impact being the one and only best way to organize.

The third evaluation used a case study method to explore individual success stories. We examined eighty-nine case studies proposed by public servants as the best examples of successful innovations in the Results program. For each case study, we analyzed the different management or design features the public servants had identified as contributing to the enabling environment for the innovations. This evaluation not only provided a more granular analysis of the program but also included selection bias, as the vignettes had been submitted by public servants involved in the program.

The fourth evaluation observed and explored the behavior of public servants in responding to the presence of performance management. This included a literature search of government documents and media reporting relating to the Results program and particularly accounts of how behavior had changed over time (from the introduction of the program).

Each of the four evaluations provides a different perspective on the program: descriptive and positive versus normative; introspection versus observation; qualitative versus quantitative; internal (public servant) perspectives versus external (media) perspectives; comparisons within the program versus over time; and developmental versus formative versus summative inquiry. Simply stated, we cannot be sure we are accurately describing why the Results program worked, but we have looked at it from as many angles as we could imagine. This diversity of perspectives and analytical reference is generally considered desirable in public administration research because it provides a more complete view and therefore more robust explanations.[8]

In combining these four evaluations, we used mixed methods for two purposes: triangulation and complementarity. Triangulation seeks to corroborate findings from different methods to overcome the limitations of each of the preceding evaluations in order to improve the validity of inferences about constructs and the strength of the justification for inquiry findings. The findings from the four evaluations were compared to look for features that more than one evaluation consistently supported or opposed.[9] Triangulation is used to compare multiple descriptions of the same phenomenon. Therefore, triangulation is only useful when that phenomenon is described in multiple evaluations and any features identified in only one evaluation method are ignored. Some of these features identified in single evaluations may represent real success factors in the Results program that may be important in trying to replicate the approach elsewhere. Triangulation is therefore likely to be more reliable than the individual evaluations and produce less spurious associations, but the findings that can be corroborated from multiple evaluations are likely to be less complete and omit several real associations. The four evaluations included a total of forty-five findings; of these, ten were supported by more than one evaluation (see table 11-1).

Complementarity seeks to elaborate or illustrate findings from one method using findings from another method or to develop a more comprehensive understanding of the constructs being studied.[10] The remaining chapters draw on the detailed findings from the evaluations to draw inferences about what worked and why. In particular, the features of success identified through the triangulation and complementarity of the four evaluations give structure to the insights in part 4 of this book.

Each evaluation used publicly available official reporting and may therefore have missed other important sources of information. Public servants often have insights into what works and what does not work that tend not to be written down. Managerial "craft" is often informal and sometimes subversive, at least in working *around* formal rules to achieve the intended goal. After publishing findings from these formal evaluations in 2016 and 2017, in 2018, we returned to those who had worked within the Results program—practitioners credited by their peers as having "made it work." Through a series of interviews, we tested the conclusions of the early evaluations. While our interviewees largely concurred with the formal findings, they embellished and augmented these descriptions with anecdotes and reflections that furnish the other chapters of this book.

The final source from which we draw is our own experience. In this book, we cannot claim to be neutral, dispassionate, or objective sources. The authors have, among them, the experience of several decades working as public servants, designing and implementing public management reforms. Ross Boyd worked on the Results program from the beginning in 2011 (as well as being involved in preceding policy work from 2007). He was a participant in many of the discussions that formed, implemented, and monitored the program. He

TABLE 11-1. Key Findings of Previous Evaluations

	COMPARATIVE (Scott and Boyd 2015)	NORMATIVE (Scott and Boyd 2016a)	VIGNETTES (Scott and Boyd 2016b)	TARGET (Scott and Boyd 2016c)
Selecting problems				
Selecting a small number of problems	n.a.	strong	n.a.	strong
Building on existing relationships	strong	n.a.	n.a.	strong
Selecting targets and measures				
Public commitment and transparent reporting	n.a.	strong	n.a.	strong
Specifying Results at an impact level	weak	n.a.	n.a.	strong
Alignment between Results and targets	weak	n.a.	n.a.	weak
Implementing collaborative arrangements				
Maximum of three agencies	strong	n.a.	strong	strong
Cascading levels of governance	strong	strong	n.a.	n.a.
Aligned accountability systems	strong	n.a.	n.a.	strong
Learning and adapting				
Fast feedback and learning	weak	strong	strong	weak
Sharing administrative data	n.a.	strong	strong	n.a.

Note: Strong = this feature was strongly supported as contributing to the success of the BPS Results approach. Weak = this feature was weakly supported as contributing to the BPS Results approach. n.a. = not applicable, this feature was not described in this evaluation.

coordinated the community of practice that shared ideas and insights about what was working and not working (see appendix 5). This book is an analytical work but also a reflective work from a long-serving practitioner.

This book therefore draws its conclusions from a variety of sources; formal evaluations, drawn together in a deliberate way through mixed-methods techniques of triangulation and complementarity; interviews with practitioners, who generously shared their stories and reflections; and the lived experience of the authors. Though drawing such inferences can never be precise or conclusive, we feel reasonably confident in asserting that the factors we describe contributed to the success of the program, especially given that they are consistent with both the emic and etic perspective. They explain how collaboration was successful even when it felt hard and why innovation and effort remained high despite the setbacks. This led to a theory that the Results program could be understood as generating and sustaining goal commitment among the public servants involved, thereby creating the conditions for public entrepreneurship.[11] The remainder of this book is dedicated to exploring this theory. Furthermore, our intention is to outline some lessons here that other jurisdictions can take and apply to solve some of the most challenging problems they face, just as we drew on the experiences of other jurisdictions outlined in chapter 3.

PART IV

GOAL COMMITMENT

Targets can be thought of as a mechanism for compelling public servants to improve performance. They encourage hard work, clarify where effort should be focused, and inspire problem solving. We call this effect "goal commitment." Goal commitment is a commonly used construct in performance management literature. It is formally defined as "a volitional psychological bond reflecting dedication to, and responsibility for, a particular target."[1] This means that people feel committed to strive to succeed, even if obstacles are encountered along the way. It has been studied extensively in experimental conditions and in applied contexts.[2] Like almost all areas of behavioral literature, the results vary. However, three general effects have been observed as explanations for what goal commitment actually does. When people are committed to achieving a goal:

1. They exert greater effort toward achieving that goal;

2. They demonstrate greater persistence in working toward that goal;[3] and

3. They create new solutions that help them get there.[4]

However, in goal commitment literature, the effect is usually applied to individuals completing discrete tasks. Because interagency working involves the *problem of many hands* where no individual can be held solely responsible for achieving the goal, interagency working literature has rarely engaged with goal commitment. Interagency working literature instead focuses on making collaboration easier by "reducing complexity and transaction costs."[5] It is not concerned with explaining how to sustain effort when collaboration is hard.

Mention of commitment more generally in interagency working literature is typically applied by different authors in slightly different ways. Ann Marie Thomson and James Perry talk about "commitments," the promises that public servants make to each other (for example, the "commitment to future action."[6] Other authors, such as Mark Imperial, also emphasize the importance of honoring agreements.[7] This sense of "commitments" as promises differs from the sense of being committed to achieve a goal. Indeed, the parliamentary system of government in New Zealand meant that public servants were limited in the explicit commitments that they could make to each other, as individual Ministers could subsequently overrule any agreements made by the public servants under them. Instead, they could only continually renegotiate provisional agreements and adapt to changing circumstances. That is, they stood on shifting sands, and relied on their commitment to achieve the goal to overcome their inability to make binding commitments to each other.

Other authors describe the importance of commitment to collaborative processes. Chris Ansell and Alison Gash found that collaboration tends to be more successful and sustainable if participating parties feel obliged to adhere to the agreed governance mechanisms. As noted in Part 1, before the Results program, New Zealand had a "sectoral" approach to interagency working. This involved commitment to collaborative governance mechanisms, but lacked the focus on achieving a goal.

In terms of being committed to each other, researchers studying interagency working frequently comment on the importance of trusted relationships.[8] Sometimes public servants feel committed to working together because they don't want to let each other down. It seems from this earlier research that relationships can sustain interagency working, but relationships come and go. Some of the problems that the New Zealand government wanted to solve involved agencies with no prior history of working together or with a history that included conflict or competition between agencies. Relationships matter, but governments can't rely on relationships when designing their programs. The idea of goal commitment as described in this book refers to a means to sustain effort and entrepreneurship across a five-year period, despite the many obstacles (which sometimes included the other public servants involved).

Goal commitment wasn't a phrase used by New Zealand public servants in researching this book. However, it is certainly consistent with the way they described their experience. The three effects of goal commitment identified above were certainly evident in the program. Public servants exerted great effort toward achieving the targets, investing their own energy in improving the lives of New Zealanders. A Deputy State Services Commissioner expressed a sense that the passion to achieve the goals sustained the program despite the obstacles that public servants faced:

> All of the Results teams met significant opposition to breaking from previously established approaches to governance, decision-making, funding, partnerships and delivery . . . The passion of the leaders and teams for improving the lives of New Zealanders was essential in sustaining their efforts to overcome resistance to working differently.[9]

Their persistence was also obvious, sustaining their efforts over five years. At the time of the 2017 refresh, the enthusiasm for the program was at high as it ever had been. Ministers remained engaged, and continually asked for more information about what was going on, and what they could do to help things improve more rapidly. Even aside from the 2017 announcement to renew the program for another five years, few reforms in the New Zealand public service are sustained for this length of time. New Zealand's Managing for Outcomes reforms lasted less than three years.

The innovations of the program described in the previous chapter, and the further innovations used as case studies in the following chapters are evidence of the constant invention and trialing of new solutions. The instances of public entrepreneurship were the by-product of clear goals, feedback and measurement systems, and discretion on how to reach the targets. Many of the novel solutions didn't work, or weren't enough on their own, and public servants had to try and try again. For example, the incidence of rheumatic fever was seen first as a detection problem, to be solved with better screening; then as an awareness problem, to be solved with novel school-based education programs; and finally as a housing problem, to be solved with better risk assessment and coordination with social housing providers.

This retrospective analysis is intended to fill the gap left for many policy experiments, which are frequently abandoned before their efficacy can be fully evaluated and understood. The Results program was one of the most significant changes in how New Zealand agencies are organized to address problems that span agencies boundaries, and how public services are delivered, in several decades.[10] It seems important to at least try and draw some lessons from it that policymakers and practitioners may apply to their work in addressing cross-cutting problems in other jurisdictions. The details of how the Results program supported goal commitment and why this matters are organized in the following chapters into a framework of three general antecedents of goal commitment: expectancy, instrumentality, and valence. These three antecedents each encompass more detailed factors to be considered when designing an interagency performance target program that builds and sustains goal commitment.

Expectancy in Goal Commitment

Most goal commitment literature is based upon "expectancy theory," which refers to the influence of desirability of expected outcome on individual behavior.[1] Generally, this is expressed as a product of the expectation of achieving the goal, and the attractiveness (rewards or sanctions) associated with goal attainment.[2] At first glance, this seems fairly straightforward and in an experimental context, it is. In the applied context of the Results program, we refer to this first element as "the likelihood of program completion." However, we also broaden this out to include aspects of goal selection such as distribution of attention, level of difficulty, and alignment between Results and targets. We have selected these as other factors that are likely to be important, particularly when dealing with a multiyear government program that spans many agencies.

Keeping It Simple

Although Part 1 outlined a confluence of several conditions that made a target approach appropriate for solving some of New Zealand's hardest problems, the approach remains limited by many of the challenges common to any target approach. Chief among these is that target approaches are most effective when used sparingly; problems selected should be few rather than many, and they should be defined narrowly rather than broadly. New Zealand was able to make progress on ten important problems in part because it focused its attention on only ten and defined them at a scale that was manageable.

In a frequently cited 1956 psychology paper "The Magical Number Seven, Plus or Minus Two: Some Limits on Our Capacity for Processing Information," Princeton researcher George Miller notes that the memory span of the average adult is seven items[3] (memory span being the longest list of items that a person can repeat back in correct order on 50 percent of trials immediately after presentation). Because those involved in the Results program were exposed to the list of Result priorities more than once, the New Zealand government was able to select a few additional items to make a round ten problems, supported by fourteen targets. This necessarily involved excluding some problems that might otherwise have been considered equally important, such as obesity, homelessness, social mobility, the road toll, or water quality in lakes and rivers. Omitting any problem risks political attack from those for whom that problem is top priority.

With only ten of the most important government priorities being selected, it was possible to conceive of the Results program as a single program in which each simultaneous experiment could be remembered and discussed by ministers and public servants. Ten is not a magic number, but it might be close. Too many more problems, at some undetermined number higher than ten, would have become impossible to remember. The only way to keep track of hundreds or even tens of problems would be with the kind of spreadsheet the government loves but that no one ever reads, especially not the public. These conditions mean that if one or two targets started to waver off track, they could be allowed to fail quietly because the relative importance of each target is minimized. Losses in one problem can be offset by gains in another. Eventually, no single problem seems quite so urgent or so critical.

Ministers and senior public servants can only direct their attention to a finite number of items. Part of the success of the Results program was that, with only ten problems, each continued to be important. None can be allowed to fail because each represents a significant portion of the whole program. The Results program required an allocation of something equally as scarce as resources: the attention and affective commitment of senior leaders. Experimental studies on goal commitment frequently assume the individual involved is only working on one task. Public servants, however, face countless competing priorities and are to varying degrees accountable for all of them. To encourage commitment to some goals, it is necessary to concentrate attention on these in contrast to other goals.

This may seem like a simplistic factor to identify as part of the expectancy of goal completion, but it has not been effectively deployed in examples from other jurisdictions, often due to the political risk of excluding some problems. Even when other jurisdictions have committed to only a few priorities, the parallel instinct is to define each priority very broadly. For example, the UK Blair government had hundreds of targets in its target approach, and the United Nations Sustainable Development Goals are defined so broadly that any possible development action could be mapped to at least one of them (for example,

"Good health and well-being").[4] Similarly, New Zealand's Business Growth Agenda had 84 priorities when first launched in 2012.

Before the Results program in 2008, the New Zealand government priorities, known as "development goals" had been "economic development," "families young and old," and "national identity." Public servants knew their project had a greater chance of success and access to resources if it aligned to one of these priorities. Soon every business-facing activity was part of "economic development," any social project was part of "families young and old," and anything left fell under "national identity." Shoehorning projects into the priorities became a well-known Wellington pastime.

Such broad priorities are no longer priorities; they are themes that group and divide the entirety of what government does. They don't provide any sense of what is important or where to start. In contrast, the mostly narrowly defined targets of the Results program made use of what systems scientist Donella Meadows described as "leverage points"—parts of the system in which making a small change could have a disproportionately large effect on the rest of the system.[5]

The target in Result 3 to reduce the incidence of rheumatic fever provides the clearest example of a narrow target enabling wide-reaching positive effects. The program team for the rheumatic fever Result had spent some time defining the problem from the perspective of those affected before committing to any solutions. The team was determined not to be biased by the "favorite solutions" of multiple public sector experts. It realized the current, internationally accepted approach (in which clinicians focused on finding solutions to the more serious condition—rheumatic heart disease) wasn't going to work; the nature of interventions had to change. Because rheumatic fever is associated with poverty, crowded housing conditions, and a lack of awareness of the disease, it cannot be solved purely as a health problem. To significantly reduce the incidence of rheumatic fever, these other broad problems must be addressed. The program team adopted a slogan for their new approach: Stop it (address the housing issues); Treat it (improve access to clinical care); Own it (engage the local organizations and communities to make progress sustainable).

It became increasingly apparent as the program matured that the impact of the rheumatic fever target would not be confined to a reduction in this disease, making the target a leverage point for solving other issues. The children of families in damp, overcrowded houses also suffered from respiratory conditions and skin infections. Both the health and the housing interventions were addressing a range of other conditions related to poor housing and family poverty. This was a health target rather than a poverty target, but addressing the conditions related to family poverty had the effect of a target to reduce poverty.

In many ways, this was the most successful Result, even though the target did not get met. Something more important had been achieved. How and why the target worked as a leverage point is one of the most compelling insights from the BPS Results program. The effectiveness of setting narrow targets to address far wider outcomes was considered by ministers for the refresh of the Results program going into 2017. As the program leader, Dr Pickin, puts it, "We didn't hit the target, but we did shift the paradigm, not only in New Zealand but worldwide. For example, Australia has recently established a rheumatic fever program that, for the first time, addresses the root causes of the disease."[6] Australia is also leading international collaboration on the issue and starting to change the international discourse. Dr Pickin puts this change down to the impact of the New Zealand program.

Part of the reason that the Results program was able to capture the interest of New Zealanders was that it was simple. Not only were there only ten Results, simple line graphs, and personal stories, but also the goals themselves were easy to understand. Sometimes this meant selecting simple goals ahead of other technically superior alternatives. "Reduce the crime rate" is a simple statement that is relevant and important to every New Zealander. By contrast, when the Obama administration introduced its "Cross-Agency Priority Goals" in the United States, one was to "expand the use of high-quality, high-value strategic sourcing solutions in order to improve the government's buying power and reduce contract duplication." More efficient sourcing is undoubtedly a worthwhile goal, but it doesn't directly affect the lives of citizens. It is unlikely to have the same emotive effect as the mission to reduce crime. It is too long to be memorable and filled with jargon that many people would not understand.

Technical experts sometimes struggle with making these trade-offs. Result 1 was originally framed as "reducing long-term welfare dependency," which was criticized as describing people who were unemployed in pejorative terms. The intention wasn't to get people off welfare but instead to help people make long-term changes to the trajectories of their lives. Government subsequently recognized that the original framing of the Result 1 wasn't quite right, but the revised Result missed on another count—it was too complicated. The language that was chosen to describe lifelong impact was "accumulated actuarial release," a concept barely comprehensible even to most policy analysts. It was also utterly dry and without emotional power. Results needed to motivate public servants, and motivate the public, which meant that they would need to be understandable and simple. The Scrabble-winning words would need to be kept out of it. For the most part, the program did settle on goals that were phrased simply and in plain English, balancing (imperfectly) the trade-offs between being easily understood and being technically precise.

Choosing only a few priorities, defining them narrowly, and picking only a few targets isn't a panacea. But it does allow the world to be simplified into smaller, more manageable chunks. It focuses effort and provides a place to start. In part, New Zealand was able to make progress because it chose only a few problems that weren't too broad, and these were articulated as simply as possible.

The Edge of Possible

A significant aspect of expectancy is the perceived likelihood of goal attainment and program completion, which indicates that the level of difficulty at which targets are set will have a significant impact on goal commitment. It's at this point that expectancy overlaps with valence (discussed later). Goal commitment tends to rise as a goal becomes more difficult, only to rapidly fall when the goal is seen as impossible. Goals are thought to be more motivating when the efforts of the individual will determine whether the goal is achieved or not; this suggests targets work best when they are still up for grabs until the last possible moment.[7] The key was to set goals at the right level of difficulty so that they would receive the greatest increase in goal commitment, driving urgency and resulting in sustained effort and entrepreneurship.

The Results program might not have perfectly set targets at the right level. Three were too easy and were revised. One was too hard. Even the program coordinator isn't quite sure how many were ultimately achieved, in a context in which "achievement" became a mix of mathematics and common sense. It didn't make sense to continue with targets that had only fallen slightly short of an artificial mark set five years earlier when most of the gains had been made. In these cases, the Result was achieved even if the target wasn't, and ministers determined that it was time to "mainstream" the work and move on to other priorities. The Results program was particularly challenging in terms of whether and when to revise the targets once they were set. Ultimately, New Zealand was rewarded for aiming high, accepting the risk of failure, and learning how to celebrate progress while remaining committed to the final goal. Such an approach might not be perfectly replicable with a more hostile or adversarial media or with a more risk-averse government.

Politicians and public servants typically like to set safe targets that are easily achieved, especially because political reporting in the media tends to follow a negativity bias. Politicians tend to be punished in the media for not meeting targets more than they are rewarded for meeting them. However, for targets to be most effective in changing outcomes, they need to carry the risk of failure. If a target is so low that it can't fail to be reached, then it doesn't alter behavior or create the urgency that would spur public servants to be innovative and try different things. International experience suggested that a success rate of 70 to 80 percent was "about right."

It is much easier to set the right level of difficulty for something if it has been completed before, preferably many times. It is much more difficult to set a goal at the right level of difficulty in the case of social problems that haven't been solved before. When President John F. Kennedy announced in 1962 that the United States would send a man to the moon within that decade, he didn't know whether it would be possible (it was).[8] When Prime Minister Bob Hawke announced in 1987 that no Australian child would be living in poverty by 1990, he didn't know whether this would be possible either (it wasn't).[9] Of course, this is a simplification because the goal in this case is not the goal. The purpose of having a target-based program is not to achieve the target but to improve performance. In his time as prime minister, Hawke failed to eliminate child poverty, but he did manage to achieve a reduction in child poverty of 30 percent, greater than any Australian prime minister before or since.

In New Zealand, it was decided that the targets for the Results program would need to be set "at the edge of possible." At the outset of the program, three targets were causing the most concern among public servants. As indicated in the previous section, in the case of Results 4, 6, and 8, ministers ultimately chose targets that were more ambitious than those suggested by public servants and were therefore considered impossible by some.

Result 8 saw significant progress for the first three years. The reoffending rate was falling at about 5 percent per year, still on track to meet the 25 percent total target. And yet, further improvements became harder each year, as the easiest gains were achieved. This was in large part because of the way the target was expressed—while the number of people reoffending continued to decrease, the percentage of people in prison who were reoffenders (the reoffending rate) first dropped and then increased as the prison cohort became harder to rehabilitate—as described in the case study of Result 8 later in this chapter. By the end of 2015, it was apparent that the efforts of the justice sector would be unsuccessful in reaching the target. Subsequently progress slowed, and ultimately the reoffending rate started to rise again, though not as high as the 2012 baseline. This suggests that targets are only motivating while they remain possible—if they are too hard to meet, they can be a source of despair.

Conversely, if they are too easy to meet, they can lead to complacency. In the case of rheumatic fever, when initial efforts were associated with a small improvement, a lower target would have left public servants satisfied with the progress they were making. They would not have felt the need to continue to innovate and to try new things to achieve a two-thirds reduction in the disease.

Across the program, public servants were generally much more conservative than ministers in suggesting what improvements were possible—for example, when setting a target for improving workplace skills and qualifications in Result 6 (see chapter 5). This links to the type of gaming known as ratchet effects, whereby targets based on previous performance can incentivize underachievement.[10] In tensions between views on what level to set targets at, public servants may have been influenced by the knowledge that they would subsequently be responsible for achieving those targets.

There is some evidence that targets tend to be more effective at improving performance if the people responsible for doing the work are also involved in setting the goals.[11] This was true in the Results program, in which selection of Results, targets, and measures appeared to work best when there was a collaborative effort, with public servants initially suggesting a range of options, ministers selecting which Results they thought were most important, and several rounds of revisions and refinements. In most cases (though not in Result 9, as discussed in part 2), expert public servants provided invaluable information on how to frame a Result to capture the most important factors affecting New Zealanders' lives. They were useful in designing measures that provided rapid and accurate insights into the problem, and they provided some useful advice on what improvements would likely be possible based on current settings and international experience. However, their incentive to under-promise meant that, in many cases, ministers were right to demand more (as in the case of Result 6). Politicians and bureaucrats each bring different perspectives and insights into setting Results, targets, and measures—the discussion of Result 8 above provides an interesting counterexample of where this did not go quite as planned.

Choosing problems that could be replaced by others once the original was solved to a reasonable degree helped mitigate the difficulties of setting targets at the right level. For example, when the percentage of children who received all their scheduled vaccinations rose from 83 percent to almost 95 percent, improving the vaccination rate was no longer seen as the highest priority for improving infant health. Instead, the 2017 refresh chose the problem of maternity care and set a target to increase the percentage of pregnant women registered with a lead maternity caregiver (midwife) to 90 percent.

Attainability of the Welfare Target (Result 1)

Result 1, to reduce long-term welfare dependence, provides an illustration of a target that was not set at the right level and indicates one of the ways this can be managed. Progress reports to Cabinet in 2013 after a year of the Results program indicated that most activity to reduce welfare dependence concerned the roll-out of case managers who actively supported individuals transitioning into the workplace. The government also adopted a much more flexible budgeting approach to how these services were allocated, within the same overall budget. These actions translated into a reduction in long-term jobseekers of 2,700 in the first year, which accelerated to a further reduction of 6,400 by March 2014. The Result was on track to achieve the target, and the rating on the reporting dashboard went from yellow (on track but changes not yet embedded) to green (on track). What had originally been considered a stretch target was on track to be achieved.

Not only was the target now considered too easy, but also there was increasing dissonance between the Result target, which counted the number of clients, and other policy changes in the social sector that were taking a more weighted approach. The Welfare Working Group, a group established to consider new policy options for New Zealand's welfare system, concluded that some long-term beneficiaries were at risk of *never* returning to work.[12] These people accounted for a disproportionately large amount of the money spent on benefits, particularly when considering the costs over a lifetime. The Welfare Working Group suggested more effort should be put into supporting those individuals identified as at the highest risk of long-term welfare dependence.

This approach became known as Social Investment. The government developed a new data infrastructure (the Integrated Data Infrastructure or IDI) that allowed data to be combined from many sources, including administrative data that different agencies held. This new tool allowed a "big data" approach to understanding how early risk factors correlate to lifelong outcomes. The government used an actuarial method to develop a valuation of the long-term fiscal liability of different population groups. The intention was to use changes in the valuation as an assessment of progress.

The Social Investment approach created new insights into how services were delivered. Significant effort had been targeted at jobseekers who had previously been in the workforce and who did not face significant barriers to returning to work. When these jobseekers did find work, success was attributed to the assistance they'd received when they may well have done so regardless (particularly with economic tailwinds). Data from the IDI showed that these were not the clients most at risk of long-term welfare dependence—in fact, the original jobseeker target included only 16 percent of those most at risk. In mid-2014, the BPS progress report to Cabinet pondered this issue:

> We think there may be better ways to achieve collective action with population groups that are exposed to poor outcomes. We have learnt from the investment approach used in the Welfare reforms that taking a more granular population level understanding of specific population groups can better target investment to areas of need. Similarly, the Analytics and Insights work by the Corporate Centre and Statistics NZ enables us to better understand how our interventions are impacting on individuals and population groups, and thus how we should change the way we intervene and/or the intervention mix.[13]

The end of 2014 progress report to Cabinet signaled the way ahead:

Social Sector Priority Ministers are working with officials to embed the social investment focus on identifying common customers and understanding future outcomes and costs to improve the quality of service for New Zealanders, particularly the most vulnerable. Investment approach concepts are being considered in and across the Welfare, Justice, Education and Health sectors.

Work has been fast-tracked on data integration and analytics. There are several streams of work underway:

- Anonymized integrated child data held at the Ministry of Social Development is being used to identify groupings of vulnerable children and their families. This work expands on the range of adverse outcomes included in the initial model, and identifies significant risk factors, including showing the number of children who have multiple risk factors at a national and Territorial Local Authority level. This analysis is a further step toward a common definition of risk factors and the most vulnerable.

- Statistics NZ and the Social Sector Board, working with the New Zealand Data Alliance, are working on a clear project plan for completing social sector data integration to form a single view of the customer.

- Work is also underway to identify the current and future costs associated with vulnerable groups to inform Budget 2015 and future budgets. The Treasury has also been asked to work with the Social Sector Board to develop an investment approach to support decisions about where to invest across health, education, justice and social services for shared population groups for Budget 2016.[14]

While many governments would have been content to cruise toward the target and claim victory, the underlying aim of the Results program was to drive improvement in outcomes rather than simply to collect victories. Therefore, New Zealand decided to review the targets to make them more challenging.

Thus, in December 2014, in the refresh of the BPS Result targets and measures, the government made two changes: the target was broadened to include all main benefits (not just jobseekers), and an additional target was set using the actuarial valuation. Broadening the target to all main benefit types increased the need to manage horizontally. One benefit group, those receiving the "Supported Living Payment" (SLP) benefit, had the highest long-term costs. However, these were not the target of the Ministry for Social Development's previous efforts, as they were not seen as able to work. Helping these people be ready and able to enter the workforce would require working closely with the agencies of the health system.[15]

The second target, based on actuarial valuations, was qualitatively different from the others. While other targets were based on simple, easy-to-understand measures, the actuarial target was not intuitive. The target measure was explained to the public as "a release in the liability means a reduction in the amount of time beneficiaries will spend receiving a benefit."[16] The actuarial estimate attempts to isolate the impact of collective government management on beneficiary numbers. Adjustments are made to remove the impact of interest and inflation rate changes on the liability and other factors beyond the control of management.

Ministers now faced an interesting conundrum: they had found a way to accurately measure and report progress on exactly what they wanted to achieve (a reduction in long-term benefit dependence) by using an estimate of future long-term cost. The problem they faced was that the public didn't understand the target (it was too technical), and the opposition accused them of a focus on reducing cost to government rather than a focus on improving outcomes for people. The use of a target based on long-term cost was effective in driving the actions of the public service but not so effective in conveying to the public what the government was trying to achieve and what progress was being made. Because the government wanted to achieve both things, that is, to drive the efforts of the public service in the right direction and publicly communicate success, it tended to use the numerical target for public communication and the actuarial-based target to drive public service actions.

The impact of the new target on the public service was immediately obvious in subsequent progress reports. The lead agency could no longer depend on improving its case management to achieve the target. It had to harness the efforts of other agencies to address the barriers to work—chronic health conditions or injuries, drug and alcohol dependence, lack of workforce skills, and criminal convictions. Matching client skills with labor market opportunities also needed a step change. The midyear 2015 progress report described it this way:

> The new target is deliberately ambitious and represents a significant challenge for the social sector, requiring greater collaboration between agencies. The diversity of the client base means reaching the target within the current fiscal context will require more than simply increasing levels of case management; it will require more targeted and different mixes of services from across government and more matched labour market opportunities for clients. It will also require active participation and support from employers, along with a stronger focus on improving clients' work-readiness. Work toward the new target involves a cross agency approach by the Ministries of Health, Education, Business Innovation

and Employment; Social Development; the Department of Corrections; Police; and the Accident Compensation Corporation.[17]

Despite progress, the target was so ambitious that many people working on it feared it would never be met. If the initial target was too easy, the new target was too difficult. A central reason for setting the target at such a high level was that it represented a political undertaking going into an election. Having claimed a 25 percent reduction in all beneficiaries over the next three years, the government had tied itself to setting an unrealistic target, at least in the view of officials who hadn't had the opportunity to give ministers their opinion before the target was announced. To some extent this was demotivational. Officials tended to see it as a political target rather than as a public management target. They were still putting up plans but started to play number games rather than trying to achieve real change.

Measuring at the Right Point—Outputs or Outcomes

It's one thing to identify at a broad level the problem you want to solve but another to precisely describe how progress will be measured. The measures in the Results program needed to be useful for management decisionmaking, motivation, and accountability. Unfortunately, there is no single rule that informs what performance information will be needed in all contexts and for all purposes. Balancing the trade-offs between measuring Results at the outputs level or the outcome level is a crucial part of setting the right targets. The Results program did this uneasily at times, but with some success.

It was easier to judge the right measure for problems that already had trend data, but none of the problems had been solved before, and therefore no one knew what the right measures would be. Some of the more effective targets were set in reference to a baseline: 30 percent fewer jobseekers, two-thirds fewer cases of rheumatic fever, and a 25 percent reduction in criminal reoffending. Other Results were able to describe a future state but include reference to the starting point: "An average of 70 percent of New Zealanders' most common transactions with government will be completed in a digital environment by 2017—*up from a 29.9 percent baseline*" (italics added). But other Results described a future target without any reference to the past: 98 percent of children starting school will have participated in quality early childhood education, and 95 percent of eight-month-olds are fully immunized. In these cases, public servants were generally given credit for the improvements they did achieve rather than being challenged on whether they had met the target. Here, the reporting format may have played a role, with a focus on line graphs rather than raw numbers. Line graphs make it easy for the reader to determine whether overall performance has improved from baseline or the historical trend. In the face of such dramatic improvements, it might seem petty to question why an arbitrary line wasn't met.

Much has been written about the selection of outputs versus outcomes as performance measures.[18] Each has its advantages. Outputs tend to be more directly attributable to individual actions and tend to involve shorter information delays. However, outcomes tend to be more intrinsically valuable; they are the things that public services are ultimately designed to achieve. Figure 12-1 shows the relationship between intrinsic value, attribution, and timeliness.

New Zealand was left with conflicting demands in selecting Results at the right level. On the one hand, the necessity of intrinsic value and meaningfulness pushed selection of measures to the left of figures 12-1 and 14-1, toward outcomes. But too far toward outcomes, and public servants don't have as much control, at least not in the short term. They have no way of knowing whether what they are doing is making a difference or whether they should change course. The public may react skeptically too—seeing these end outcomes as too far off or as too far removed from concrete action. On the other hand, timeliness, attribution, and instrumentality pushed selection to the right. But too far toward outputs and the public service may end up optimizing the production of something that isn't very useful. Optimizing an output is only valuable if that output makes a difference to the community.

This was part of an ongoing discussion in the New Zealand public service, which had been undergoing a focus shift from outputs to outcomes over a period of a decade, led mostly by the New Zealand Treasury and the Office of the Auditor-General. Ultimately, decisions about the program measures fell somewhere between outputs and outcomes. The debate about the merits of

FIGURE 12-1. Intrinsic Value, Attribution, and Timeliness

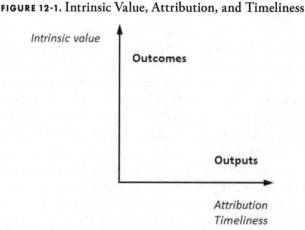

Source: Scott, R., and Boyd, R. (2017). *Interagency Performance Targets: A Case Study of New Zealand's Results Programme.* IBM Centre for the business of government.

each, along with the role of terminology in guiding behavior, contributed to the program design feature of referring to "results" rather than outcomes. Although this was a departure from recognized terms in mainstream public management literature, it was part of a deliberate intention to drive greater focus on action. Use of the term "Results" in the program was orchestrated in part by a "Results team" that was tasked with finding a way to advance performance in New Zealand's public management system. The team was established within the State Services Commission in 2010, before being transferred into the newly formed BPS Advisory Group secretariat in the Treasury in 2011.

In terms of explaining how outputs contribute to intermediate outcomes and then final outcomes, intervention logic or logic models can provide some clarification of the causal relationships at play.[19] However, logic models can also add complexity, which causes problems when communication with the public is an important factor for success. In the production model of public services, inputs (money, people, authority) are converted by the activities of departments and agencies into outputs (goods and services).[20] These outputs in turn contribute to societal outcomes. Public servants rationalize their actions using logic models that explain the causal links between inputs, activities, outputs, and outcomes (see figure 12-2).

Criticism of the program in the media around the 2017 change of government included claims that the program had been skewed too far toward outputs (see more detailed discussion of these in the "Media Critiques" section of chapter 8; see also discussion of outputs and outcomes in the chapter 1 section on "New Public Management Reforms in the 1980s"). In reality, most Results were targeted at what are referred to in New Zealand as intermediate or short-

FIGURE 12-2. A Production Model of Public Services

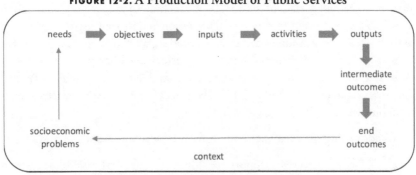

Note: This figure simplifies and adapts several different versions of the production model. In this instance, we have removed labels for the relationship between these different production stages. For example, the relationship between inputs and outputs is often labelled "efficiency," and the relationship between outputs and outcomes is often labelled "effectiveness."

term outcomes, broadly meaning any point in a series of causal steps that link outputs to end outcomes.[21] For example, to measure a more skilled workforce (in Result 6), ministers chose the proxy or lead indicator of qualification attainment rather than the end outcome of productivity, innovation, or economic growth. Qualification attainment changed more quickly, and was easier to measure and attribute, while still being a reasonable proxy for a skilled workforce.

Some of the Results could also be described as "co-production outputs." Co-production describes the involvement of citizens in the creation of public value, through contributing to the design and implementation of public services.[22] In New Zealand, outputs are considered co-produced when the value is created by the public's choosing to engage with the service. For example, in Result 3, immunization rates depend on parents deciding their child should be vaccinated and then engaging with the public service to ensure this happens. Though vaccinations themselves can be considered outputs, increasing the immunization rate represents an intermediate step between offering the vaccination service and the ultimate goal of reducing the incidence of preventable disease. The immunization rates cannot be increased (in a voluntary system) without some contribution by the parents, and therefore the public service is challenged to make these services appealing and accessible.

Other Results, like the crime rate (Result 6), or the rate of rheumatic fever (Result 3), were much closer to being end outcomes. This was particularly the case in these examples because of the interconnectedness of underlying causes for the problems. Progress in addressing problems like these can rarely be directly attributed to a single action, and public servants working to solve them relied on a range of information sources to understand what was and wasn't working and then adapt.

It should be noted that this is not the same conclusion reached elsewhere. Gemma Carey and Patrick Harris emphasize performance information as a management tool for adaptation.[23] They conclude that outcomes change too slowly to be effective in managing collaboration and instead suggest a focus on activity measures to show whether collaboration is happening. Carey and her colleagues have studied how interagency performance has been managed in Australia, looking particularly at the Australian federal government's "Social Inclusion Agenda" launched in 2007. The Social Inclusion Agenda set six long-term outcomes:

1. addressing the incidence and needs of jobless families with children;

2. delivering effective support to children at greatest risk of long-term disadvantage;

3. focusing on particular locations, neighborhoods and communities to ensure programs and services are getting to the right places;

4. addressing the incidence of homelessness;

5. bolstering employment for people living with a disability or mental illness; and

6. closing the gap for Aboriginal and Torres Strait Islander Australians.

Simply having these goals, Carey and colleagues reported, was a first step in giving a sense of purpose to interagency working: "By having the Agenda you go some way to ensuring that the reforms that are undertaken and what the government is doing aligns with those general principles—just because it's there it helps."[24] But the goals were so distant that they weren't effective either for accountability or adaptive learning. For example, closing the gap for Aboriginal and Torres Strait Islander Australians was expected to take many years, perhaps generations. The activities such as improving access to health and education services, which public servants could undertake in working toward this goal, could not directly be linked to improved quality of life or lifelong outcomes. This led to Carey's suggestion that Australia should return to a focus on process measures.[25] Our research indicates that there are challenges in managing in the way Carey and Harris proposed and that instead there is a middle ground between distant end outcomes, which lack feedback and attribution, and process measures, which lack intrinsic value and can lead to "collaboration theatre."[26]

Many of the case studies from the Results program show managers using performance information to make adaptive decisions to progressively solve complex problems. For example, in Result 1, data on long-term unemployment helped prioritize effort to a smaller group of clients. In Result 2, near-real-time data on early childhood education enrollment rates meant that providers were able to quickly experiment and evaluate different approaches. In Result 3, data on the incidence of rheumatic fever showed that early efforts to treat the rheumatic fever as a health-screening problem or as a public information problem were effective but insufficient to achieve the desired change. For management decisionmaking, targets need to have short lag times between action and observed effects, intrinsic value such that improving the measure results in an improved outcome for citizens, and good synecdoche with the underlying condition.

Having good synecdoche with the underlying problem was particularly important because imperfect measures are vulnerable to criticism for reflecting improvements that did not actually occur in the underlying problem. Targets are only useful if an improvement in the measure is also associated with an improvement in the underlying societal condition being measured. For the most part, this was avoided in the Results program, wherein all but three of the initiatives relied on a full count of the actual incidence of the problem: assaults against children, workforce qualifications, and ease of doing business.

For example, assuming that record-keeping is accurate, the number of childhood vaccinations reported as delivered by the registered health professionals is a good reflection of the number of vaccinations received by New Zealand children. Conversely, the number of reports of family violence is not a good reflection of the true rate of family violence, because campaigns to reduce family violence result in greater awareness and an increase in the number of reported cases.

At the beginning of the program, Result 4, to "reduce assaults against children," was in a state of flux. A new agency was established to improve outcomes for vulnerable children. This new agency adopted an operating model based on "social investment" by which decisions on potential actions would be based on an assessment of the anticipated reduction in the long-term cost (liability) of poor outcomes suffered by an identified group of vulnerable children. Ministers decided that framing Result 4 in terms of the social investment model wouldn't "retail" and reverted to a simple count of incidence of child abuse, despite full awareness of the technical issues with the target (chief among these being that successful steps to solve the problem would increase social awareness of abuse and therefore improve reporting rates, and would initially make progress toward the target harder to achieve).

This meant that the measure of violence against children had to rely on substantiated cases, which reflects a combination of the underlying incidence of violence and the likelihood of those assaults being reported. Using assaults against children as a measure not only reflects the acute and immediate setting in which abuse occurs but also societal attitudes and intergenerational family dysfunction that can take many years to change. Result 4 was also the measure perhaps furthest toward being an "end outcome." This was the Result for which the target represented the smaller proportional change—halting the upward trend in assaults against children and reducing it by 5 percent. This is not the sort of problem for which government can put in a short burst of activity and then declare the problem solved and move on to something else.

Measures for workforce qualifications and ease of doing business with government were both assessed through a survey and therefore represented a random sample of the population. These measures tended to vary slightly between successive surveys due to sampling error. However, there is no reason to believe that this error predictably or consistently inflated the reported outcome.

In the case of Result 9, ministers and officials took steps to address the synecdoche problem. The issue was that the target measure did not indicate that any progress had been made toward the desired outcome, despite that interaction with government was improving at a transactional level, particularly for online transactions. The government was not willing to change the target or target measure, which was a political decision; any change to publicly facing targets would be seen as the government resiling from its commitments, whatever the real reason. The government's response was instead to publish other measures alongside the lead target measure. Measures of service satisfaction, service performance, and digital service availability, based on data from existing surveys, were reported from mid-2015. The rating of progress was still based on the target measure and remained unchanged, but a rich array of data better described what was actually going on.

The issue of poor synecdoche for some of the target measures used highlights a design feature of the BPS Results program. In attempts to keep things simple by having only ten priorities and fourteen target measures, the measures would never be able to tell the full story of progress toward the outcome. Accuracy could have been improved by having multiple measures, but this would introduce complexity and reduce clarity of purpose. Clarity of purpose and of desired outcome drives action, which was what the government sought through the program, more than an accurate reflection of the state of play. There were casualties from this approach, chief among them being the demotivating effect on some officials, but the benefits outweighed the costs.

The exact balance of these different considerations for setting measures at the right point will vary by the nature of the problem, the jurisdiction, and the timing. The Results aimed, imperfectly at times, to balance being easily understood with being technically precise. They were somewhere in the gray area between outputs and outcomes. Other problems, in other settings, might call for slightly different choices, valuing some considerations over others. In any case, selecting the right goals involves striking a difficult balance between simplicity, meaningfulness, and attribution.

Difficulties Measuring Service Delivery (Results 9 and 10)

From the outset, Results 9 and 10 were referred to simply as Result 9 and Result 10 rather than being referred to with Result descriptors. This was partly because they didn't involve natural sectors of agencies with existing names (such as the justice sector), but it is also partly because the descriptions of the outcomes were poorly framed. Although they were useful signals to what the government wanted to achieve, they were not easy to measure. This was damning for a program that depended on target measures to determine success.

There is some variation between the two Results here. Officials working on Result 9 were initially frustrated at being handed down a target that was difficult to both measure and achieve. Conversely, Result 10 did meet the standard for being an effective publicly facing Result and target—it was clearly expressed and seen as being important, and the data for the measure were easily collected and understood. The problem was instead that officials working on Result 10 thought that the target was too transactional—a coarse approach to measuring improvement that was a proxy at best.

From the outside, the problems seemed disastrous and demotivating, but internally the goal commitment of public servants carried the program through. The team leader for Result 9, Linda Oliver, perhaps surprisingly described the target selection as "an inspired choice" because it demanded cultural change from both government and business—the shift to a customer focus rather than a focus on service delivery.[27]

The best way forward in Result 9 also turned out to be ignoring the target to a certain extent, focusing on "shifting the indicator needle" in the right direction, regardless of how unachievable the target might have seemed. Of course, this meant that the progress rating remained stubbornly on "Amber," indicating some gains but issues still to be resolved. The program was widely considered unsuccessful from the outside, but whatever the shortcomings of the targets, the resulting insights about customer experience of government were a critical development.

They were heavily influenced by the pain points research described earlier in chapter 10 on public entrepreneurship, which found that customers were not currently at the center of government's digital services. Customers were frustrated at having to integrate government services across agencies for themselves, sometimes even between digital and non-digital channels. In the end, these customer views were paramount. A customer focus for government services may seem normal now, but the research had never been carried out before. The methodology developed in the program that was able to account for effort, satisfaction, and sentiment within its measure of customer centricity proved to be a game changer and was picked up by agencies throughout government.

The research was able to shake up a focus on agency views of their products and services and shift the paradigm of how government conducted its business. Through the surveys of business every six months to determine progress toward target achievement, the Result 9 program team picked up that large business transformation projects often led to increased customer dissatisfaction with government, even if service delivery improved. The team was then able to flag for agencies what responses they should expect to business improvement actions. One of the lasting innovations from the Result 9 program has been the practice of establishing customer satisfaction units as critical parts of business transformation projects.

By mid-2015, Result 9 had finally established target measures, and the data were indicating progress toward the target. Unfortunately, the data were, at best, fickle. The Result 9 program was taking steps to make it easier to transact with government in areas like filing tax returns online, but there were often long lags between service delivery improvements and changes in customer satisfaction. Also, in responding to the survey, businesses tended to bank any gains and forget them, focusing instead on the difficulties caused by new legislation that they found irksome and unnecessary. In 2016, business owners, grumpy about the burden and additional cost to business imposed by new health and safety legislation, answered the survey negatively, and the measure of success for Result 9 started going backward. Anecdotally, progress was good, but the data said otherwise.

The temptation was to write it off as a poor target, but the new focus on customers meant that the customers were always right. The program clearly needed to focus on the aspects of interacting with government that businesses were still complaining about. Officials explained in a paper to Cabinet that progress toward the target was negative because businesses were upset about recent legislative changes, which was clouding their ability to see the advances the program had made elsewhere in making it easier to deal with government. Despite agreeing with this assessment, instead of allowing it to serve as an excuse, the responsible minister was then able to lead a discussion about how to address the imposition of legislation that was not landing well with business. The onerous measures required by the new health and safety legislation were important—they saved lives—but maybe the legislation could be designed to be more user-friendly. Officials were asked to return with solutions.

What followed provides an insight into how target measures mismatched to the underlying problem can still be used effectively to make progress (the importance of ministerial responses to data is discussed in more detail in chapter 14 on valence). In discovering this new problem unrelated to the effectiveness of government online services, agencies altered the way they carried out regulatory change. Instead of relying on the public consultation phase to iron out any issues, they now involved representatives of the end users (in this case, businesses) in the design phase, using them to test the workability of proposed legislative changes.

In Result 10, the target drove online uptake, and reasonably good progress was made, but officials were unhappy for all the right reasons. Similar to Result 9, the lack of alignment between Result 10 and its target led to ambiguity about the actions that agencies should take. With this level of uncertainty, failure was in the cards. But again, the perception of the Results with the leaders responsible for delivering them was instrumental in overcoming this. Result 10 senior leaders were able to determine a future vision for online service delivery that provided the basis for a clear set of actions. They saw the Results as a means to a different end from what the target pointed toward—a much more meaningful end.

Despite improvements to online service delivery, Result 10 leaders wanted better evidence that the increased volume of online transactions actually meant that it was getting easier to deal with government online. By the end of 2014, an additional measure was introduced into the progress reports every six months from an existing survey called Kiwis Count. Kiwis Count is a regular survey of a cross-section of New Zealanders that collects data on the population's satisfaction with a range of public services. Two questions were added to determine whether it was getting easier to access government services online—one based on experience of digital transactions and one based on perception. Over several years, the perception of ease of digital transactions increased slowly (from 64 percent in 2013 to 66 percent by 2016), whereas the experience of ease of transacting digitally was always higher and increased faster (from 67 percent in 2013 to 78 percent in 2016). Volume increase did turn out to be a good proxy for increase in the ease of digitally transacting with government.

The measure from Kiwis Count was useful for supporting the trend evident in the other measures, but it was not as useful for driving action. This is because of the same vulnerability to external factors described above, which may influence reports of ease of interaction. For example, people who are unhappy about a change in entitlement are unlikely to be able to separate this unhappiness from a perception of how easy it is to access it. Additionally, the causal link between changes and data was stronger for administrative data than for survey data—change in online service delivery causing improvement or deterioration in uptake over a few months provides a strong feedback loop on which to base further improvements.

In both Results 9 and 10, initial difficulty with poor synecdoche between targets, measures, and underlying problems were overcome with iterative processes led by public servants with clear visions for the improvements they were actually trying to make. They were able to spark interagency conversations about how they could work together to improve the customer experience of transacting with government, and they counted perceptions of increasing ease as successes for the program. Regardless of challenges, the targets still drove action. As Linda Oliver put it, "If you don't have targets you don't get anywhere."

Likelihood of Program Completion

The continuation of the program is a significant consideration in the likelihood of goal attainment. In goal commitment literature, it is assumed that the goal, once selected, does not change. However, this condition cannot be assumed in the public sector, particularly not for goals that span multiple years. Programs that span many years run the risk that government priorities will change, and goals set now may not be relevant in five years' time.

Sometimes public servants are characterized as being change averse.[28] Perhaps a better description is change-weary, or even change-wary, because many new features are not fully implemented before the next change is introduced. Governments introduce new policies and programs with great fanfare, and then attention gradually wanes as it is diverted to shiny new objects elsewhere. The constant churn of new programs means that sometimes it feels to public servants like they are running just to stay still. For a public servant, a rational response to a new announcement is a cautious wait-and-see approach. It is prudent to hold back, and not fully commit to implementing the new program, in case that decision is soon reversed. Or even more likely, a new priority supersedes the previous announcement. Ministers know this and complain that the public service does not leap into action when told, except when external events demand it (such as in response to a crisis). But ministers, too, are reluctant to be too concrete in their commitments so they may later claim that what happened was exactly what was intended.

The big challenge for the New Zealand government in setting targets in 2012 was that to ensure commitment of public servants, it had to commit itself. By publicly committing to targets, setting dates for completion, and reporting progress in a transparent manner, the government created a rod for its own back.

Typically, there are three possible outcomes for a program—it succeeds, it fails, or it is changed. Governments tend not to like failure and are criticized by the opposition and the media if they do so. This means that, usually, the likely outcomes are limited to succeed or change. But by committing to achieving targets and reporting on progress, the government increased the political cost of exiting the program.[29] This made changing the program more difficult. While the government was able to revise three of the targets in 2014 to make them more difficult, other changes were effectively ruled out because the political costs would be too high. It was not politically possible for the government to abandon the program, soften or hide the reporting, or revise the targets to make them easier to achieve.

When public servants saw that politicians were unable to change the program, they were left with only two options—succeed or fail. And since politicians weren't keen on the latter option, public servants felt a sense of urgency to fully commit to the program.

The New Zealand government was aided in this attempt by some fortuitous timing. While it had effectively tied its own hands, such that it would have been punished politically for abandoning the program, a future government would not feel so compelled. When the Results program began in 2012, there were more than two years until the next scheduled election held in September 2014. The incumbent National Party was performing well in opinion polls, and it seemed likely that it would be reelected. This meant that from the beginning of the Results program in 2012, it seemed very likely that the same government would be in charge when the program ended in 2017.

When the government chose new goals in 2017, it did not have the same benefit of timing. Another election would be held in September of that year, and the anticipated outcome was too close to call. Public servants would be prudent to hold off fully committing to achieving the revised goals until the outcome of that election was known. The National Party was defeated at the 2017 election and replaced by a new government led by the Labour Party, which had a different set of priorities. These electoral considerations will differ over time and between jurisdictions. However, the general principle remains: public servants are unlikely to commit to achieving a goal until their political masters have committed themselves. To generate commitment, sometimes it is necessary for politicians and policy makers to tie their own hands.

Progress and Setbacks for the Reoffending Target (Result 8)

Progress for Result 8 was initially rapid thanks to a strong following wind. Reduction in crime was a worldwide phenomenon in this period, attributed to a range of contested and not fully understood factors such as better approaches to reducing crime, better technology, and population aging. In reporting progress in mid-2014, the justice sector acknowledged this global trend but then pointed to reduction in data most resistant to improvement in the past, such as a reduction in violent crime and a reduction in the reoffending rate of those who had been in prison (rather than on community sentences). By the middle of 2014, two of what had originally been considered stretch targets had already been achieved—the target for total crime and youth crime. By the end of 2014, during the refresh of the targets and measures, the government increased the reducing crime target from a 20 percent to a 25 percent reduction in crime.

Amid success and congratulation, omens of trouble lay ahead, particularly in recognition that further gains would get harder as the targets moved closer to being achieved. As it happened, the 2014 midyear progress report marked the high point for the reducing reoffending target. The end-year report showed an increase in reoffending over the previous two quarters. The rating was changed to yellow (following discussion in Cabinet Committee), for "on track but changes not yet embedded."

The immediate response by the justice sector was to bolster programs to support rehabilitation, such as alcohol and drug rehabilitation and family violence programs. It didn't help. There was further deterioration in the reoffending rate over the next quarter. The progress report began to explain some of the problem: the number of reoffenders had continued to fall, but the target measure was the reoffending rate, which essentially measured the "churn" of offenders.

By the end of 2015, the rating had gone to amber—"progress but issues to resolve." A new line was added to the graph in the dashboard so that it showed an upward trend for the rate of reoffending but a downward trend for the total number of reoffenders. The Cabinet progress report recognized "problems with how well the headline measure for the target reflects actual reoffending" and went on to describe it this way:

The reoffending rate is a combination of two measures. These two measures are:

- the rate of re-imprisonment for people leaving prison, within 12 months of their release; and

- the rate of reconviction for community-sentenced offenders, within 12 months of starting their sentence.

Policing activity has diverted the less serious cases out of the justice system, so there is now a larger proportion of people more likely to reoffend and a smaller proportion of first time and lower-risk offenders in the Corrections populations. This has put upward pressure on the reoffending rate, as there are fewer people who offend each year (which affects the denominator in the reoffending rate calculation), while those people who do offend are more likely to reoffend (which affects the numerator in the reoffending rate calculation).[30]

Officials in the justice sector had worked more collaboratively to improve outcomes and had reduced both the crime rate and the numbers of reoffenders. They felt like they had succeeded, but it looked like they had failed because they were saddled with a target that was framed in a way that meant it could never be achieved. They wanted it changed to something sensible, like a reoffending rate based on the total population, not just offenders in the criminal justice system.

The government recognized that it had saddled itself with a problem but refused to change the target. Instead, it published more data to show what was actually happening. This was, at least in part, a political decision—if it changed the target, the public credibility of the program would be reduced. No matter how well explained, the public, assisted by opposition parties and the media, would see it as a cover-up for policy failure.

Interestingly, the opposition, when it was voted back onto the Treasury benches in 2017, viewed the reoffending target as one of the best. But it wasn't the target that the opposition was referring to—it was the focus on this problem. By then the prison population had expanded significantly, mostly because of policy changes, in particular, tightening bail and remand conditions. The deputy prime minister of the previous government had labeled imprisonment a failure of society and a moral outrage. The incoming government agreed—this was a problem that needed to be addressed. It had to be a central priority of government.

On balance, while it was an unfortunate measure on which to base a target, the reoffending target was effective at focusing effort on an important issue. This speaks to the difficulty of developing effective measures and targets for high priority, publicly facing issues. The target should seek to maximize the benefit for people, communities, and society and, at the same time, provide an acceptable level of risk for the government. The reducing reoffending target was a failure if the objectives of the program were to make the government look good. It was a success if the objective was to improve lives.

Taking Aim

So we see that expectation of goal attainment is made more complicated in the New Zealand context of the Results program and includes considerations not just of the level of difficulty but also of simplicity, the point of measurement, and the likelihood of program completion. Restricting the program to only ten Results, worded in plain English as much as possible, made it easier to get buy-in to the program across public servants, ministers and the public. Setting the targets at the right level of difficulty and at the right point between outputs and outcomes meant that public servants were motivated without being disheartened and could track the impacts of their work. Having dedication to the program at the highest levels of government, including public reporting on progress to the targets, gave public servants the certainty they needed to overcome their wariness of a new program.

13

Instrumentality in Goal Commitment

In relation to goal commitment, instrumentality refers to the level of control over outcomes. When looked at in the context of the Results program, instrumentality includes consideration of actor selection in terms of the number of agencies involved, existing and new relationships, and governance and accountability arrangements. This chapter is about organizing to solve problems when responsibility crosses multiple agencies, the public management problem of agencies not acting collectively when they needed to. The lead agencies responsible for coordinating this were dealt a tough hand, and they struggled. Through this struggle, New Zealand learned a great deal about the "managing" part of managing horizontally, about how to work together and how not to work together.

As with expectancy theory, discussion of instrumentality requires some adaptation for a public sector context. Experimental studies discussed earlier describe discrete tasks wherein the individual is directly in control of whether the goal is achieved. In public administration, the direct activities of public servants are frequently only indirectly related to the intended social outcome. For example, a "good" employment program may fail to reduce unemployment if the economy stalls. A "good" health promotion program may fail to change behaviors if it coincides with a media story to the contrary. Furthermore, even when public programs make a difference, that difference can have a delayed effect. Improved early childhood education might improve lifelong learning outcomes. Efforts to reduce smoking might reduce cancer rates for decades to come.

Targets have been criticized for discouraging collaboration.[1] If accountability tends to be individual, effort tends to give priority to those things for which an individual will be held responsible. A focus on measurable performance discourages those cooperative and helpful behaviors that are more difficult to measure and ultimately to attribute. This is a specific example of the distortionary effect of effort substitution.

Narrowing the focus of public servants to the performance measures for which they are responsible can be effective if the problem can be neatly divided in advance. Each target in the UK Delivery Unit could be attributed to an individual leader—the principal of a school was accountable for education outcomes and the manager of a hospital accountable for health outcomes. In this case, effort was focused, pressure to perform increased, and the tendency to help others decreased because responsibility was targeted individually.

But not all problems can be divided in this way. As noted earlier, some problems are "wicked," wherein each attempt at a solution changes the understanding of the problem. Wicked problems involve the intersection of health, education, social, and economic problems and cannot be solved by these sectors acting alone. Some students cannot achieve good education outcomes because of their home and family environment. Some patients cannot achieve good health outcomes because they return to poor housing conditions.

Conversely, targets are, by their very nature, set in advance—they are something to work toward. They do not, and cannot, anticipate the ways that public servants will need to coordinate and cooperate to solve wicked problems. The lessons explored in this chapter do not constitute clever *a priori* design features by the New Zealand government intended to overcome this difficulty. Instead, the groups responsible for all ten problems each organized themselves differently to work toward the targets. Over time, through trial and error, and through a community of practice, certain models were shared and became popular.

The mechanisms for holding public servants to account for single-agency actions are straightforward in theory, for example, via statutory reporting requirements and select committee reviews of department performance or by individual ministers answering to Parliament for the resources, issues, and agencies for which they have direct responsibility.[2] However, the practice is not always so easy. Indeed, accountability, even when it only involves the actions of an individual, is complicated.[3] In an interagency context, it is even more so, often emerging as one of the biggest challenges.[4] Accountability has a range of definitions, relating to blameworthiness, liability, answerability, and account giving, and Bob Behn has described it as an "ambiguous abstraction." Behn notes that accountability involves an accountability *holder*, someone who holds someone else to account, and an accountability *holdee*, the person being held to account. Accountability holders seem to always want more accountability but struggle to define what it means. But for accountability holdees, "accountability (frequently) means punishment."[5] This has been the case in many target-based regimes, notably the target regime introduced under the Blair government in the United Kingdom, often called "targets and terror" (also discussed in chapters 2, 3, and 14). As evident in the examples in this book, accountability does not always mean punishment. In relation to the Results program, we define accountability more broadly, to mean the obligation to explain and justify one's actions and accept responsibility for them.

The basic definitional problem of studies of accountability in the public service is centered on three questions: whom should public servants be accountable to, for what should they be accountable, and how should they be held to account? This chapter touches briefly on what public servants can be held accountable for but mainly focuses on how and to whom. In the public service, the latter two questions are entangled, as the various methods of holding public servants accountable are usually linked to whom they are being held accountable by.

Regarding what public servants should be accountable for, the tension is between accountability for actions (process), goods and services produced (outputs), or the Results achieved (outcomes). In the interagency context, accountability for processes can lead to all manner of activities that look like good collaboration but that don't produce Results. For example, in the early 2000s, New Zealand agencies were encouraged to form interagency groups to discuss their shared outcomes. This was originally organized under the banner "Managing for Outcomes," and when this term faded from use, these groups became known as "sector groups." Participants in these groups were frustrated that their meetings lacked purpose and that they were "collaborating for collaboration's sake."[6] These public servants were accountable for interagency working to the extent that they were performing the behaviors that we associate with good collaboration. Behaviors and associated artifacts like forming working groups that meet regularly, having terms of reference or charters, and jointly producing documents that map their interdependencies or commit to some shared vision or aspiration were held up as evidence that the groups were collaborating well. While there were likely some benefits from sharing information and developing greater familiarity with public servants from other agencies, interagency working was in part a performance to please accountability holders. Within the New Zealand public service, such behaviors have earned the nickname "collaboration theater."

Whether for processes, outputs, or outcomes, public servants are assigned responsibility for something and then later held to account for what happened. In New Zealand, this historically took the form of "purchase agreements" and later "output plans." But this is only one form of accountability—"legal accountability," positioned as one of many by Romzek and Ingraham:

1. Legal accountability involves substantiation against compliance with established mandate, such as statutory reporting documents, fiscal audits, and select committee hearings.

2. Hierarchical accountability is based on the relationship between individuals with different power levels, like the relationships between ministers and chief executives, or between the commissioner and chief executives.

3. Professional accountability is based on arrangements with high autonomy based on internalized norms of appropriate practice.

4. Political accountability requires responsiveness to key external stakeholders, such as elected officials, client groups, or the general public.[7]

In each of these kinds of accountability, a distinction can also be made between individual accountability, whereby individuals must accept responsibility for their own actions, and collective accountability, where individuals must accept responsibility for actions performed by the group, including those they themselves did not participate in. For example, in the legal accountability described first above, interagency working multiplies the complexity of holding individuals to account. In a single-agency context, public servants are accountable for their own actions and typically also for those taken by other public servants who report to them and over which they have hierarchical control. But interagency working involves multiple parties making decisions together and acting in a combination of separate, joint, and interdependent ways. It can be difficult to disentangle the actions of one party from another to assign individual accountability; therefore, accountability as assigned in interagency examples is typically collective accountability.

Different jurisdictions have tried to assign accountability for interagency working in different ways. The examples in this book include attempts at holding individual agencies (and their leaders) accountable for their respective contributions to interagency working; attempts at holding individual agencies responsible for the degree to which their behavior can be characterized as collaborative or whether they put the collective interests of government above their individual agency interests; attempts at holding groups of agencies collectively accountable for how well they seem to be working together; and finally, attempts at holding groups of agencies collectively accountable for what they achieved. In this respect, we can also distinguish between "felt responsibility," which is a psychological construct, and "causal responsibility," which is a descriptive positivist construct. We want public servants to feel responsible for solving problems and therefore try their hardest to solve them, even when it is not strictly "fair" to blame them for the success or failure.

Three important paradoxes or tensions are inherent to working horizontally. First, there is a tension between limiting shared responsibility to a few agencies and leveraging the full range of available resources and expertise. Second, very little happens without somebody pushing ahead, and yet the presence of a leader makes others feel less responsible. And finally, while mature, trusting relationships make horizontal management easier, the best way to build trust is through shared experience of successfully working together. Some of the more useful and innovative responses to these tensions are outlined below in sections about managing group size, signaling equal responsibility, and developing relationship maturity.

Managing Group Size

In single agency problems, the agency already has the control it needs to be able to change its operations to address the problem. However, most of the issues in the Results program required multiple agencies to make changes and integrate solutions across each other's portfolios, in which they did not necessarily have the right level of control. Some of the Results could be achieved with only two or three agencies working together, and these tended to find progress easiest because collaboration was easier with fewer agencies. However, serving the public interest, or trying to do so, means that even agencies that start from insalubrious conditions, with low prospects of success, have to make the effort. In some cases, these agencies can try to make do with substitute conditions and strategies; they can adapt.

Some of the cases began with a large number of agencies (greater than three) but were able to make good progress by selecting a small number of critical partners as a core group and involving others on an as-needed basis. This was achieved using tiers of involvement. In these cases, collaboration was limited only to those agencies that needed to redesign their services together. Other agencies were involved as needed for information sharing and cooperation. Two examples (described below) used a tiered governance structure to limit their core governance group to two and three agencies, respectively.

Five agencies contribute to boosting workforce skills: the Ministry of Education, the Tertiary Education Commission, the Education Review Office, the New Zealand Qualification Authority, and the Ministry for Business Innovation and Employment. The Ministry of Education, the Education Review Office, the Tertiary Education Commission, and the New Zealand Qualification Authority have a long history of working together, and the Ministry of Education has led this work. Therefore, these four agencies were comfortable that the Ministry of Education could speak on their behalf in a governance partnership with the Ministry for Business Innovation and Employment (even this is a simplification—the Ministry for Business Innovation and Employment itself represented several economic and business-facing agencies, see figure 13-1).

Governance arrangements for boosting workforce skills experienced some

FIGURE 13-1. Governance Tiers for Boosting Workforce Skills

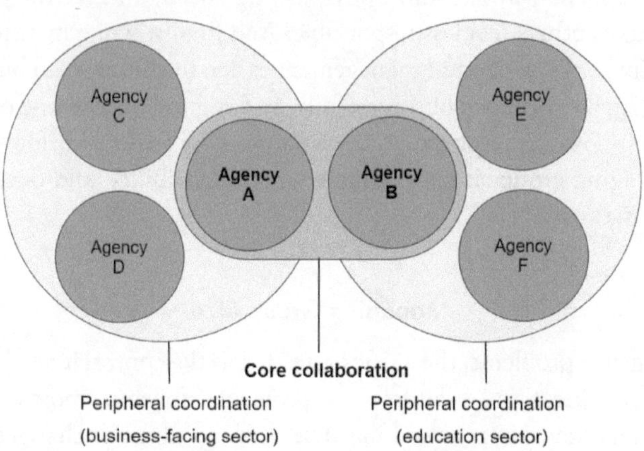

Core collaboration

Peripheral coordination   Peripheral coordination

(business-facing sector)   (education sector)

Note: Agency A = Ministry for Business Innovation and Employment; Agency B = Ministry of Education; Agency C, D = other business-facing agencies; Agency E, F = other education and qualification agencies.

Source: Scott, R. J., and Boyd, R. (2015). "The New Zealand Better Public Service Results: A Comparative Analysis Linking Inter-Agency Collaboration with Outcome Performance." In *Proceedings of the 2015 Australia and New Zealand Academy of Management Conference.* ANZAM.

growing pains, and the solution described above emerged over time (as described in chapter 6). In contrast, the agencies in the justice sector were already referring to a "big three" long before the Better Public Services Results were announced.[8]

Justice sector chief executives faced a conundrum because stemming the flow into the criminal justice pipeline depended on preventative work by several of the social sector agencies. Responsibility for reducing reoffending was allocated to six all together: Ministry of Justice, Department of Corrections, New Zealand Police, Serious Fraud Office, Crown Law Office, and Ministry of Social Development. The Ministry of Justice was included for its obvious role in developing and maintaining justice policy and administering other bodies like the courts, Public Defence Service, and Legal Aid. The Department of Corrections covered prisoner, parolee, and other offenders' compliance, while the national New Zealand Police force were charged with keeping the peace, preventing crime and enforcing the law, and maintaining public safety. The Serious Fraud Office was involved in its capacity as investigator of financial crimes, bribery and corruption, and the Crown Law Office in its capacity as the government's legal adviser and home of public prosecutors. The Ministry of Social Development was included particularly because of its work with children and young people and on family violence. Furthermore, successful reentry into society following a prison sentence also depended on other agencies to provide income support, housing, employment skills and employment opportunities, and reducing drug and alcohol dependence.

But the justice sector had already learned that including all these agencies in a governance group would make it too unwieldy to be an effective decisionmaking unit. To maximize the effectiveness of the Justice Sector Leadership Board, only the "big three" were needed to make joint decisions about expenditure and collective operations, redesigning their frontline services to work better together. These agencies were Ministry of Justice, Department of Corrections, and New Zealand Police. To maximize connections with other agencies, all of which had a role to play in reducing reoffending and achieving the targets, the board established a regular forum to meet with them at both chief executive and deputy chief executive level. This provided the opportunity to share information and coordinate activities as and when they overlapped (see figure 13-2).

In both cases, tiered governance was a viable model for reducing the number of core partners while at the same time keeping available, both technically and politically, other agents who might be useful on an *ad hoc* basis. Their expertise is on tap, and they don't feel (too) angry about being excluded.

Unfortunately, this wasn't quite the reality of the arrangement for the jus-

FIGURE 13-2. Governance Tiers for Reducing Crime and Reoffending

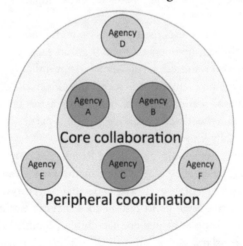

Note: Agency A, B, C = Ministry of Justice, Department of Corrections, New Zealand Police; Agency D, E, F = Crown Law Office, Serious Fraud Office, Ministry of Social Development.

Source: Scott, R., and Boyd, R. (2017). *Interagency Performance Targets: A Case Study of New Zealand's Results Programme.* IBM Centre for the business of government.

tice sector. In the first instance, it had been the agencies responsible for other Result areas that sought support from the police, courts, and corrections. For example, the school qualification target was unlikely to be reached unless youth who were disengaged from the education system were instead removed from the youth justice system and returned to school. As progress toward the reoffending target stalled, the justice sector began to reach out more urgently to agencies that controlled the levers needed to reduce reoffending—the health agencies to reduce drug and alcohol dependence, the education agencies to develop workplace skills, and the social development agencies to support reintegration into the community.

But the justice sector found that when its cases did not contribute to the Result areas for the other agencies, justice sector "clients" fell to the bottom of the priority list. Justice sector agencies struggled to provide criminal offenders with access to the services they needed to address those challenges that contributed to them offending in the first place, as well as reoffending. The solution was for the Department of Corrections to directly purchase several of the services it needed, usually from third-party (nongovernment) providers, and build up its own workforce capability (for example in addressing mental health issues). It is questionable whether this was a positive outcome; it wasn't exactly an integration of service delivery. If anything, it was a further fragmentation of service delivery that extended outside government as well. But the problem was that accountability for achieving the criminal offending targets was set too clearly within the justice sector. The level of control had been balanced out across the big-three agencies, but there was little impact more widely across government.

Tiered governance is a response to a tension within horizontal management between responsibility (members of a small group each feel more responsible for the outcome) and resources (typically a large number of agencies are each able to influence the problem). This is where the universal nature of horizontal management is problematic. Some literature emphasizes broad participation.[9] In the literature on networks, for example, different parties can bring resources that are not originally known or anticipated.[10]

Several examples of this appeared in the Results program. The Ministry for Pacific Peoples is the smallest department in the New Zealand government, with twenty to thirty employees. It was somewhat of a surprise then when this ministry made such a large contribution to achieving Results 2 and 3. The Ministry for Pacific Peoples helped connect public servants from larger departments into Pacific Island communities in cases in which these communities were disproportionately affected by the problems.

But large groups are also problematic. The Ringelmann Effect is a well-known phenomenon from psychology.[11] The more members there are of a group, the less any one person feels responsible for the outcome of the group.

This was originally observed in the game "tug of war" in which each additional participant resulted in less effort by all participants. In horizontal governance, a large group means it is very difficult to assign shared responsibility in the manner discussed in the previous two chapters.

This is observed more generally as "diffusion of responsibility" in which an individual is less likely to act in situations in which there are others who might also act.[12] The individual assumes that others are responsible for taking action or have already done so. Experiments by John Darley and Bibb Latané showed that bystanders were less likely to help someone suffering from a seizure if others were present. Daniel Wegner and Donna Schaefer measured that this effect is magnified when the group is larger.[13]

The diffusion of responsibility is reported to have five major (negative) consequences.[14] Groupthink causes individuals to feel less responsibility for ensuring the quality of decisionmaking because they assume that others are doing so. The awkwardly titled "risky-shift" describes a tendency for individuals to be willing to acquiesce to risky proposals because they do not feel responsible for the outcome. Social loafing describes individuals exerting less effort in a group situation (such as in the Ringelmann effect above). The bystander effect describes the phenomenon wherein nobody acts because everyone assumes that others will. Finally, the presence of bystanders tends to inhibit helping behavior of others by normalizing inactivity.

Large groups also have higher coordination costs, particularly when (as is often the case with collaboration) consensus agreements are required. While the examples above were able to make good progress by limiting participation to just three agencies, New Zealand has also been host to attempts at horizontal management involving eleven parties.

Take, for example, the natural resources sector. This was an attempt at horizontal management by the New Zealand government, outside the Results program, to address environmental problems. The group size has always been large, but it is clear that some members are more responsible for solving certain problems than others. The Ministry for Primary Industries and the Ministry for the Environment will always feel, and be held, more responsible for the quality of fresh water in rivers and lakes than will the agency responsible for keeping a land information registry (Land Information New Zealand). Yet, in a broadly inclusive group, progress can only proceed at the pace of the slowest member.

Such arrangements give rise to what could be called an "animal farm" governance arrangement, after the George Orwell novel of the same name: *all agencies are equal, but some are more equal than others.* Collective commitment and urgency will only be achieved when each of the core group feels equally responsible.

Digital Services Governance (Result 10)

The group of agencies involved in Results 9 and 10 was defined by the basket of online service transactions that were included in the target. Richard Foy, tasked with leading the Result 10 program, referred to these agencies as the "lucky eight." [15] He established a new governance group for them called the Digital Services Council and was clear that he needed service delivery leaders in the room, not "techies." These were second- and third-tier managers from different parts of government, brought together from across government to form what Foy described as "a multi sectoral system team." This council was the engine room for Result 10 and was given significant permission by its chief executive group, which convened quarterly to oversee progress. The Digital Services Council was supported by a program group located in the Department of Internal Affairs and funded in cash and in kind by the contributing agencies. In-kind secondments proved important for the viral change model Foy adopted:

> People were exposed to new ways of thinking and different methodologies. They became part of the "movement," supported the vision and became part of the viral infection of the system we looked for by returning as ambassadors to their own agencies.

In contrast to the other Result areas, Result 10 had no ministerial group to provide a mandate and instead tended to be driven from the ground up. This proved difficult at times because the mandate needed to be won and maintained rather than being conferred from above. Ultimately, the mandate was won on the back of strong leadership, bringing agencies together to achieve Result 10 as part of a contribution to a broader vision for the future.

Foy was assisted in this by his own boss—the chief executive Result lead Colin MacDonald. MacDonald was also a functional lead in the position of government chief information officer, a role in which he oversaw the development of an ICT strategy with integrated, citizen-centric service delivery as its vision for the future.[16] It was recognized that the Digital Services Council represented the interests of the agencies directly working toward the Result 10 target, but a wider group of agencies would need to be around the table to develop the ICT Strategic Plan if the scope of the work were to be digital transformation across the whole government.

Traction started when these strands of work (originally operating as separate parts of the Department of Internal Affairs), along with work on data use Statistics NZ led, were combined under one governance group—the Digital Government Partnership. The digital design improvements in ICT interoperability and security of information provided the technical basis for the service transformation Result 10 required. While this new governance group broadened the oversight of data and digital functions, it was large and complex. Five governance groups reported into the Digital Government Partnership, and it suffered from poor connectivity among them. Clearly, there are no silver bullets when trying to make horizontal management work, especially when many agencies are involved.

Signaling Equal Responsibility

There's no denying that hierarchy, through "command and control," is an efficient way to make decisions, but that approach doesn't cut it in a fragmented world where power, resources, knowledge, and other means to solve problems reside with multiple individuals and organizations. This environment instead requires "the process of building consensus or obtaining the consent or acquiescence necessary to carry out a program in an arena where many different interests are in play."[17] Interagency governance is particularly difficult because, as noted by Blackman, its actors "must get change to happen through allocating tasks to others in their own and other related organizations, typically under conditions which are not entirely of their choosing."[18] In these situations, the interagency governance challenge is very much to "sustain coordination and coherence among a wide variety of actors with different purposes and objectives."[19]

When designing accountability systems for maximizing goal commitment to interagency performance, policy makers must balance individual and collective responsibilities. Multiple agencies required to work together to achieve the outcome makes it difficult to determine how responsibility should be shared and attributed and who should be praised or blamed for what occurs. The "problem of many hands" means that individuals cannot be directly and solely responsible for whether the goal is achieved.[20] In the design of the program, policy makers must determine how to include those who control all the necessary resources while not diffusing responsibility too broadly. The distribution of responsibility will influence the attractiveness of achieving the goal. An individual public servant might feel less committed to achieving the goal, and therefore apply less effort or creativity, if they think that someone else will get the credit or the blame. Equally, an individual might feel less committed if their contribution doesn't matter or is only a minor part of a bigger effort.

Some academics deny that shared (collective) responsibility is possible; methodological individualists like Robert Downie claim that only individuals possess moral agency:

> Collectives do not have moral faults, since they don't make moral choices, and hence they cannot properly be ascribed moral responsibil-

ity. For there to be moral responsibility, there must be blameworthiness involving a morally faulty decision, and this can only occur at the individual level.[21]

Equally, normative individualists like Stephen Sverdlik doubt that shared responsibility is fair:

It would be unfair, whether we are considering a result produced by more than one person's action or by a single person, to blame a person for a result that he or she did not intend to produce.[22]

Ultimately, it is less important whether it is philosophically possible for a group to be responsible for an action or fair for that group to be held responsible. When managing horizontally involves trade-offs between contributing to the shared goal and to each agency's separate goals, it's more important for public servants and politicians to understand and implement the settings that will bring about enough cooperation among disparate players to get things done. While it may not be possible to say that a group was responsible, in a sense of moral agency, it is certainly possible to say that multiple individuals *feel* a duty, obligation or, yes, responsibility to collectively achieve a desired goal. This feeling of shared responsibility can influence behaviors, resulting in greater cooperation within the group and efforts to influence others within the group to achieve the shared goal. In the Results program, it was helpful for teams being held to account for their leadership of the program to feel that other agencies and teams were also held to account for their contributions to target achievement and provide better public services.

In its reform of the public sector through the Results program, the government sought to drive different behaviors in the public service. Earlier public sector reform had created strong vertical accountabilities between individual chief executives and their responsible ministers, with incentives that required and rewarded action such as delivering on the portfolio requirements of a minister and that assigned clear accountability for expenditure required by the Public Finance Act. New Zealand public servants had been trained in a system in which single-person responsibility is taken as an article of faith.

These arrangements were effective for solving problems that were contained within a single agency, but they did not provide incentives for agencies to collaborate to solve problems that crossed agency boundaries and ministerial portfolios (see also horizontal funding in chapter 6). Any attempts at assigning shared responsibility were typically rebuked by the reflexive use of popular idioms: "When everyone is responsible, no one is responsible," or put more graphically, "one hand to shake, one throat to choke."

The effect of the BPS reform was to lay expectations for interagency collaboration (in other words, horizontal actions) over the top of the existing (vertical) accountabilities. But working horizontally is not easy; horizontal and vertical management interests are often in tension. After many years of indoctrination into a single-point responsibility system, skepticism of collectively felt responsibility persisted. Although chief executives and their agencies initially responded positively, when the going got tough, they tended to revert to acting in line with vertical accountabilities. Public servants remained alert for signals as to which agency would actually be held responsible. Decisions made collectively at agency level were easily trumped by decisions made by an individual minister and the agency that reports to that minister.

Many of the top-down design features as covered in this book could be seen to contribute to this uncertainty of public servants as to the real lines of responsibility. Such features include those that made a performance target system appropriate; the setting of the Results, targets, and measures; the reporting requirements; and some of the accountability structures such as the appointment of a "lead" chief executive to convene and organize the other participating agencies.

Indeed, some of the accountability structures would much more appropriately be described as "governance cascade" than as horizontal governance.[23] For example, for each Result area, a steering group of chief executives from the core agencies met infrequently to set overall direction and to agree to delegate working responsibility to a group of second- or third-tier leaders. These operational groups met much more frequently (usually every week or every two weeks) to manage a work program. Working groups were set up to solve specific issues. Sitting above it all was an informal ministerial group that could make important decisions to resolve important trade-offs. Results 9 and 10 originally didn't have the corresponding ministerial group to provide governance oversight, which resulted in difficulties when such trade-offs were required. For Result 1, the ministerial oversight group was called the Social Priorities Ministers Group, and a strengthened version of the Social Sector Forum at the chief executive level, supported by a newly established group of second-tier officials.

These arrangements were more effective at some levels than at others. At the top level of governance, chief executives had the necessary strategic conversations—what changes are we making? What is our vision for the future? How will we get there? Further down the governance cascade, members of steering groups were at varying levels within their agencies and did not necessarily have the right mandate to be able to make quick and efficient decisions.

But the more complete story accounts for how public servants at lower levels organized themselves in response. In more formal terms, the rest of this section concerns the governance structures public servants adopted that do qualify as horizontal management. Our use of the term horizontal management refers to the high-level process of working across agencies, regardless of the vertical hierarchies we acknowledge were also at play.

Several experiments with different approaches to governance were tried as the Better Public Services reform was implemented. Architectural and design forums yielded many lessons about how to work across the public service, powered by the government's expectation of interagency work. These were organized by central agencies in response to program team needs and in their support capacity for governance and funding expertise. One such forum was a workshop of people involved in the "improving interaction with government" Result area, which identified several systemic issues.

Ministers were paying attention to the difficulties of interagency decision-making in functional leadership and the Results program, and the head of State Services was determined to improve horizontal leadership by chief executives. This culminated in a 2013 discussion between the central agency chief executives and State Sector Reform ministers (particularly Deputy Prime Minister English) and a commission to central agencies to address the issue:

> Ensuring effective governance and associated working arrangements for multi-agency work are crucial for the achievement of BPS Results, and we have commissioned further work on alternative forms of governance that may be used by the public sector to reduce the transaction costs incurred through cross-agency negotiations over direction, timing, and funding of change.[24]

Some lessons had already been learned from earlier experiments with horizontal governance in New Zealand. The natural resources sector group of chief executives provided key insights into system governance from 2008 to 2015. The group had learned the importance of having people around the table with the ability to remove members' vertical management "hats" at the door and don their horizontal management hats, making decisions for the common benefit. They also needed the authority to make the necessary decisions, without the need to refer everything up to the higher levels of governance. Delegation to increasingly lower levels had proven the enemy of effective decisionmaking by horizontal governance groups.

Breaking down the walls between agencies was considered a challenging but essential part of delivering an interagency program. The 2015 midyear progress report to the Cabinet revealed increasing interest from ministers in how progress for some of the Results was affecting others:

> It is apparent that the achievement of some Results is more critical than others because they [the Results] provide a foundation for improved outcomes in other areas. The Education Results (Results 2, 5 and 6) in par-

BOX 13-1. Result 9 and 10 Workshop with Central Agencies to Identify System Issues

Key problems to be addressed:

- Decisions are hierarchical, drawn out, and require constant negotiation. There are too many decision points, both within and across agencies, in a context in which agencies have different priorities, processes, and time frames.

- Constant negotiation & managing trade-offs—like "working in treacle." How can we move beyond coalition of the willing so that cross-agency working is the way government does business?

- Cross-agency work is seen as a priority for agencies charged with leading this work but not for others—including for ministers.

- Reluctance from people to come on board; they want proof of the benefits to their agencies before they will commit. Strong incentives for individuals to put their agency first rather than the system benefit.

- Funding (financial and asset) decisions are difficult to achieve:
  - How resources (including funding) are reprioritized
  - Building assets in "good faith" . . . who pays?
  - Lack of certainty of funding in a three- to five-year funding horizon

What we are learning:

- Need for early clarity of vision (future state) to get agency commitment. Clarity is needed over multiple horizons—what's in the next phase and the one after that? "If you know where you are going, there is less haggling on the journey."

- Alignment of ministers is important.

- The leadership needed for a matrix model (collaboration requirements imposed over a silo accountability system) depends on ability to influence/persuade and to live with ambiguity.

- Individual agencies need processes to ensure that their planning/resourcing is aligned with their commitments to the system vision/future state.

ticular provide the basis for improved employment and justice outcomes. The opposite also holds, and people not engaged in ECE or achieving entry-level qualifications are more likely to become the "clients" of the justice and social development sectors.[25]

However, this was not enough to address the difficulty of the education targets in driving the improvement in interagency work envisaged by the designers of the program—the education targets themselves were too easily achievable within the education "family." The dependencies for the education targets were more of a pipeline, wherein achievement at each level of the system improved based on participation and achievement at the previous stage—achievement at school improves if children have participated in quality early childhood education, a base-level school qualification is necessary for students to achieve success in tertiary education, and a base-level tertiary qualification is necessary for young people to participate in higher education and skilled work.

Although the Ministry of Social Development contributed to reengaging vulnerable youth in education, this activity was not driven by the social development agency's support for the school qualification target. As noted by a Ministry of Education official:

> The school achievement target was seen as an education target; there was little ownership by other agencies. Involvement in a governance group focused on the contribution of education outcomes to the economy may have helped to improve the connections between [education and economic] government agencies, but failed to make the breakthrough that may have been expected.

The education pipeline only served to improve linkages within the education system, increasing engagement and achievement at crucial points. It had little impact on interagency work because there was no ownership of the education Results from outside the education "family."

Conversely, the teams making the most progress in the Results program were those that had embraced the interdependent culture of the program and saw each other as equals. They were putting significant effort into crafting governance arrangements that signaled equal responsibility. As Oliver describes it (for Result 9), what this shift looked like was co-design of improvements by those agencies affected, jointly signing up to get the work done, rather than a single agency developing a business case over several months and trying to impose it on others. In Result 3, the signal of equal responsibility was employed by the rheumatic fever Result team to ensure the sustainability of the successful program once the team was no longer able to continue the work. The team did this by effectively handing over control to district health boards, making sure the boards would own the desired outcomes and proposed solutions and would commit to them beyond the end of the program's funding.

The State Services Commission recognized the importance of this equal and collective ownership and moved to a system of assigning indivisible responsibility of the kind Sverdlik would likely decry as unfair. This was part of a shift that had begun before the Results program reform. The central agencies of the New Zealand public service (the Treasury, the State Services Commission, and the Department of the Prime Minister and Cabinet) were moving away from perceptions of themselves as the "control agencies" of earlier years. Increasingly they saw themselves as enablers, responsible for designing a public management system that supported agencies to provide the services the public demanded and needed. One of the metaphors developed at the time was of central agencies as player-coach—involved in the game and providing constructive suggestions—rather than as referee blowing the whistle on the sidelines, controlling the game.

The development of the "corporate center" of government, as the central agencies re-characterized themselves, was a way of signaling equal responsibility at the system level.[26] They "walked the talk" of horizontal governance, setting up the structures that would enable it. They governed horizontal governance—meta governance that controlled the environment of action in the public sector rather than controlling that action directly. They exercised their meta-governance/leadership role by creating the enabling conditions for agencies to do things differently—working with them to remove barriers to effective horizontal management rather than designing and imposing solutions from the center. They were working across government-wide structures, processes, norms, rules, and policy frameworks in several meta-governance functions for the Results program:

- Mandating (for example, legislative changes)

- Facilitating (for example, the BPS Results & functional leadership)

- Resourcing (for example, BPS seed funding)

- Partnering (for example, with functional leaders)

- Endorsing (for example, recognizing good practice—a key to the success of the BPS Results)

The concept of stewardship is central to meta governance, defined as "using every opportunity to enhance the value of the public assets and institutions that have been entrusted to care." This means maintaining trust in government and building a culture of innovation and integrity in policy advice as well as ensuring financial sustainability. This mode of operation emphasizes relationships, embraces complexity and ambiguity, and supports other leaders in their roles. It relies heavily on influence, in many cases working outside regular lines of authority. The central agencies were able to connect strategy and effort, finding ways of persuading broad participation in transformational action and steering the whole public service.

They demonstrated this in their use of a "co-production" approach for the program itself. They set up a secretariat for the Better Public Services Advisory Group, initially located at the Treasury and later at the State Services Commission, made up of policy analysts and managers from the three central agencies. Members of this secretariat worked alongside the lead agencies when the idea of organizing around a few priority outcomes or results was first mooted by the BPS Advisory Group, and central agency chief executives invited their chief executive colleagues to run a trial of the approach in their sectors. For each sector, a lead chief executive was tasked with working with their colleagues to identify the one or two critical results that they needed to work collaboratively on if they were to successfully improve outcomes for New Zealanders. The lead chief executives were also asked to develop one or two measures against which they could measure success and to decide how they could best organize themselves to deliver the result(s).

As the agency responsible for the selection, development, and performance management of public service chief executives, the State Services Commission took on the responsibility for developing the capability for horizontal leadership and supporting chief executives and other leaders in these challenging roles. Chief executives in these roles still had their usual appointed responsibilities of running their agencies and supporting their ministers' policy objectives. The Results program retained this strong linear accountability from agency to minister and overlaid an additional responsibility to act collectively. Furthermore, all the chief executives remained functionally equal, with no decision rights for "lead" executive over "contributing" executives even where this distinction existed in labels. In a situation in which they had no real control over their peers, leading through influence was the only tool available.

Signaling equal responsibility is likely to be an important lesson for many types of horizontal management, collective governance, and interagency working. However, specific practices are highly context-dependent, and the examples presented below should therefore be taken as illustrative only.

One example of the symbolic commitment to equal responsibility can be found in the use of secretariat groups. The ten Results used secretariats in different ways, including by assigning them responsibility for providing policy analysis and advice, reporting progress through a shared measurement system, and coordinating governance groups. The most successful BPS Results featured secretariats that were jointly resourced through the temporary provision of employees by all participating agencies. Where a secretariat was resourced and hosted by one agency, this symbolically raised the relative responsibility of that agency and signaled to others that they would be held less responsible. For example, the Social Sector Governance Group was initially supported by a secretariat staffed from the Ministry of Social Development, and some participants felt that this lessened the sense of commitment by other agencies. In the middle of 2014, the social sector transitioned to having a jointly resourced secretariat.

The justice sector's governance board met every two months, which was insufficient to drive the joined-up actions needed to achieve ambitious targets. The designated lead of the Result area—the chief executive of the Ministry of Justice—agreed with the new board to establish a Justice Sector Group, led by a deputy chief executive. The establishment of this "backbone unit" was a critical success factor. Participating agencies felt reducing crime and reducing criminal reoffending were shared responsibilities. It was a shared secretariat, located within the Ministry of Justice, but composed of officials from the other justice sector partner agencies—police and corrections.

The Justice Sector Group was a strategic policy group, not an administrative group. Its role was to advise the Justice Sector Leadership Board on strategic and investment decisions for the justice sector. It had capability in policy, strategy, investment tools, data analysis, forecasting and modeling, research, and evaluation. In public management terminology, it is a policy hub rather than a program office. A capable policy hub is future focused and can set direction; it can generate, examine, and act on evidence; and it can drive innovation and action. It is the engine room of reform. Program management has a place, either within the hub or linked to it, but public management reform requires changes in behavior more than changes in planning and organization. Reform is a strategic policy function.

US-based consulting group FSG has studied horizontal management cases over the past twenty years and concluded that the most important factor for determining the ability of a group of organizations to deliver "collective impact" is the presence and performance of a "backbone function" provided by a single lead agency.[27] Similarly, studies on networks suggest the importance of a "network administrative organization."[28] The use of jointly resourced secretariats suggests that this support can be provided without appointing a single leader. There is a tension between equality and individual leadership. It may be that the initial designation of a "lead" chief executive was necessary to get the program up and running. But over time, the importance of equality has become clearer. Following the Results program, the New Zealand government has taken increasing care to signal this, with new horizontal management programs featuring independent chairs for the steering group and a new organizational form for independently hosting a secretariat.

One of the legacies of the Results program was the insights from several experiments in governance undertaken by each of the Result leads. As described earlier, governance arrangements were not prescribed, but developing effective governance arrangements was one of the requirements for the Result Action Plans. To ameliorate the "light fuse and stand back" approach by the central agencies to both governance and funding, the central agencies established small teams (led by one of the central agencies, but comprising all three) whose job it was to assist the Result lead agencies with system issues (the Result 9 and 10 workshop described earlier in this section is an example of joint problem-solving of system issues). The BPS Results coordinator also convened the agency teams responsible for achieving the Results for Community of Practice workshops to find solutions to common system problems by sharing their experience (see appendix 5).

Subsequently, aspects of system learning in governance and funding were adopted in other areas of system design, for example, through establishment of the Social Investment Board in the social sector. Here, big data emphasizes the interdependencies between and among agencies, providing a strong rationale for joined up thinking and action. The chief similarity with the Justice Sector Leadership Board is that the Social Investment Board comprises a small subset of social sector agencies with "skin in the game"; its members can make binding decisions that impact more than one agency. However, in other ways, the Social Investment Board represents the next generation of designing for collective responsibility. It has a stronger mandate from being established by the Cabinet, and it has an independent chair (the State Services Commissioner rather than one of the social sector chief executives). It also has a stronger "backbone unit"—a departmental agency with its own chief executive, hosted by the State Services Commission.

In 2018, the State Services Commission published on its website a System Design Toolkit that described eighteen models for managing problems that cross agency boundaries based on the level of trade-offs involved.[29] The approach used in the Results program was one of these models, given the name Shared Responsibility. Having similarly concluded that contingency theory applied to horizontal management, SSC suggested, the Shared Responsibility model was most appropriate for problems involving moderate policy and resource trade-offs and requiring a few agencies to work together. If each agency doesn't need to sacrifice, or must sacrifice only slightly, this can be managed by voluntary coordination and "reciprocal altruism" (acting for the benefit of others in the general sense that such kindness will be returned).[30] If the sacrifices are so significant that they threaten the ability of an agency to perform its core functions, the State Services Commission recommends a return to hierarchy—in its language, a "superordinate minister" to make the most difficult decisions.

In this case, the term trade-offs is a convenient shorthand. It is not meant to imply that there are a fixed range of possible resource allocations and that all changes to benefit one goal must necessarily come at the expense of another. Amartya Sen would instead describe the matching of relative importance and significance with allocation across multiple dimensions—in which case there may be new allocations that are mutually beneficial.[31] But in the practice of interagency working, agencies certainly *feel* that sacrifices must be made, either in pursuing individual goals at the expense of shared goals or vice versa. Social scientist Bernd Marin describes such trade-offs as an example of agencies having interests that are in opposition to each other: *Without interest opposition, coordination would be unnecessary. Without interest interdependence, coordination would be impossible.*[32]

In this light, managing horizontally is about creating shared or interdependent interests that are so powerful that they overcome the drivers of managing vertically. The Results program engineered, and indeed its successes relied on, a strong sense of personal affective commitment among senior public servants to achieving each Result. In such a context, it proved imperative that everyone feel that sense of urgency and that no one feel like a bystander. Within the "core" group described in the previous section, everyone was equally responsible.

This constitutes felt accountability—individual leaders feel committed to achieving the Result because they feel an obligation to several different parties, including ministers, Parliament, the State Services Commission, other agencies and branches of government, each other, and the citizens they serve— sometimes as individual recipients (often via the media) as well as to abstract ideals like professional standards and other norms and conventions. Behn concludes, "To whom must public servants be accountable? The answer is everyone."[33]

However, Linda Oliver points out that the Results program, and Results 9 and 10 in particular, was just the start of interagency working in New Zealand. She believes that while there have been "fundamental changes" to the way government agencies operate, there is still a long way to go. "We still don't have horizontal decision-makers in place to make the big horizontal plays. It is still too difficult for our chief executive to be the horizontal decision-maker on behalf of his/her colleagues."[34]

Mobilizing Communities for Early Childhood Education (Result 2)

When resources, knowledge, and other problem-solving tools are spread across a range of individuals and organizations, it becomes ever more important to engage the right groups. Although the preceding section mostly dealt with these issues in terms of central agency governance at the meta level and then at agency level, this case study illustrates similar principles in operation at the community level, as facilitated by NGOs. This case study is included with a view to enabling practitioners to learn from the rich experience of the

NGO/community sector in facilitating shared responsibility. In the community sector, shared responsibility typically arises as a response to felt problems (as opposed to felt responsibility). While this is a natural response from local actors to the problems in front of them, the following case study nevertheless provides an example of what a focus on improving outcomes looks like at the community level. In the Results program, the role of government agencies was to encourage, facilitate, and support these ventures (for example, by providing government property and resources). The program's framework created an environment where mobilizing all resources, including those at the community level, would be necessary if the targets were to be met.

The need to mobilize resources at the front line was a constant demand of the ministers who drove the BPS Results program. In a speech to Australian and New Zealand public servants, Hon. Bill English put it this way:

> Your front line matters a lot more than your management. So the way we are approaching fiscal consolidation almost without exception involves much more substantive engagement of frontline public servants, appealing to their intrinsic motivation about what they want to achieve and working to provide them with the decision tools that allow them to be flexible and come up with better solutions.[35]

He often also pointed out that the immediacy of the problem was a spur to action in communities:

> There was some tension between government departments about the hierarchy of frontline staff between departments, and who could tell who what to do. And it was suggested in our Cabinet committee that one way to resolve that would be to hold a meeting outside a home where a child was being beaten up inside because if you could hear the screaming, those government departments would decide in an instant what their priority was.[36]

In the area of Result 2 for increasing participation in early childhood education, the necessity of involving a village to raise a child provides a clear impetus for such a practice of interagency collaboration. In Gore, the "village" came together in mid-2014 to form the Gore Kids Charitable Trust, made up of representatives from the local Playcentre, Parents Centre, and Toy Library. In the words of Trust member Shelley Lithgow, "Our whole philosophy is 'it takes a village to raise a child.'"[37]

Over the course of two years, the three organizations of the Trust purpose-built a "kids hub" to fulfill the need for new facilities in the area. The Hub, described as "bright and beautiful," provides early childhood education spaces as well as shared community rooms—including an office, consultation space, and meeting room—available to be hired by organizations working with children. The Hub complements other local early learning services, accommodating Playcentre sessions, Barnados and Parents Centre courses, music groups and cooking classes, and health and well-being classes and appointments in the community rooms. The connection between the three organizations of the charitable trust through the Hub had the additional benefit that each organization saw significant increase in their memberships.

Ministry of Education ECE adviser in Otago, Kurt Chisholm, says: "It is a hub in the truest sense of the word because it has come together from these three different groups, from the planning to the fundraising. It really is a genuine community project." Full community involvement is also evident in the local council having gifted the long-term lease of the Hub's site, while the charitable trust would continue fundraising to build the Hub's playground, which would in turn be gifted back to the community.

Lithgow notes that the Hub is careful not to "duplicate any service that is already in the community." She went on to discuss the heartening experience of developing connections across the community:

> Many of the families that use the hub use multiple services. We're trying to ensure that when parents have time off work or study, they have somewhere to play and learn alongside their children, and develop relationships with other families.
>
> It's an amazing, big space. We put in a closed sleep room, so it's fantastic for families that are coming with babies in tow. The very young children can safely sleep in this room so parents can be hands-on and as involved as possible with their toddler.
>
> Whether you need somewhere to come and have a coffee and talk to other parents about, say, toilet training, or whether you need support from a range of different organisations, you can access the whole lot from here.
>
> We believe it can be a lonely journey for people, bringing up their children. And it can be a hard journey, at the best of times. So what we're trying to do is create a space where all families are welcome.

In Kaikohe, Te Kohekohe drop-in center serves a similar purpose in mobilizing the "village" around children. Again, the center is facilitated by a trust—Puawai o Kaikohekohe Trust—which runs a playgroup five days a week for preschoolers, alongside a weekly Puhi weaving group. The latter is why the walls of the center are so beautifully adorned with woven art and why it smells of freshly cut harakeke (flax). The drop-in center is one response to a survey undertaken by Trust member Kelly Yakas on behalf of the Early Learning

Taskforce. The survey identified three central unaddressed needs in the region: "There was nowhere in the Far North town where mothers felt comfortable to breastfeed, there were no public nappy changing facilities, and Kaikohe lacked a playground that was safe for preschoolers."[38] In Yakas's view, the survey also highlighted the importance of early childhood centers having the right "vibe" for parents to enroll their children—more so than other factors like cost or commitment. "Parents needed to have the right feeling about a place, to feel comfortable to hang out and to play and learn alongside their children." The drop-in center has met these community needs by being warm and welcoming and building the "right feeling or vibe of aroha and manaakitanga."

Other local initiatives resulting from the survey were street play days every two weeks near the children's playground, with free Wi-Fi; advice and information for parents offered through the center on alternative forms of early childhood education; linkages with health services; and an additional playgroup run in conjunction with Kaikohe East School to ease the transition from early childhood education into school. Within a year of being set up, the targeted playgroup for four-year-olds had captured eight children who had not previously taken part in early childhood education, setting them up for school with a Reggio Emilia approach that meets them on their own terms, responding to individual strengths and interests. Staff from Kaikohe East School help bridge the gap between ECE and school by visiting the playgroup, reciprocated by visits of the children to the new entrants' class at the school. Two users of Te Kohekohe services had positive feedback to share:

> You can see and feel the positive energy buzzing around the children, parents and families as they weave and kōrero. People are making connections and building relationships. Sharing kai and kōrero. They are helping and guiding each other. They are learning customs and values by listening to the kuia.
>
> The centre provides physical, spiritual and mental well-being. There is no other place in Kaikohe that offers this environment. *[Playgroup mum and weaver Makareta Jahnke]*

> As a parent living on the outskirts of Kaikohe, Te Kohekohe playgroup is very beneficial. It is a free, fun and safe environment with a very positive vibe.
>
> The opening hours are great, 10 am to 2 pm five days a week, allowing us to come and go as we please, with no pressure. I have a 14-month-old son who is breastfed. Feeding and changing him in town used to be very challenging. Te Kohekohe provides facilities for feeding and changing. There is also a separate baby area with age-appropriate resources to

help empower me as a parent and help him further develop his social, emotional, and fine and gross motor skills, which are very important in those first three years of brain development.

Te Kohekohe is a positive and great environment to be in. It is a great asset to the Kaikohe community. *[Leigh]*

More broadly across New Zealand, an education program called Poipoia te Mokopuna is delivered in sixteen locations by fifteen organizations. The program is intended to deliver tailored early learning for Māori children under three not currently engaged in education or kōhanga reo that is aligned with *Ka Hikitia—Accelerating Success 2013–2017* and based on the national curriculum *Te Whāriki 2017*. Those delivering the program through contracts with the Ministry of Education are encouraged to take a "one-size-fits-one" approach, adapting the program to meet the needs of the communities they operate in.[39]

In the Seaview region of Wellington, the Māori section of an organization called Naku Enei Tamariki delivers the Poipoia te Mokopuna program, managed by Kerry Dougall. The organization as a whole supports a range of whānau with different needs, ranging from those who have had involvement with Child Youth and Family services and may be struggling with poverty or addiction through to those trying to cope with a sense of disconnection from community, culture, or iwi. Naku Enei Tamariki's delivery of the Poipoia te Mokopuna program is targeted at whānau whose most urgent needs have been addressed and who have turned their focus to best meeting their children's needs, many of whom were not yet born at the time. Dougall gives the example of a young pregnant woman who had somewhat lost touch with her identity; she didn't speak te reo, knew some of her whakapapa, but was disconnected from her community:

She was pregnant when she came in, and so one of the things we did with her and her Pākehā partner was that we all talked about what would happen with the whenua—placenta—after the baby was born. Traditionally it would be gifted back to Papatūānuku by burying it, for her growth and sustenance. So, we spent a bit of time working on that kōrero, and as a whānau learnt a karakia which they recited at the burial of the whenua after baby was born. It was an opportunity for her to reclaim some of what it means to be Māori by this traditional observance.

This had a massive effect. One of the outcomes we didn't realise would come from it was the involvement of the mother's Pākehā partner and his whānau. The two cultures really came together for the benefit of the child.

Building interconnectivity across the community is a core tenet of Māori culture, and colonization has had substantial negative effects on connectivity in many Māori communities. This gives the work of gathering a village and signaling equal responsibility a unique mandate in Aotearoa New Zealand. Dougall says that Naku Enei Tamariki work has "developed groups within different communities; what we do is connect Poipoia te Mokopuna whānau with each other . . . [to] meet every fortnight . . ." The program is also tied to a number of more formal outcome measures such as "whānau are more confident in their role as their children's first teachers" and "parents read and talk more with their children." Dougall's insights in this area are that confidence is often a significant barrier to these outcomes:

> A lot of the whānau that we work with have come from a background where there's been abuse, or similar. Sometimes the parents we deal with don't see themselves as having much self-worth. So, a big part of what we do is to pull out and acknowledge the strengths that whānau have.
>
> We encourage that for example through waiata, karakia, or we might give books to whānau. What we don't ever do is hand over some book or something, and say, "see ya." Everything we do is about modelling, and about us constructing a relationship with whānau.

Leadership

Although it may seem contradictory to the importance of signaling equal responsibility, the difficult levels of control involved in interagency working can also be managed with strong leadership. The success of the Results depended as much on effective leadership as they did on having mechanisms like priority outcomes, targets, and action plans. The ability of leaders to build a strong team, focused on a compelling vision of success, was important for the achievement of many of the Results. Equally important were local leaders who didn't wait for directions from the center and effectively mobilized resources at the front line.

Early on in the program, a review of the arrangements for Results 9 and 10 offered some insight into the importance of leadership:

> Delivering a cross-agency programme is an extremely challenging task, and government and agencies are still learning how to operate within this new way of working. What is clear is that strong leadership is required to manage the high number of senior stakeholders and ensure that the programme delivers outcomes that satisfy each stakeholder. Ultimately, the agencies will be responsible for delivering the change driven by the programme and ensuring their buy-in will be crucial.[40]

The Results program provided the mandate and expectation for chief executives and ministers to exercise collective responsibility and collaborative leadership, but success required the ability and willingness of leaders to operate in these roles. Especially given the context of no additional powers and no additional funding, the paradigm change of achieving results across government was a leadership challenge rather than an organizational challenge. It required transformational leadership to change the way people looked at problems and acted on them. Examples of this abound in the Results program (see discussion of public entrepreneurs in chapter 10), which is why this section mentions many such leaders by name.

One of the most important aspects of leadership is the ability to build the right team for the job. Across the Results program, the most successful teams were small and agile, prepared to innovate, and empowered to make decisions and take immediate action. Richard Foy in Result 10 described his job as "building a coalition of like-minded and right-minded people," a job that got more difficult as he tried to introduce more collaboration and teamwork below second-tier manager level.[41] Kararaina Calcott-Cribb was appointed to lead the Early Learning Taskforce set up by the Ministry of Education. She recruited people "with the ability to make things happen; think outside the square; think bottom up; ask questions about what works and then do that."[42] Strong, distributed leadership was important. All members of the taskforce were valued as leaders in their own right based on the belief that hierarchies don't work in situations in which you're working with communities.

Dr. Chrissie Pickin in the rheumatic fever part of Result 3 also established a strong team around her, chosen not only for their skills in program and change management but also for their abilities to engage and collaborate and for their positivity. She had inherited a small initial team but had rapidly moved it on when it became apparent that most of the team actually thought that making progress to reduce the disease, let alone meet the ambitious target, was unachievable. In this case, the success of the program relied more heavily on effective leadership than on sound governance. When asked what characteristics were needed to lead such a program, Dr. Pickin used descriptors such as "collaborative, focused, agile—adopting a test, learn, and adapt approach; and tenacious, staying the course in the face of conflict."[43] Dr. Pickin had her own entrepreneurial qualities, being both innovative and strategic, a public servant with a passion to make a difference and the ability to wrangle other agencies.

Much of the joining up for the rheumatic fever Result was done locally (particularly in Auckland) and relied on ongoing personal relationships and problem-solving workshops. An interagency reference group helped the team test ideas, and an interagency program board helped get support for housing initiatives that addressed the needs of high-risk families, but linkages based on personal relationships at a local level were the key to achieving results.

Local linkages were also made between the early childhood education Result and the immunization Result (which was working with many of the same families). It started when the Ministry of Education, which was also struggling to reach the last few percentage points needed to achieve its target, set up a "hard-to-reach communities" strategy that enabled it to work with gang-affiliated communities and families previously inaccessible to government agencies. By the end of 2015 when the interim immunization target had not been achieved, the Ministry of Health began actively working with the Ministry of Social Development and the Ministry of Education to locate the children overdue for immunization. The Ministry of Health also engaged with the college of midwives to ensure that messages about immunization were getting to hard-to-reach families during pregnancy. In a better connected public service, the immunization team would have started to work with the early learning task-force much earlier, but as target achievement grew more difficult, interagency cooperation improved. This was less about effective design from the center than it was about local leaders stepping up when the going got tough.

Likewise, it would be misleading to attribute the shift to more effective interagency work in the early childhood education Result to effective governance at a national level. In reality, the Social Sector Board at chief executive and deputy chief executive level had a wide remit, met infrequently, conducted business formally, and operated at a high level. It tended to deal with reports rather than driving action, took a long time to make decisions, and proved to be too far removed from what was happening on the ground. Conversely, along with having a strong change methodology (as described in chapter 10 on public entrepreneurship), the Result 2 team was able to make progress thanks to more effective leadership at a lower level, with service providers and practitioners joining forces.

The ability to provide a vision for the future is another critical part of effective leadership. As noted in one of the program reviews for Results 9 and 10, "program leadership needs to be able to create and communicate a compelling vision for a diverse set of stakeholders . . . and an end-to-end roadmap for the program."[44] The recommendation was to develop a future state operating model, securing agreement for the vision of the future and how to get there. By the end of 2014, papers outlining a "blueprint" for Result 9 and both a "blueprint" and higher level "road map" for Result 10 were provided to the Cabinet.

But it takes effective leadership to translate a paper-based vision and plan into action. Richard Foy, the person delegated by the chief executive of the Department of Internal Affairs to be responsible for establishing and leading the Result 10 program, seized the opportunity that inclusion in the Better Public Services Results program offered. He had been working with two other main agencies to improve and align digital initiatives across government with limited success. Talking digital transformation was easy; getting action to achieve it was an entirely different matter. The Results program provided "a platform to hold agencies to account," permission to try different things, and momentum that he could use to progress the real agenda; he talks about "starting a movement," "having the belief," and "telling the story."

The focus of the Result 10 governance group, the Digital Services Council, could easily have been simply transactional, getting more public service interactions online and achieving channel change. But Foy took the opportunity presented to work differently and talked about transformational change across government. In his words, he set about working toward a vision of "system-level transformation of service delivery and customer services." It was a vision that was bigger than an individual agency's vision or strategy or technological change program. The intention was to change the customer experience of government—the way in which customers interact with government.

The leadership approach required "guiding and leading" to get others to buy into ideas and concepts—leading through influence as opposed to "command and control." Foy, a talented communicator of ideas, was able to provide this sort of leadership. Foy started with a two-day vision-setting workshop and then went on to build rapport with every member of the Digital Services Council through one-on-one meetings, setting the tone for the journey they were on by using words such as "exploratory," "discovery," and "emergent." The early meetings of the council were perhaps not as tidy and planned as the members may have expected, but they were energizing, uplifting even.

Given the difficulties in the Result 9 and 10 teams in terms of managing group size, it is a real testament to Foy's leadership of Result 10 that people on the Digital Service Council "kept turning up"; this was his measure of success. The fate of many such groups is that they start with second- and third-tier managers, but if these people don't see the value of attending the meetings, they will send progressively lower level delegates who don't necessarily have the authority to make decisions on behalf of their agencies. But the agencies involved had "skin in the game"—they contributed funding to keep the program running and stayed at the table to ensure they had maximum benefit from this expenditure. They knew they risked missing out on something if they didn't turn up. They benefited from the recognition that success brought, whether through effective practice or new technology (what Foy refers to as developing a "new shiny thing"). Most important, they stayed at the table because they bought into the vision; they wanted to change service paradigm across government for the benefit of New Zealanders.

On the back of strong leadership and successful service innovation, Result 10 made steady progress toward the target of 70 percent of the most common transactions with government being online. The progress rating of yellow (on track but changes not yet embedded) was maintained, and by the beginning of 2016 had gone to green (on track).

Local Leadership for the Vulnerable Children Target (Result 4)

These case studies from Result 4 provide examples of the importance of local leadership, which can be much more powerful and effective than central leadership and which was an important feature of the program across many Results. The use of local leadership also supported the public entrepreneurship of the program through design approaches like co-design.

In New Zealand's northernmost and subtropical region of Tai Tokerau, concerns about the social and economic conditions of local children and young people provided a call to action for Child, Youth and Family (CYF).[45] The close-knit community of Kaitaia had been shocked by two high-profile cases of sexual abuse with multiple child victims, while other challenging cases in the area over the same period included clusters of youth suicides. Given the challenges of living and working in this specific environment, CYF recognized the complications of lumping Tai Tokerau into the agency's northern region, which also included the substantial population of Auckland. To strengthen local leadership and to better support local staff, CYF set up a new leadership team dedicated specifically to Tai Tokerau as the region spreading from Te Hana to Cape Reinga. The regional director of the team, Marion Heeney, noted that the end goals of the team were to strengthen service provision by ensuring a closer match to the needs of this specific regional context.

The new regional team was able to develop organizational culture and form strong community partnerships. Recognizing the hard work of the roughly 60 full-time-equivalent social workers already serving local communities from Whangarei, Dargaville, Kaikohe, and Kaitaia, CYF contracted local iwi Te Rarawa to situate one of its social workers at Kaitaia College to provide dedicated care for the students. Building on this through a partnership with Te Aupouri Social Services, the new team expanded the Social Workers in Schools program from five schools to thirty, improving 2,500 Tai Tokerau students' access to support.

In another example of local leadership, Tai Tokerau CYF signed a memorandum of understanding with Te-Runanga-a-Iwi o Ngapuhi to ensure that a joint decision would be made about vulnerable Ngāpuhi children, placing them in care with other Ngāpuhi whānau as much as possible.[46] Ngāpuhi children made up around a quarter of all Māori children in state care—around 470 at the time. Reconnecting Ngāpuhi children and young people with their cultural heritage was also intended to help in cases of criminal offense. As noted by Ngāpuhi Iwi social services manager Liz Marsden, Ngāpuhi young people needed to be able to grow up "knowing who they are and where they belong." In Marion Heeney's words, this was "a huge step forward for Ngāpuhi tamariki. We believe it will really make a difference for vulnerable Ngāpuhi children if they are able to safely maintain iwi and marae connections and receive support from their wider whānau and community."

Strengthening connections to marae was also identified as a contributing factor to achieving the best outcome for children and young people in other regions, leading to a practice of holding family group conferences (FGC) or "hui-a-whanau" on marae at the request of those involved.[47] This allowed CYF staff to tap into the tikanga and cultural responsiveness of the marae to build positive and meaningful connections with the wider family/whanau of vulnerable young people. Liz Marsden says that marae-based hui provide a way to "safely challenge [whānau] to get their children back by sorting out their issues and making home safe for their kids." The connection to tikanga Māori principles and values of peace can help eliminate barriers and abate violence or arguments. Marsden sees "a real potential to reduce numbers coming into care, and to reduce their duration in care, by being involved early. We want a continuum of support, from families putting their hands up for help to referrals by statutory agencies." As much as possible, those involved try to intervene before crisis points are reached.

In Auckland, Papakura Marae CEO Tony Kake supports the marae-based hui and is positive about the outcomes it enables by immersing whanau "in ancestral connections, wairua and tikanga," empowering and putting them at ease. It is his hope that "whanau get a sense of neutrality by being on a marae." Auckland Region project specialist Danny Thompson acts as a kai korero (facilitator) alongside social workers at the hui to develop robust plans and ensure clear communication. He believes the hui and the broader relationships with marae that they represent are part of building capacity for social workers working with Māori. He says, "It's about working in partnership; it's about working together." He goes on to say, "We've been able to navigate our way through the most difficult and complex Māori cases and achieved good outcomes for mokopuna." Thompson shared a case study vignette of his own, contributing to the State Services Commission's online success stories from the Results program:

> I was recently asked to assist a C&P coordinator and social worker to meet the cultural needs of a whanau who there were a number of concerns for. The father was known by NZ Police and Police were asked to be on standby during the pre-FGC hui-a-whanau held at site due to the risk of the whanau becoming volatile.
>
> The whanau were resistant to our processes and colluded that the concerns were not valid. However, they did agree to hold the FGC on Manurewa marae and for myself to attend to support their cultural needs.
>
> Supported by Manurewa Marae kaumatua and the kai mahi for the

father, we were able to move through the FGC without any issues, and an agreed plan was formulated to transition the rangatahi back into the care of a whanau caregiver. The environment of the marae and those who led the culturally led process, supported by the social worker and coordinator, are what made the difference for this whanau.

Developing Relationship Maturity

This section explores relationship maturity and trust in interagency working and applies social psychology to explain the effect of the social identity of public servants on cooperation. Part of how this operates is through a feeling of accountability to peers, which functions as a normative behavior. Icek Ajzen's theory of planned behavior suggests that decisions to act are a product of the interaction between a person's own attitudes about the behavior, controls that influence the behavior (such as public servants' varied lines of accountability), and the person's beliefs about how others will view their behavior.[48]

The normative power of the group is a source of accountability less frequently discussed in public administration literature. Proximity is a significant contributor to influencing behavior, which is relevant in the case of the Results program because many of the groups involved met repeatedly—often weekly—over the five years.[49] In repeated interactions like this, public servants may exhibit what James Kahan described as interactive rationality.[50] In game theory, each interaction provides an opportunity to learn about and influence the likely future behavior of the other players. In games like the famous "prisoners' dilemma," the only way to win the game is by all parties trusting and cooperating. The best way to predict (and therefore trust) cooperative behavior is by establishing a pattern across repeated interactions.

In the context of the Results program, this was evident in the way the chief executives of departments appeared to exhibit more cooperative behaviors over time as they started to refer to each other as a single team, though it is difficult in this case to disentangle cause and effect. Unsurprisingly, collaboration appeared to be easier where there were existing relationships. The longer the partner agencies had been trying to work together, the more likely they were to be able to create the cognitive, emotional, and political ties that facilitate collaborative work.

However, this does not explain why some groups with long histories found progress more difficult than others did. Nor does it explain how some without prior history were able to develop momentum. At this point, the nearly fifty-year-old continuum of "closeness" may provide some of the contextual adaptations so often missing from the universal bent of horizontal management literature.[51] There are versions of this continuum in over thirty studies on horizontal management, all with differing language. A common variant identifies five types of interagency working: coexistence, communication, cooperation, coordination, and collaboration (see figure 13-3), whereby communication is the simplest form of interagency working and deep collaboration is the most complex and intimate form of horizontal management.

In this typology, the distinction between these different models of horizontal management is the extent to which the agencies align their goals, strategies, and work. Coexistence does not imply any (structured) horizontal management and may be the default setting of many government agencies. Communication involves a simple sharing of information about what each other is doing. Cooperation allows an aligning of some aspect of a policy or service delivery to allow each agency to achieve its separate goals more effectively. Each agency continues to be responsible for the services that it delivers. Coordination involves the realignment of existing activities toward the better achievement of overlapping goals. And collaboration implies that goals are aligned and that there may be joint design or delivery of policies and services. Each step along the continuum is thought to represent an increase in relationship complexity, and the implication is that more complex relationships are more difficult and should only be attempted when needed.

This played out clearly in the Results program, as the most rapid progress was made between those organizations with a history of successful cooperation; after all, the government had been trying to improve outcomes in these ten areas for some time. BPS Results 1 to 8 involved agencies with a prior history of working together under the Managing for Outcomes initiative and

FIGURE 13-3. Complexity Continuum of Horizontal Management

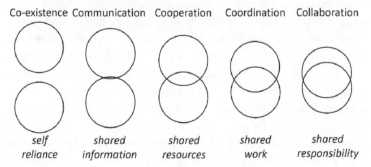

Co-existence Communication Cooperation   Coordination   Collaboration

self   shared   shared   shared   shared
reliance   information   resources   work   responsibility

Source: This version of the continuum draws most heavily from two previous versions, those by Eppel et al. (2013) and by the Nous Group (2013): Eppel, E., Gill, D., Lips, M., and Ryan, B. (2013). "The Cross-Organisation Collaboration Solution? Conditions, Roles and Dynamics in New Zealand." In: O'Flynn, J., Blackman, D. and Halligan, J. (Eds). *Crossing Boundaries in Public Management and Policy: The International Experience.* Routledge, 47–63. Nous Group. (2013). "*Collaboration between Sectors to Improve Customer Outcomes for Citizens of NSW.* Research report prepared for the NSW Public Service Commission. Nous Group.

resulting sector groups. Some of the successes of the Results program may well be attributed to these developmental stages having laid the groundwork. In discussion with the managers and practitioners involved, there is anecdotal evidence to support this explanation for the immunization portion of Result 3. However, the practitioners involved acknowledged that this likely explained only a small change in the measured outcome and only in the initial stages of the five-year program.

In Results 7 (reducing crime) and 8 (reducing criminal reoffending), the "justice sector" had been building progressively closer relationships since 2003, beginning with information sharing to understand the progression of individuals through the "justice sector pipeline" and then cooperation on a variety of initiatives culminating in pooled funding for innovation projects. When the Results program commenced in 2012, the agencies in the justice sector were able to quickly move to co-creating and co-delivering services, such as the frontline collaboration of the Hutt Valley Innovation Project described in chapter 5.

Ultimately, it is unlikely that the improvements in all ten Results initiatives can be explained by prior actions. Correctly predicting positive delayed effects in ten of ten initiatives would represent an extraordinary level of foresight. Indeed, the mixed rates of progress observed for some of the other Results suggests that a deeper interpretation of the continuum is required to describe the experience of participating agencies. This was particularly in those groups with significant prior interaction but where there was less evidence of prior successes, such as Result 2 (early childhood education) and Result 5 (high school graduation rates). Working together for a long time hadn't built trust, in part because those past interactions hadn't always been successful. This indicates that each step closer along the continuum requires greater mutual trust as a prerequisite because the consequences of being "let down" by your partners become greater, but it also presents an opportunity to build greater trust as a consequence of success (see figure 13-4). For example, while communication may not require significant amounts of trust to be already present, it provides an opportunity to demonstrate trustworthiness.

Engaging in communication does not require significant trust in the other agency to successfully deliver. As long as proper privacy and confidentiality is maintained, the ability of one agency to deliver is typically not significantly affected by what another agency does with its information. Cooperation only requires that agencies endeavor to use their shared information to operate in a more aligned manner. Each agency continues to maintain full responsibility for its services, and a failure of the one agency to deliver on its commitments usually has only a small impact on the others. It requires a moderate amount of trust to cooperate, and successful cooperation can build trust.

It is only when agencies coordinate that they start to really depend on each

FIGURE 13-4. Trust

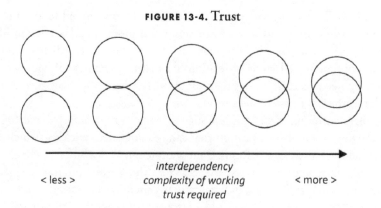

interdependency
< less >   complexity of working   < more >
trust required

Source: See source for figure 13-3, this volume.

other. Coordination involves modifying existing services such that they work better together. One agency will not willingly change its practices unless it is confident that the shared approach will work. A failure of one agency affects and interferes with the actions of another. Coordination requires significant trust to implement. Collaboration takes this even further, involving the co-creation of solutions for which agencies are then jointly and indivisibly responsible. A failure of one agency is a failure of all agencies. The highest degree of preexisting trust is required for agencies to feel comfortable committing to collaboration.

As the counterpoint, the greatest initial obstacles, more kindly referred to as growing pains, were faced by groups with little prior interaction. Result 9 (better for business) and Result 10 (digital services) participating agencies had to work hard to build even the basic levels of trust necessary to get started. The Ministry for Business Innovation and Employment and the Department of Internal Affairs took the lead, respectively, in trying to facilitate eight parties of strangers to develop a shared vision for the future. They were able to start with projects that required lower levels of mutual dependence—an information-sharing project developed in partnership between the Ministry for Business Innovation and Employment and the Inland Revenue Department. The Employer Registration Project allowed business owners to register as an employer at the same time they incorporated their company.[52] It also served to build the first stages of trust between those two agencies, allowing them to prove their trustworthiness by delivering on what was promised.

Although the agencies continued to work closely together to coordinate their respective business transformation programs, their broadly participative collaborative endeavors were ultimately not as successful as their less grandiose ideas around the edges were (their "road map" and "blueprints" remain unfulfilled). This is not to say that all interagency work should follow a natural progression (from left to right) of closer and more complex relationships. Rather, it suggests that it is worth considering whether intermediate outcomes are appropriate for all levels of relationship maturity. Perhaps if agencies feel that they need to collaborate, they should first ensure they can successfully work together in a less complex form.

Other communication literature suggests trust can be built by focusing on "quick wins"—small-scale projects that can be completed quickly—which was a methodology used by the Result 9 program team, as described in chapter 10 on public entrepreneurship. Experiences from the Results program suggest a slight correction to this idea, indicating that a small collaboration project may require more prior trust than would a large information sharing project. This is partly indicated by experiences from the justice sector prior to the Results program, whereby the pipeline concept acted as a forecasting service to share information about what the police and the courts were doing that would affect the Department of Corrections. This built trust and confidence among the agencies that then provided the basis for more active collaboration and interventions like custodial change management.

Similarly, some quick wins from Result 9 that were used to generate momentum with an associated increase of trust and confidence were relatively simple information-sharing projects. For example, the ONECheck tool launched in 2012 on the business.govt.nz website involved communication across the New Zealand Companies Office, Intellectual Property Office of New Zealand, and the Domain Names Commission to allow businesses to check the availability of company names, domains, and trademarks with one search. The tool was one of the most popular features of the business.govt.nz site.[53] The sharing of information from registers held by three different agencies did not present any significant risks or result in any interdependencies that would require trade-offs and therefore did not require much prior trust. Conversely, flagship programs like the New Zealand Business Number and RealMe required collaboration across the whole system and created dependencies between agencies and may have been attempted too early in the process.

That does not negate the broader point—working horizontally requires a bias for action. Because horizontal management requires trust, the tendency of public servants is to begin cautiously, and "feel each other out." Each of the examples above involves building trust by working together in some way. The New Zealand government encouraged (some would say forced) this bias toward action through the requirement that each of the ten Results submit, within three months, an action plan for what tangible actions each would take over the first year of the program. Chapter 6 describes how the justice sector used its Action Plan to get started. A template used for the Action Plans is included as appendix 1, to be adapted for use by other jurisdictions as needed.

Digging deeper into the formation of trust, it's not just proximity and experience of collaborative success that contribute—social identity also starts to play a part. This has been described as a three-stage process in which individuals first organize social information by categorizing people into groups, individuals then give these groups meaning through social comparison and, finally, individuals identify themselves with these categories (or not). The norms of the groups that individuals define themselves as members of have a much greater effect on how they behave than do those from outside the group.[54]

Of course, identity is complex, and not all comparisons are equal. This is expressed in the Bedouin saying, "I am against my brother, my brother and I are against my cousin, my cousin and I are against the stranger."[55] Public servants each have a variety of social identities, from personal and professional lives, that overlap and interact. Social identities from their personal lives may include groups like family, nationality, ethnicity, gender, sexuality, religion, political views, hobbies, fandom, and so on. Social identities from professional life may include professions, teams, organizations, and the broader group called the public service. For simplicity, this chapter only considers the relative importance of identifying with the agency and identifying with the horizontal group responsible for achieving the Result.

Through a series of experiments, Marilynn Brewer and others have observed that the order, or relative importance, of each group membership is important.[56] Groups with a "differentiated group identity," in which individuals identify more with a subgroup than with the whole group, were less cooperative than were those with a stronger "superordinate group identity," wherein individuals identify more strongly with the whole than with the subgroups, and were able to manage resources more effectively (see figure 13-5).

In New Zealand, at least since the New Public Management reforms of the late 1980s and early 1990s, there has been an emphasis on the identity of agencies, with a focus on individualized branding and developing a strong and

FIGURE 13-5. Cooperation and Social Identity Complexity

= Less cooperation

Differentiated group identity: Social identity stronger with subgroup than whole

= More cooperation

Superordinate group identity: Social identity stronger with whole than subgroup

Source: Scott, R. J. (2019). "Public Service Motivation and Social Identity." Presented at the International Research Society for Public Management annual conference, Wellington.

distinct organizational culture. In this respect, social identity provides a new theoretical basis for understanding the challenges of managing horizontally. Not only must public servants reconcile differing interests, with real sacrifices needing to be made, they must also overcome a much stronger sense of identity with their agency rather than with the group working toward a shared goal. This is illustrated using the example of the three agencies working together on Results 7 and 8—the New Zealand Police, the Ministry of Justice, and the Department of Corrections—or collectively termed the justice sector (see figure 13-6).

In an interview, a leader of the justice sector described how meeting every two weeks for five years created a sense of trust (what Kahan would call "interactive rationality"). But they also described something deeper—a sense of shared identity. Public servants working for each of the three agencies would describe themselves as "members of the justice sector." Similarly, recommendations from the Result 9 "health check" report were for the Result team to "develop its own sense of identity" and possibly to "physically relocate all program resources to a new environment designed for collaborative working."[57]

A previous section described an innovation from the justice sector whereby the three agencies would provide consolidated advice to their ministers on issues that affected each other. On one occasion, in early 2015, one agency reportedly broke this norm and provided separate advice to its individual minister. It was quickly rebuked by the group with the simple statement "that's not what we do," and from several accounts, that was enough to restore the previous cooperative practice (the terms of reference for the group were also subsequently revised to clarify expectations). Statements about who *we* are and what *we* do or don't do can be important drivers of behavior within a group with a strong shared identity. In their text on "identity economics," George Akerlof and Rachel Kranton give the striking example of social identity altering behavior in an elementary school.[58] The headmaster recognized that he

FIGURE 13-6. A Hypothetical Example of Differentiated Group Identity

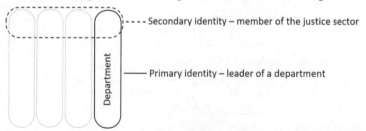

Source: Scott, R. J. (2019). "Public Service Motivation and Social Identity." Presented at the International Research Society for Public Management annual conference, Wellington.

had succeeded in reforming the appalling conduct at the school when he saw a student stop a fight with the words: *"We don't do that in this school."*

Horizontal management inevitably incurs significant transaction costs, primarily the time commitment of many of the most senior public servants in the country. But this commitment of time contributed to a newly forged shared identity, and as trust increased, transaction costs declined somewhat. The behaviors of public servants in interagency groups could be the subject of a whole other book; for the purpose of this book, it is enough to say that work seemed to progress more quickly as public servants from different agencies developed closer relationships with each other. Throughout the five years of the program, public servants remained committed to making it work. Although they were reluctant to go on the record to discuss relationship breakdowns, several remarked that the targets provided a reason to keep going. The lessons of the Results program as presented in this book are less about making horizontal management easy and more about making the impetus to overcome those challenges—the goal commitment—stronger than the difficulties of interagency working. The beauty of the Results program was that it worked even when trust was reduced and collaboration was hard.

Trust and Continuity in the Justice Sector (Results 7 and 8)

The justice sector is a clear choice for a case study of relationship maturity, just as it was the most natural cluster of Results. As discussed in the section on managing group size, the three large departments (Ministry of Justice, New Zealand Police, and Department of Corrections) largely held responsibility for the targets of reducing crime and reoffending, supported by smaller agencies. The "big three" agencies had first started working together in the early 2000s, analyzing the relationships between their interventions and activities. This analysis and recognition of interdependence resulted in the concept of the justice sector "pipeline," which formed the basis for successful collaborative operations well before the Results program was introduced. Scott et al. (2019) describe the pipeline as a metaphor that helped the justice sector retain lessons from its earlier experiences and therefore sustain a long-lasting collaboration.[59]

The justice sector was formalized as such between 2007 and 2012, building on earlier information sharing dating back to 2003. The justice sector group had well-established governance systems, with the chief executives of the Justice Sector Leadership Board meeting monthly and deputy chief executives meeting fortnightly. Given its head start, the justice sector was able to quickly change the way it operated to organize around achievement of the offending targets when it was given responsibility for them in the Results program. Early progress toward target achievement was also rapid. From the first progress report the rating was Green—"on track to achieve the target"—for both reducing crime and reducing reoffending.

Those involved said that one of their key success factors was that the pipeline concept provided a clear rationale for the necessity of the sector's collaboration. One public servant from the justice sector pointed out the need to "work out what are the things that will pull it together, what are the things that will keep it together, and what are the things that will transcend the personal relationships over time." Others noted that the "natural" or "fairly obvious pipeline" meant they were "naturally linked in" or bound together "more than any other sector."

The justice Results depended on preventative action—reducing crime and stemming the flow into the pipeline. For people in the prison part of the pipeline, improving outcomes depended on rehabilitation and reintegration into society following release, rather than reentering the pipeline:

> The criminal justice system pipeline starts very much in the policy area then policing and then courts and then on to corrections, so there's a natural synergy across the sector.
>
> [It] very much is about understanding how the pipeline operates, understanding how people come into the system, how they exit the system, what happens to them when they're in the system, and what are the different points of intervention we have.

The pipeline metaphor provided good explanatory power for the linear dependencies between the components of the justice system, including "custodial management of offenders, the relationship of policy to operations, and the interdependency of resource allocation and business planning between departments." Aphra Green noted a "collective belief in what we are doing that is greater than our agency selves," which is not inherently an enduring condition.[60]

Another factor that set the justice sector apart from others was that it was predisposed to adhere to processes. A dedicated secretariat helped embed this by maintaining normative agenda, decisionmaking, monitoring, and reporting processes. This meant that this sector was able to achieve incremental progress, sometimes through relentless optimism in the face of repetitive meeting "every fortnight or every week [over] a number of years." This was reiterated by another justice sector public servant:

> I think the thing that I see quite a lot in the Justice Sector is people working together week after week, and it kind of sounds a bit simple, but actually it is about meeting a lot, talking a lot, establishing relationships a lot, and doing things that are purposeful in those meetings.

Sticking Together

Accountability in cross-cutting problems is made more difficult by the problem of many hands. The Results program succeeded in making small groups of public servants feel equally responsible for achieving something. As groups learned to trust one another, they were progressively more willing to enter dependent relationships and modify their own activities to fit into a stronger whole.

A few of the governance arrangements actually preceded the Results program, and most have survived its end. During this time, all the senior parties have been replaced, and yet the arrangements persist. Returning to the justice sector (Results 7 and 8), there were no current members (at the time of writing) of the Justice Sector Leadership Board who were members in 2012, let alone in the earlier phases of interagency coordination dating as far back as 2003. Individuals had been replaced in the group through promotions, resignations, and regular rotations, and new members were inducted by the remaining members into the established operating norms and values. Interviews conducted in 2018 revealed similar language used by current justice sector employees and justice sector employees from the early 2000s.[61] The need for continuity now informs the State Services Commission's approach to leadership deployment, with efforts to stagger rotations to ensure that there always remains a stable core to maintain the culture of a successful governance grouping. As previous manager in the justice sector group, Paul O'Connell, noted:

> The more you can solidify processes that outlive given personalities, then so long as everybody doesn't change at once, you've got a chance that the process and "the way things are done around here" endures beyond a given individual.[62]

14

Valence in Goal Commitment

Valence is a term used in discussion of goal commitment to refer to the value or perceived contribution of achieving a goal or target. It is sometimes discussed as "mission valence" in public administration scholarship, especially in terms of the motivational effect of "making a difference."[1] Mission valence can be thought of as a public servant's perception of the attractiveness of a mission[2] or the alignment between that mission and their personal values.[3]

This tends to be obvious at the front line. Examples might include teachers who care about the education of their students or nurses who care about the health of their patients. However, policy makers and public managers also seek out work that aligns with their values and are motivated by making a difference. Just as a teacher is motivated by making a difference in the lives of students, so too might the chief executive of the Ministry of Education be.[4] Yet this spirit of service to the community, so obvious in the attitudes and behaviors of public servants, often receives scant attention in program design.[5]

In the context of the Results program, goal commitment was clearly influenced by the valence of the Results themselves and the way the intrinsic motivation of public servants was buttressed by reporting practices and the use of data. The New Zealand Results program was popular and motivational for public servants throughout its five years. In part, this was due to public servants feeling like they were making a difference and being praised for this by the media. But with this focus on improvement, the final success or failure in achieving the target was diminished. Focusing on improvements or on achieving the final goal each involves trade-offs and results in different behaviors.

Intrinsic and Extrinsic Motivation

Experiments described in goal commitment literature assume that following the completion of the task, an individual is directly rewarded or punished. According to "loss aversion" in prospect theory, punishment is more effective than reward. Amos Tversky and Daniel Kahneman's famous experiments in the 1970s observed that people would place a higher value on something they already had (and might lose) than things they might gain.[6] This was interpreted as suggesting that sanctions would be more effective than rewards at driving performance. In the case of public servants, the implication was that fear of reputational loss is more powerful than the potential for reputational gain.

Linking target regimes to punishment and sanctions has traditionally been effective. In the Soviet system, speculation held that such sanctions could mean death or disappearance (see subsection on the Soviet Union target regime in chapter 2). Under the UK Delivery Unit, the consequences were less dramatic but negative nonetheless. Underperforming individuals (or rather, the leaders of underperforming units) were sanctioned for poor performance, either through being fired ("targets and terror") or through being publicly humiliated as a poor performer ("naming and shaming"). The prime minister's Delivery Unit had combined the theory of loss aversion with the "knights and knaves" dichotomy, which is also a prevalent construct in public administration. The dichotomy appeared as early as the 1700s when David Hume rhetorically divided members of a group into "knights," virtuous and altruistic in their intentions, and "knaves," self-invested and amoral.[7] As Hume saw it, it was very difficult to determine in advance who was in which group, and he therefore proposed that all people must necessarily be treated as knaves to prevent knavish behavior, regardless of whether they were. In the Delivery Unit, the theories were combined to great effect, resulting in a system to root out knavish behavior by punishing poor performance.

If a unit didn't perform up to a required standard, it was publicly highlighted as a poor performer, a practice that became known as "naming and shaming." If an individual leader was unable to improve the performance of their unit over time, the person was fired, earning the regime the title "targets and terror." Those involved believe that this created a sense of urgency and commitment to improvement, and the practice certainly drove home the need for strong attribution between the actions within the control of the leader and the measured result. It would be neither fair nor defensible to fire someone for events out of their control. This forced the UK regime toward the right-hand side of figure 12-1, this volume, with measures of activities and outputs like "hospital waiting times."

Use of such severe negative consequences for poor performance in the United Kingdom may not have been sustainable. It reportedly left the public service demoralized and fearful.[8] Sir Julian Le Grand eventually realized that fear was only useful for improving the worst performers—driving performance from "awful" to "adequate." There came a point at which "flogging the horse harder" did not produce additional results. By the time the approach was abandoned, those parts of the UK civil service most affected by the targets were reportedly deeply demoralized, and Tony Blair remarked "I bear the scars on my back" from years of conflict.[9]

It is no wonder then that target regimes around the world tend to be unpopular with public servants, seen as managerial tools that get in the way of public servants' higher calling. They have been criticized for decreasing both morale and intrinsic motivation over time, as public servants focus more on achieving the target and less on making a difference.[10] This links back to chapter 12 on expectancy, whereby it is important to select measures that fall at the right point between outputs and outcomes. Figure 12-1, this volume, which illustrates outputs and outcomes in terms of their intrinsic value, can also be depicted in terms of how meaningful a goal might be to public servants as compared with its instrumentality—the relationship between the work of the individual and its effect on achieving the goal. Public servants feel they have more control over outputs (instrumentality) but find outcomes more meaningful (see figure 14-1).

Meaningfulness refers to perception of the goal's value. In the Results program, targets were meaningful because they related to problems that were important to New Zealanders, were priorities of government, and were framed at an intermediate-outcome level such that they could be seen as intrinsically valuable (in contrast to output or activity measures).

FIGURE 14-1. Meaningfulness and Instrumentality

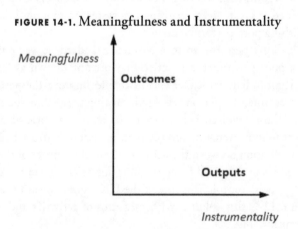

Source: Scott, R., and Boyd, R. (2017). *Interagency Performance Targets: A Case Study of New Zealand's Results Programme.* IBM Centre for the business of government.

To be sustainable, it was clear that New Zealand's interagency performance programs must be compatible with a spirit of service to the community. New Zealand started with the "knights and knaves" dichotomy but, in stark contrast to the UK Delivery Unit, did not forget about the motivations of "knights." Where proponents of new public management suggest that the assumption that all public servants act out of rational self-interest is "a useful lie," the New Zealand perspective leaned toward a more complete and more human-ist understanding of motivation. The New Zealand government assumed that public servants were not motivated by producing goods or services (outputs) but instead by the outcomes to which they contributed. This meant that it was important that the Results program was not purely a rational exercise but was instead designed to capture the imagination of public servants and encourage them to maximize their effort, urgency, and commitment

This required an acknowledgement of the ways in which both intrinsic and extrinsic motivations in the public sector differ from those in the private sector (which are often assumed in the goal commitment literature). As discussed in chapter 13 on instrumentality, part of this difference is because account-ability in the public sector is complicated. Public servants are accountable "to everyone"—ministers, Parliament, the State Services commissioner, peers, and the public. And in accountability documents presented to Parliament, they had to demonstrate how their contributions aligned with and contributed to the work of others.

Public servants are thought to place much greater weight on intrinsic moti-vations to serve the community than employees in other sectors.[11] As Orange puts it, "The very idea of public service is a call to intrinsic values of service to our community."[12] Recognition of this fact has long held a place in the New Zealand system, with Gladden's 1945 requirement of the public service to be "imbued with a spirit of service to the community" making its way into the long title of the State Services Act 1962 and purpose statement of the State Sector Act (1988).[13]

The importance of intrinsic motivation to public servants has a correspond-ing effect on their extrinsic motivations—the rewards and sanctions that will drive them. When compared with the private sector, employment in the public sector typically involves a lesser role for performance-related pay.[14] Instead, rec-ognition and reputation tend to be strong motivators for public servants. For many senior public servants, their reputation for doing a good job and helping their community plays an important part in their sense of self.[15]

People are capable of holding a range of interests and motivations that can be encouraged or discouraged by their environments. Motivation crowding theory provides evidence that appealing only to the self-interested motivations of "knaves" can crowd out "knightly" motivations.[16] The Results program had inbuilt recognition of the fact that knavish behavior is often in the minority and that the dichotomy is not an absolute or a permanent classification. In performance meetings with their employer, the State Services commissioner, chief executives were rewarded with performance bonuses for the collective performance of the Results to which they contributed, but performance bonuses were ultimately eliminated because they were thought to crowd out intrinsic motivation.

Ultimately, there was a far greater place in the Results program for rewards than for sanctions or punishment. Pedagogical theory on achievement motivation suggested that learning, experimentation, and innovation—the hallmarks of entrepreneurial behavior—would be encouraged when success was praised and when innovators were able to quickly move on from failures.[17] There would need to be a balance between the urgency to act and the freedom to create. Orange also noted the importance of intrinsic motivation for driving dynamism, which he identified along with trust and responsiveness as the "essential characteristics of an effective civil service," especially in a complex and highly mutable world.[18] Similarly, Le Grand concluded that while fear was effective in driving conformity, it could not drive innovation.[19] The fear of being on the bottom of the ranking table was motivating those at the bottom to try to replicate the practices of those at the top (or at least the middle). This wouldn't have worked in New Zealand, because the problems selected for the Results program did not have known solutions, and therefore there was no best practice to conform to. New Zealand public servants would need to innovate, not conform.

The program reporting gave rise to a practice of "naming and faming" rather than "naming and shaming." In meetings with ministers, no one was punished for falling behind on progress to achieve their targets. Instead, they were subject to greater scrutiny and more intense questioning. The focus was on learning. Ministers wanted to know what the barriers were to things improving and how these barriers could be removed; they simply wanted to be confident that everything possible was being done. This was particularly effective because it tapped into the intrinsic motivations of public servants who care about their reputations and base their identity and self-esteem, at least in part, on the notion that they are doing something valuable for their community.

Having the interest and occasional attendance at board meetings of the senior ministers involved in the program, including the deputy prime minister, provided a boost to Result teams. These meetings were opportunities for the teams to share case studies from their work and present data proving the impact they were having. For example, the early learning taskforce from Result 2 told ministers that lack of money was not the problem—a huge amount of funding was going to disadvantaged areas—the problem was the siloed way the funding was used, flawed operating models that were not family centric, and programs that were not sustainable once the agencies withdrew (because agencies hadn't strengthened the communities they worked in). Ministers were interested in what was happening, asking questions like "Why didn't we know about this before?" Their interest had a profound impact on both the motivation of the team and the mandate for their work. In Calcott-Cribb's view: "This is what drove us."[20]

Ministers' response to poor progress in the data was typically to work out what was really happening and constructively address the issues presented. This approach meant that casualties from inaccurate or misleading measures were limited. If officials had been publicly "beaten up" for failure to achieve a target when the fault was with the way progress was measured rather than lack of action on their behalf, dysfunctional behavior (such as gaming the numbers) would probably have resulted. A trusting relationship between the government and the public service was a key ingredient of success. Equally, success of the BPS Results increased government's confidence in the public service to deliver, leading to greater involvement of officials in the refresh of the program discussed in chapter 7.

At the end of the program, public servants were even more enthusiastic and committed to achieving the Results than they had been at the beginning. They reported that the targets had a "galvanizing" effect on them and served as a "rallying call."[21] Orange noted that "the Results spoke to the key drivers of why many of the people working on the Results had become public servants in the first place."[22] Public servants changed their behavior not because of the consequences of failure to achieve a target, but because they believed it was the right thing to do, because it improved people's lives. Foy describes it as "hacking government from the inside," the idea that people motivated by doing the right thing for the public could sabotage the bad ways of working and promote good practice.[23]

At the end of the day, even when the targets weren't quite met, their impact was to change the way the public sector operated to achieve results. They managed to lift public sector morale and belief in what could be achieved. People involved in the program were motivated and energized by success and wanted to be part of it. As Calcott-Cribb put it:

> I loved this job. It was the highlight of my career. We did some really big things and cut through existing ways of operating in the public sector. People are still talking about what we did. [24]

Thus, the attractiveness of goal attainment must be viewed both in the context of the extrinsic motivations traditionally assumed in goal commitment literature as well as the intrinsic motivation of public servants to meaningfully serve the community. Unsurprisingly, the reality of the complex social problems discussed in this book is more complicated than the theory.

Emotive Vignettes about the NCEA Target (Result 5)

The concerted effort made throughout the Results program to frame progress in terms of impact on individuals contributed to the development of public interest and therefore to public servants' sense of commitment. In Result 5, case study vignettes published by the State Services Commission included substantial quotes from people directly affected by the program's interventions. Conversations centered on data drove a particular focus on individuals for the Result 5 target to increase the proportion of eighteen-year-olds with NCEA Level 2. Schools began to focus their attention on students performing below the standard required by the qualification, organizing one-on-one meetings with the students and their families to identify stumbling blocks and implement plans for maximizing their educational achievement.

Broader capability for schools to develop and offer courses that had greater relevance to their students' needs, often grounded in the world of work, became a significant contributor to the success of these plans. For many students, coordinating with trade education providers through the Trades Academy or Vocational Pathways programs reinforced the relevance and importance of gaining a qualification and improved student attitudes to their own learning. The programs are able to provide more hands-on and employer-relevant learning that is aligned with real-world jobs or further education and training opportunities. The students involved benefit from connections with prospective employers, community organizations, and service groups.

In a particularly emotive section from one of the case study vignettes, Massey High School principal Bruce Ritchie described the motivations of him and his staff in supporting these linkages to vocational pathways.[25] For them, the target is about more than just ticking boxes and changing the statistics. They are truly moved by students achieving things that they might never have thought possible and by the pride that those students' parents have in them. Ritchie gave two poignant examples of how the programs were touching students' lives:

> One student on work experience from the Academy burst into tears in a review, saying that they were the only person in their family who had ever had a job. They now have part-time work and an offer of full-time work once they complete the academy.
>
> One at-risk student, unlikely to remain in school, attended the Academy and now has employment in an apprenticeship. The student returned to thank the school and inform students how important the academy was. We encourage this—it has happened in about a dozen cases already.
>
> Partnering with vocational and trades academies, and the arrival of

the Vocational Pathways programme, are two of the most significant changes made for New Zealand's students in recent years. Both are changing pupils' lives, and their futures.

There are similar stories from other schools using the Vocational Pathways program, integrating it with the existing Gateway program that supplemented NCEA with workplace learning. At Ruapehu College, the school's Gateway coordinator Liz Hall describes the effect of helping her students start on pathways to their future careers: "When I see a student go on to do something they really want to do, it's great. It's very heartwarming."[26]

Sentiments of dedication to improving student outcomes and the resulting personal satisfaction expressed by teachers were also included in the reporting on a collaboration effort that brought together twelve schools in West Auckland to form a Community of Learning (CoL). The CoL was intended to improve teaching quality and raise the level of achievement for students as well as broaden career opportunities for teachers and principals. In another case study vignette on the initiative, the deputy principal of Waitakere College and leader of the Waitakere CoL Shona Smith noted, "a genuine commitment from all teaching staff to lift their knowledge and practice of culturally responsive pedagogy," as well as support and commitment from the school boards of trustees.[27]

Part of the CoL's plans was to consult much more directly with students about what their needs were and how they could best be supported to achieve. As Smith put it, "Our students are our success story, and we want them to share their journeys and dreams. Our job is to listen, enhance their stories, support their journeys, and help them realize their aspirations." Smith went on to express the scale of the challenge in discovering "what actions and interventions in practice will make a difference to student achievement" and vehemently confirming the commitment of those involved, saying on behalf of the CoL: "We will definitely give everything we have to ensure our achievement challenges are realized and the journey for our entire CoL community is inclusive and rewarding. . . . We are working as a team rather than as islands, and we will gradually understand what is possible at each school—we know we can't do everything!"

Reporting

Naming and faming individuals is more complicated in New Zealand than in some other countries. New Zealanders are often embarrassed to be given workplace awards, and "tall poppies" may be the subject of resentment or cynicism.[28] The Results reporting achieved naming and faming through a rather more indirect mechanism. In the beginning of the program, successes were described in largely impersonal terms. The dashboard would include a few lines about a new program that had been launched and a figure regarding its effectiveness. But progressively the reporting became more personal; the stories became more localized and more specific.

There were still no awards or individuals praised for their achievements. Instead the reporting focused on telling the stories of individual New Zealanders whose lives had been improved through local innovations (see appendix 4 for examples). This had practical benefits in allowing innovations to be emulated elsewhere in the program, forming the basis of a new best practice.[29] But it also had a motivational benefit in rewarding those who tried new things, as the public servants who had helped the individual New Zealanders started to be named in reports, pictured in the case vignettes, or interviewed in the videos. For example, Fati, the Youth Service case worker was mentioned in the story of Sam, an at-risk youth, whom he had helped by being flexible and resourceful (see chapter 6 for the full story). This was the start of the "faming" in naming and faming. Because the public servants were famed almost incidentally, the program managed to avoid much of the backlash that can accompany direct reputational rewards.

That said, given that recognition proved to be a stronger lever for change than holding people to account, publishing case study vignettes and videos were not the only way in which collaborative values were rewarded by central agencies. Examples of collaborative action were also entered into the national public sector awards, with award winners and other nominees recognized at a glittering ceremony and dinner. Recognition was given not only for innovation but also for demonstration of public service values such as working collaboratively and focusing on improving people's lives. The State Services minister and State Services commissioner have put a change in values, particularly strengthening the spirit of service, at the center of the next wave of reform in New Zealand's public service, as described in the previous chapter.

Aside from the benefits of naming and faming, the program reporting also garnered the support and interest of the public. It did this to a much greater extent than previous centrally run programs had, mostly because the reporting was easy for the media to pick up and use in ways that were engaging and interesting to their audience. As Calcott-Cribb explained, they were able to tell compelling stories from the program because they "felt the heartbeat of it so much."[30] Every six months, the government would release visually interesting progress reports in a concise and consistent format that was easy to understand, alongside individual case studies that would highlight progress with a more personal touch. Progress toward the target was published online with a "traffic light" rating that showed whether the target was on track to be reached and analysis about why or why not. Each release every six months was accompanied by a burst of media coverage.

This public attention contributed to the government's sense of commitment. It could be challenging for the agencies responsible, but it drove significant change. The program was based on having a few priority outcomes set at a level at which compelling data could be used to drive action. The progress reports were the acid on agencies to deliver; they were the mechanism through which individual ministers and chief executives could be held accountable. If the public was less interested, it would have been easier to quietly modify or shutdown the program if things didn't go well. It also likely contributed to the motivation of public servants to be seen to be making a difference in things that matter to New Zealanders.

It is remarkable that the program was described so near universally among public servants, ministers, and the media as a great success, despite the fact that only about two-thirds of targets were achieved, and in only one case (Result 5) was this unambiguous. The answer may be in how the New Zealand government reacted to failures and how it framed improvements that ultimately fell short of the target. Instead of putting providers in competition with each other as the United Kingdom had done in its star rating system for hospitals and ranking system for schools, the Results program encouraged providers of different services to work together. Instead of judging below average schools and hospitals as failing, New Zealand assessed progress toward the somewhat arbitrary targets.

For example, in Result 1, the target to reduce the number of people continuously receiving Jobseeker Support benefit for twelve months by 30 percent doesn't make any judgment about the current level; was the number of people currently receiving Jobseeker Support benefit for longer than twelve months too high? Is a 30 percent reduction good? How many are a "good" or even "acceptable" number of able-bodied working-age people to be continuously out of work for over a year? Some of these questions are unanswerable. But the 2011 baseline was deemed too high, and the 30 percent reduction target was set based on what the edge of possible was—the greatest reduction that the government could reasonably hope for over that period rather than on a level of benefit reception that would be considered acceptable.

Because the target is expressed as an improvement from a baseline rather than as the achievement of an acceptable standard, interpretation of the success or failure to reach that target is very different. As it happened, the Result 1 target was easily met, but the immunization target for Result 3 was not. Early progress in the immunization part of Result 3 was solid, increasing at about 1 percent a quarter. The immunization rate of eight-month-olds reached 89 percent by March 2013 and 93.5 percent by December 2014, well on track to achieve the interim target of 95 percent by the end of 2015. But in March of 2015, an unexpected drop in immunization of 0.6 percent was the first indication that reaching this target would not be smooth sailing the whole way. Ultimately in 2017, the rate stopped just short of the target of 95 percent.

Such progress can either be reported as a success, in improving immunization rates, or a failure, in missing the target. In the program, any progress toward the targets was typically expressed as an improvement. This is also how the progress was picked up by the media, and public servants were celebrated for having reduced the number of unvaccinated children by almost two-thirds. Whether the targets themselves were ultimately achieved, public servants were given credit for having made improvements in persistent and important problems. This in turn made public servants feel like their work was valuable and recognized. The Results program showed that targets don't have to be associated with terror.

Part of the reason the targets garnered public interest was the conscious effort to frame the Results as describing something intrinsically valuable and important to New Zealanders. It is easy for governments to lose perspective and get caught up in strategies, road maps, working papers, inquiries, and reports, which all mean very little to citizens, especially those who are the most vulnerable and in greatest need of government assistance. This was the case with the US Cross-Agency Priority Goals, also mentioned in the discussion of expectancy. When the Obama administration set the goal to "expand the use of high-quality, high-value strategic sourcing solutions in order to improve the government's buying power and reduce contract duplication," it is unlikely it had in mind connecting with the public. This goal was set for an internal audience—a technical goal to clarify objectives for public servants.

But public servants are not unfeeling automatons, and the Results program recognized that they are typically motivated by a sense of wanting to help their community. To appeal to "knights," the Results needed to be framed so it was clear that they were about making a difference for New Zealanders.

The Results program was a very high-level and strategic construct. It could easily have been described in terms of "cross-agency working groups" or "taskforces." Instead, it was described as something very practical and real, something that was connected to people in the community. It was a reporting mechanism for government performance that focused less on government and more on the communities that it served.

Minister Response to Rheumatic Fever Progress Data (Result 3)

Many of the Result areas made stilted progress as it became evident that the remaining few percent that needed to achieve the targets were from the hardest to reach families. There were similar bumps for the rheumatic fever target; when the Cabinet considered progress mid-2014, it found there had been a small *increase* in the incidence of rheumatic fever. There were several possible explanations for this, the most favorable being that improved detection and awareness of the disease led to a higher rate of diagnosis. The progress rating for the biannual report to the Cabinet was Amber (progress, but issues to resolve). When the Department of the Prime Minister and Cabinet and the Prime Minister's Office were presented with reports outlining the lack of progress so far, they were concerned, but ultimately trusting. They were prepared to listen and accept Dr. Pickin's (leader of the rheumatic fever prevention program) assurance that they were still on the right track (or rather that there was no other track that had more or better evidence behind it).

The central agencies had made it clear what the Result team was being held accountable for. As Dr. Pickin put it, "It wasn't just for achieving the target; we were being asked to work differently, to think differently. Even if we failed to achieve the target, we could shift the paradigm and make progress. There was tight monitoring, but always a focus on 'what have you learned and what is transferrable?' "[31] Furthermore, "The central agencies didn't panic when the rate increased instead of declined; rather they listened to the reasons for this and backed us to stay the course." The strong interest and support of the prime minister and other senior ministers, whom Dr. Pickin described as "tough, bright, and consistent," helped make sure the program didn't falter.

Even after the trend changed and the program team started to make progress, Dr. Pickin insisted that the rating remain Amber. This was partly an acknowledgement that the data were volatile, but it was also because the target was for a two-thirds reduction, and even the current trend would not achieve that. Had the target been less ambitious, Dr. Pickin and her team might have relaxed. Instead, they continued to push for improvement through the initiatives discussed later in this chapter. The response to a remarkable improvement in the data was, yes, this is good progress, but more effort is needed if the target is to be achieved.

In addition to retaining the support of ministers when progress was tough, rather than being punished, the determination of Dr. Pickin, her team, community organizations, and the district health boards were rewarded with public recognition in success stories on the Better Public Services webpage and in the "learning from what works" section in the midyear 2015 progress report to the Cabinet. The methodology of the Results program was very much to focus on improvement rather than to seek out and punish failure. Every opportunity was taken to celebrate innovative actions that led to improvement. Striving to achieve an ambitious target is a powerful motivator provided the targets function more as an instrument for improvement than for accountability.

Data, Feedback, and Learning

While a spirit of service to the community is an important motivator for public servants, sometimes it can be difficult for individuals to see how they're making a difference. While frontline staff can understand their impact through the lives of the service recipients, for public managers, the changes can be more abstract. The use of lead indicators and timely data provided a way for public managers to make sense of the relationship between their work and outcomes for New Zealanders.[32]

The focus on data was inspired by the approaches of the -Stat systems described in chapter 3. Over the course of the program, the use of data grew in maturity and effectiveness. Sharing data became a way to identify hard-to-reach families and link them with government services. The senior manager in the Ministry of Education responsible for coordinating the education Results observed in an interview that the introduction of the BPS Results changed the conversations within the Ministry of Education.[33] They were increasingly data conversations—analysis of areas of nonachievement and nonparticipation, raising questions about what it would take to make a difference in these areas. These conversations involved strategic policy teams, data and analytics teams, and specialist action teams, which became involved in joint problem-solving to an extent that hadn't happened before the program. As the maturity around data conversations grew, a deeper understanding developed about how agencies should operate as a system.

Similar observations were made in the justice sector, wherein Aphra Green observed that "Data permeated everything we did . . . performance information drove the business . . . it was a powerful driver of change."[34] The targets were not necessarily focused on the right things, but the data "drove the right conversations." In Green's view, data were the basis for chief executives being able to sit outside their businesses and collectively decide what they should do differently in their own agencies and together.

Conversations based on evidence and data were also powering the Social Investment work. This approach is broadly described as a combination of four features: putting people at the center, using data and analytics, investing early, and improving outcomes for vulnerable populations. Putting people at the center means being driven by improving the lives of individuals – particularly those who need government support – moving government from service-centric to person-centric ways of thinking. Delivery of better services becomes based on a better understanding of what services people are currently receiving, the cost and effectiveness of these services, and identification of any gaps. This is where using data and analytics comes in—taking advantage of advances in data infrastructure and analytics to understand how services have affected peoples' lives. Investing early means using these insights to determine what conditions need to be addressed early in their lives if individuals are to change the paths they are on and achieve better long-term outcomes. Improving outcomes for vulnerable populations means focusing on the groups of individuals that share characteristics and early investments to change their trajectories and improve long-term outcomes.

This approach was hugely influential for identifying the drivers of long-term disadvantage, helping public servants determine what was working and what actions would be needed to change the life outcomes of New Zealanders. Ministers were able to ask how to most effectively allocate resources across the social sector, using knowledge of what specific interventions would have the biggest rate of return in the longer term to make better budget decisions. Part of this was understanding how particular policy areas were performing and how they interrelated. For example, was it better for the government to spend an extra dollar in youth justice or in education to reduce crime levels? The approach added discipline to evaluation of the evidence, applying "big data" analysis to population groups. An example of this analysis is provided in the box 14-1.

Government was thinking about outcomes in terms of related social issues, drivers of cost, and long-term benefit for individuals:

We know there is a link between early childhood experiences and adult mental health, drug and alcohol abuse, poor educational outcomes and unemployment. Too many children are at risk of poor outcomes because they do not get the early support they need.

The human and financial costs of not facing up to these challenges are too high. We know that remedial spending is often less effective, and more costly, than getting it right the first time.

Early intervention brings benefits in terms of reduced imprisonment and arrest rates, higher employment, and higher earnings later in life. By doing better for vulnerable children, we could set them on a pathway to a positive future and help build a more productive and competitive economy for all New Zealanders.[35]

The integrated data infrastructure and social investment approach were crucial for revealing ethnic disparities that allowed program teams to better target their interventions. For example, New Zealand data on early learning showed participation rates for Māori and Pasifika children, and children from low socioeconomic areas, were significantly lower than for other population groups. Ethnicity data featured in reporting for all the education Results, in which the lead indicator for the target was broken down into population groups to show the ongoing disparity. From the beginning the catch cry was "we cannot achieve the target unless we raise the levels of participation and achievement for Māori and Pasifika kids."

The justice sector was an early adopter of the IDI/social investment approach, aided by the Ministry of Justice having a central leader who strongly supported the approach and led the development of parts of the theoretical framework. While it had the potential to determine the best points of invest-

Characteristics of children ages 0–5 years at risk of poor outcomes

A small number of key characteristics (or indicators) observed in agency administrative data are highly correlated with poorer outcomes as young adults:

- having a finding of abuse or neglect or having spent time in care of child protection services;

- having spent most of their lifetimes supported by benefits;

- having a parent who has received a community or custodial sentence; and

- having a mother who has no formal qualifications.

Children with these characteristics were more likely to have poorer educational attainment, to be long-term welfare recipients, and to serve custodial sentences. Compared with children with none of the four indicators, children ages 0–5 years with two or more of the four indicators are:

- eight times more likely to have contact with Youth Justice services before age 18;

- three times more likely to leave school with no qualifications ;

- six times more likely to receive benefits for more than two years before the age of 21;

- ten times more likely to spend time in jail before the age of 21; and

- four times more likely to receive benefits for more than five years when they are between 25 and 34 years old.

Source: Adapted from the New Zealand Treasury analytical paper, "Characteristics of Children at Greater Risk of Poor Outcomes as Adults," February 18, 2016.

ment across the whole of government, social investment was challenging for those who envisaged a loss of control over "their" resources and core business and an increasing accountability for liability they considered to belong somewhere else. Facing this situation, the justice sector confined its analysis to crime prevention spending, which wasn't such a threat to other agencies' core business. The benefit of the application of social investment methodology to the justice sector was better understanding of the impact of crime, reoffending, and victimization on society and how to reduce harm through preventing people entering the justice system and from returning to it.

Toward the end of the program, the Social Investment methodology started to have a positive impact on interrelationships beyond the justice sector. It began to be a new way in which the justice sector could influence other agencies to support the justice sector outcomes, by providing those other agencies with evidence of how interventions would help from other perspectives, not just the crime perspective.

Results 9 and 10 maximized on the program settings that allowed for learning and adaptive management with external reviews of their arrangements. Given that they were the Result areas that were struggling the most to make progress early on, they were also the Result areas that had the most to learn. They were commissioned by ministers in the end-year 2013 progress report to the Cabinet to conduct "further work on alternative forms of governance" that would help address their cross-agency negotiation problems.[36] Their external reviews were one of the responses to this. Result 9 called its review a "health check," whereas Result 10 called its an "independent quality assurance." Both reviews provided valuable insight into the challenges and possible solutions to whole-of-government programs, equally useful to the central agency people involved in public sector reform and the leaders of the programs.

The Result 9 health check was carried out by Deloitte and offered a range of insights on governance, level of control, leadership, and program culture. The Result 10 independent quality assurance report was carried out by the Caravel Group and identified similar problems, suggesting many of the same solutions. The insights from these reports are discussed elsewhere throughout this book in the chapters they relate to more closely.

The progress reports every six months to the Cabinet became the chief mechanism by which to surface what was being learned from the program as a basis for improving practice across all the Result areas. For example, the beginning of the 2015 Cabinet report provided the impetus for Results 9 and 10 teams to identify the main constraints to service integration:

- *Leadership and governance:* Inter-agency governance processes are layered and complex; vertical priorities trump horizontal priorities; and there is a lack of clarity over multiple priorities.

- *Information:* There is limited information sharing between agencies and no consistent approach to identity verification.

- *Funding:* Baseline funds are tied to core agency delivery, with little incentive to improve customer experience, and legacy systems absorb and tie up funds.

- *Culture and behavior:* No one is accountable for the customer experience, and the cumulative impact of multiple services across multiple agencies is not understood or managed.[37]

Armed with this information, the lead agencies, supported by the central agencies, were able to step up to change these settings based on their new insights. Some of their solutions are discussed elsewhere in the sections on governance and horizontal funding.

Linking Health and Housing Data to Reduce Rheumatic Fever (Result 3)

Another crucial part of using data in the program was in the early stages, with problem definition, and parts of the program that would affect expectancy, like target and measure selection. One of the successes of the Result 3 rheumatic fever program was that it started out with a theory of change explicitly based on evidence. The Result team was looking to see how it could predict what would happen and how it would know whether its theory was holding up. The team took a "test and learn" approach rather than undertaking a lengthy evaluation that would delay action for eighteen months (as proposed previously, but not accepted by a minister who wanted to take immediate action). As noted in chapter 5, the rheumatic fever program already in place had focused on instances of rheumatic heart disease. When population health adviser Dr. Pickin was recruited into the Ministry of Health, she refocused the program on reducing the incidence of rheumatic fever, as the target required.[38]

The intervention logic developed for the program was acknowledged to be based on the best available evidence. The team had even delved into London-based research from the 1930s and 1940s that had originally linked strep A to the onset of rheumatic fever and also had linked the strep A and consequent rheumatic fever to overcrowding. In one "experiment," a chief health officer created space between beds in a military hospital, where the disease was rife, and this immediately reduced the incidence of the disease.

It was well-known that untreated infection with certain types of group A Streptococcus (strep A) is associated with the onset of rheumatic fever in susceptible children. However, it was not known why Māori and Pasifika children in New Zealand had such a high rate of rheumatic fever. The working hypothesis, developed by the program through engagement with researchers, clinicians, and communities, was that Māori and Pasifika children in New Zealand had a high rate of rheumatic fever because they had more strep A sore throats and that when they had them, they were not treated adequately or rapidly. The two main aims of the program became to reduce the number of sore throats being experienced by high-risk children (STOP IT) and to identify and rapidly treat the sore throats being experienced by high-risk children (TREAT IT).

The first stage of the program built on the existing services for the early detection of and rapid access to treatment of strep A sore throats in children in very high-risk areas. This was combined with innovative health promotion activities in high-risk populations to raise awareness of rheumatic fever and its link to sore throats. Free throat-swabbing clinics were established first in schools and later in community settings in high-risk areas to ensure that the throat disease was identified and treated early. This was considered particularly important at the time, as primary health care for children over six years of age (the highest risk age group for strep A and rheumatic fever) was not free, and there was a known reluctance of poorer families to use primary health care for "minor" conditions such as sore throats. The learning from the program was later used to successfully advocate for an extension to free health care for children.

Dr. Pickin's understanding of population health was put to good use in the program, refocusing the school throat-swabbing clinics on areas with the greatest number of cases rather than the highest rates. At an individual level, it made sense to set the clinics up in small areas of the highest rates, but the "prevention paradox" meant that most cases of rheumatic fever were occurring in areas of moderate risk. Parts of Auckland (particularly South Auckland) had a moderate rate of incidence of the disease compared with some rural areas, but the high population densities meant that these were where the greatest numbers of rheumatic fever cases came from. To meet the target, the team had to expand its efforts in these areas.

The team then started to dig into the possible environmental factors contributing to the disease. Team members began asking questions about what lay at the problem's root cause. Why were children contracting strep A in the first place? Why did Māori and Pasifika children have a higher incidence of the disease? Like the link to strep A sore throats, the link to overcrowding had long been known, but unlike strep A, overcrowding had never been put at the forefront of a program to reduce rheumatic fever. Remarkably, the Result 3 team's predicting and testing outcomes from actions taken to address this root cause in its theory of change appeared to be a world first.

Because this theory of change also included social activation and multi-agency engagement; the rheumatic fever team had built strong links up through the district health boards with community-based anchor organizations. This allowed the team to visit homes in disadvantaged areas, discovering that the overcrowding wasn't always structural (that is, caused by the houses being too small for the number of occupants); rather, it was what the team termed "functional." Families were crowding into a single room to sleep because houses were cold and damp and/or they could only afford to heat one room. Clearly, this was a disease related to poor housing and poverty. Poor housing was concentrated in Māori and Pasifika communities—and was related to income.

Having gathered the evidence, the team set about applying it to the problem. The first hurdle was that health and housing services are delivered separately in New Zealand, and the administrative data for housing and health were not adequately connected. To allow decisions on the provision of social housing to be informed by rheumatic fever risk, the health and housing information had to be combined. The second hurdle was then mobilizing resources on the front line. A partnership with two nongovernmental community-based anchor organizations—National Hauora Coalition and Alliance Health Plus—was created as a pilot initiative in response to a tender to form the Auckland Wide Healthy Homes Initiative (AWHI).

This initiative identified families living in substandard housing with children known to be at high risk of contracting rheumatic fever. The families were then supported to identify their needs for reducing overcrowding, and a range of interventions was coordinated by AWHI. These included initiatives to improve the warmth of the home, to provide beds and bedding to discourage co-sleeping, and a fast-track referral to the Ministry of Social Development for financial review, which in turn worked with Housing New Zealand to fast-track the social housing assessment and allocation process.

Having established the process in one part of New Zealand, and having learned significant lessons on implementation, the Ministry of Health identified high rheumatic fever incidence District Health Board areas and worked with them to introduce Healthy Homes Initiatives (HHIs) in all high-risk areas. Partnering with others was clearly critical to the initiatives, which had brought together a range of organizations that shared the desire to improve the quality and warmth of homes. These included those interested in environmental sustainability, reduction in poverty, and community health, along with housing. The HHIs both facilitated identification of families in need and harnessed the collective impact of interested organizations to ensure rapid, coordinated, and effective action.

The impact appeared significant—a 25 percent drop in new incidence of rheumatic fever was reported to the Cabinet six months later (in the 2014 end-year progress report). The rating remained Amber—officials knew that the data were volatile (because of the small number of people involved), and it was too early to be confident about an established downward trend. Then in 2015, the end-year progress report to the Cabinet reported a 45 percent decrease from the baseline. The reduction was even greater for Māori (54 percent reduction) but less for Pasifika children (27 percent reduction). There were also geographic differences, with by far the largest decrease occurring in South Auckland.

Success in addressing unacceptably high rates of rheumatic fever thus depended on use of evidence (data and information) to determine where and how to intervene along with the use of a measure or indicator to determine whether the theory of change was correct.

Conceptualizing Data as the Justice Sector Pipeline (Result 7)

The justice sector pipeline concept had been useful as a starting point in the planning phase of program, providing a rationale for the agencies at different stages in the pipeline to work together (see Case study: Results 7 and 8 in chapter 13). The pipeline came into its own again in conjunction with the focus on data. Early in the program, data revealed how small changes in one part of the pipeline affected other parts of the pipeline. For example, an increase in the use of speed cameras by the police affected criminal court processes by increasing caseloads, while speeding up court processes increased the reoffending rate because prisoners cycled through faster. Digging into the data using "microanalysis" enabled agencies to gain a greater understanding of each other's business, driving better connections between agencies within the justice sector pipeline and beyond it. Agencies started having conversations about impacts and exploring the underlying drivers that would begin to reveal how the justice sector performed and where the levers were. The conversations gradually deepened to develop a common understanding of how the justice system operated, including principal interdependencies. This in turn led to significant shifts in how the sector did business, from making changes to police operation and charging practice through to different practices in courts and prisons.

The impact of enforcing road safety rules on the wider operation of the justice sector provides a more specific example of how data analysis was applied to the justice sector pipeline to understand the drivers of crime. Analysis of the data showed that traffic offenses were the highest volume offense type convicted and reconvicted through the courts. In 2014, traffic charges composed about a quarter of all charges the justice sector dealt with, 43 percent of traffic infringement tickets issued by police were unpaid and referred for enforcement; and approximately 21 percent of criminal reoffending was for driving while disqualified.

Ministers and officials were concerned that traffic offenses had become a pipeline into the criminal justice system. The policy settings did not appear to be properly aligned. Traffic policy supports road safety, and the enforcement approach by police improved road safety outcomes and assisted in the reduction of health and rehabilitation costs associated with road trauma across government. However, some of the rules related to traffic offenses appeared to be overly rigid, did not encourage compliance, and left little scope for discretion by decisionmakers, leading to churn and escalation through the justice system. For young people and people on low incomes, these settings caused particular disadvantage. Some young people were driving without licenses because poor literacy skills meant they had failed the written test or couldn't afford the cost. Others had lost their driver's license, struggled to regain it, were reconvicted, and ended up paying fines they couldn't afford or even progressed to the prison system.

This data conversation led ministers to ask the justice and transport sector officials to reconsider road safety and driver licensing policy settings, with a view to supporting all of the justice sector's desired outcomes – reducing harm, reducing the volume of people entering the criminal justice system, and reducing reoffending.

Making a Difference

The culmination of getting program settings for expectancy and instrumentality right was that public servants were clearly able to see the value of the work they were doing in the Results program for New Zealanders. The program was able to tap into their intrinsic motivations to make tangible differences in the lives of those they were serving, reinforced by reporting that also framed the program in these terms. Even the less public-facing reporting for the program—to the Cabinet and for the program leads—provided crucial data for public servants about how their interventions were working (or not) on the ground, allowing them to adjust their work as needed.

Since 2016, there has been a more deliberate and concerted effort by New Zealand central agencies (particularly the State Services Commission and its commissioner, Peter Hughes[39]) to acknowledge and nurture the intrinsic motivation of public servants.[40] The phrase "a spirit of service to the community"[41] has been included in the foundational legislation of the public service since 1962, but the relative emphasis has changed over time.[42] In particular, the reforms of the late 1980s emphasized extrinsic motivations. The "New Zealand model" of new public management (NPM) was based heavily on public choice theory and assumed that public servants were rational self-maximizing individuals who could be managed by extrinsic incentives.[43] By contrast, the evolving public service paradigm (still forming at the time of writing) is based on a more explicitly organizational humanist perspective, acknowledging the range of values and motivations that public servants bring to their work.[44] Several initiatives consciously "name and fame" public servants, to celebrate service and encourage innovation, with new awards programs,[45] videos, and social media posts.[46] Major New Zealand public service leadership events focus on how leaders can further nurture a spirit of service to their community in their employees.[47]

Conclusions

We knocked the bastard off.

—*Sir Edmund Hillary on conquering*
Mount Everest, May 1953[1]

Many important social problems cross agency boundaries, and working effectively to solve these problems is not easy. After almost thirty years of trial and error (since 1989), New Zealand's Results program proved to be a remarkable success in this regard. However, in discussing the program with various public sector leaders, it became clear that this success did not come easily.

Much of the literature on working across agency boundaries focuses on the transaction costs associated with coordinating multiple parties. In prior efforts, these costs were enough to derail an interagency initiative. When public servants ran into obstacles, they stopped. Although public sector leaders note that many of the obstacles they faced in working across boundaries remain, throughout the program, they forged ahead in their collaborative efforts despite the obstacles in their way. The Results program had sufficient impetus to jump over obstacles or to smash through them. The central argument of this book has been that this impetus, and the general success of the program, was largely due to the program's ability to inspire goal commitment among public servants, resulting in effort from participating parties that persisted over four years without any sign of decline.

The various antecedents and determinants for goal commitment have been explored throughout this book, considering the specific aspects of the New Zealand Results program that may have contributed to the sustained effort of those involved. We have been particularly interested in how the Results program overcame the typical design flaws usually associated with interagency working and with target regimes, namely, that collaboration can lack purpose, urgency, feedback, and accountability and that targets can encourage gaming and cheating, discourage collaboration, and decrease morale.

It is one thing to know that goal commitment tends to be higher when the goal is "at the edge of possible" but another to understand how public servants react when the goal is too easy or too hard. How can public servants manage the tension between staying the course with a "bad" goal versus shifting the goalposts to something more suitable? Similarly, it is one thing to know that goal commitment tends to be higher when fewer parties are held responsible but another to understand what happens when too many are involved. How have public servants tried, failed, and succeeded in reducing the number of agencies to a core few while keeping the resources of other agencies available when needed? And it is one thing to know that entrepreneurship is more likely when successes are "named and famed" but another to understand how public servants react to seeing their work highlighted. How can public servants balance positive and negative consequences for performance?

Although we were not able to provide definite answers to the questions above, we have illustrated how New Zealand public servants have approached the problem and how their attempts played out. Our understanding of New Zealand's Results program is based on close daily observation during the five years of the program, formal evaluations, and interviews with key stakeholders. It is from our reflections as practitioners and the reflections of those other New Zealand public servants who worked on the program. Our hypotheses were tested with practitioners in comparable programs across three continents. Our conclusion is that the Results program was the right program for the right time. It changed the way the public sector worked and equipped New Zealand public servants with a range of new tools for solving complex problems, tools that could be deployed as needed.

Given that New Zealand borrowed so liberally from other jurisdictions in designing the Results program, it seems only fair that we should try to explain for government executives in other jurisdictions how New Zealand was able to create and sustain goal commitment and encourage public entrepreneurship to innovate solutions. These are commonly held aspirations in countless other programs, and other jurisdictions have sought the lessons from New Zealand's Results program. New Zealand public servants, including the authors, have been approached by governments all over the world to talk about their successes. The lessons have been shared through bilateral discussions with governments from Australia and the Pacific, Europe, Asia, Africa, and North and South America. Administrations from many parts of the world have visited New Zealand's public management laboratory, and some envy what they see but struggle to transfer the ideas to their own contexts. Overcoming this requires dialogue—working with other nations to try to understand their context and trying to adapt the lessons from the Results program to meet their needs.

As outlined in part 1, New Zealand's Results program was a specific program designed to address the specific context of the New Zealand public service at that time. It makes sense that it would be difficult for a practitioner audience to simply pick up the program design, implement it in another jurisdiction, and replicate its success. But at a general level, aspects of the context and problem setting are comparable to other problem settings in countless jurisdictions around the world. Progress was made relatively painlessly on problems where responsibility is easily attributed to a single agency. Other problems are more "wicked"—spanning multiple agencies and with much less predictable solutions and outcomes. The context of fiscal constraint will also be familiar to other jurisdictions.

At a general level, the solution, too, is a common one. Governments need to know what they are trying to achieve to focus their efforts, adapt, and modify their activities on the basis of performance information and then assign responsibility and accountability. Although the program cannot be blindly copied, we try to identify and present some of the more generalizable principles for which New Zealand's experience provides illustrative examples.

The following are some of the more transferable features of New Zealand's approach that contributed to goal commitment, sustaining the program over its five years. While each may need to be adapted to fit local contexts, these practice insights are presented as suggestions for addressing persistent cross-cutting problems:

- There were only a few Result areas and only a few more targets than that, each of which was worded as specifically and simply as possible. This increased the relative importance of the targets and made them memorable.

- The targets were set in balance between outputs and outcomes, meaning that they related to issues that were important to New Zealanders and the government of the day. They appealed to public servants' intrinsic motivations but were still attributable and provided short enough lead times for feedback loops.

- The targets were set at a difficulty level at which they were ambitious enough to drive urgency but not so much that they caused despair.

- Narrowing participation to the core agencies meant greater felt responsibility for each party and that links to other agencies maintained availability of resources.

- Restriction of additional resources forced the mobilization of existing resources—not only resources in government agencies but also the resources of communities and nongovernmental agencies.

- Co-design of the Results approach (including the data and targets and the action plans) by ministers, chief executives, managers, and a raft of public servants combined with cascading governance ensured that accountability was felt down through agency hierarchies. This was not a program designed at the center and rolled out to unwilling government agencies—agencies and individuals owned the ideas and the actions.

- Collective responsibility drove a focus on achieving results rather than avoiding blame. Wide distribution of ownership, and recognition of success, motivated public servants to perform and achieve evermore astonishing things.

- Public reporting indicated that the government itself had fully committed (tied its own hands), leading to a sense of irreversibility and of urgency.

- A strong expectation to take action, try new things, and learn from them permeated the program. This was a government impatient with elaborate strategies and endless research to find the right answers before starting anything.

- A focus on successes and learning rather than on failure generated positive energy, sustaining morale and motivating those involved.

- Use of data revealed the nature and extent of the challenges, becoming both the driver of action and the proof of success—it told public servants where to apply their efforts and whether the action taken was having an impact or if they needed to try something different.

These insights offer tested steps for selecting Result targets, reporting, and governance arrangements. That is not to say that applying these lessons will lead to easy success. New Zealand's Results program was not perfect. Some measures worked better than others. Some targets were set too high or too low. Only about two-thirds were ultimately achieved. We hope, in writing this book, to have conveyed a balanced view of what worked and what didn't. The book is intended to show the messy, complicated craft of working to solve complex social problems. The intention was not to describe New Zealand's experience with rose-colored glasses.

But New Zealand was able to make progress and improve performance in all ten of the important and previously intractable problems it selected. And public servants remained committed to solving these problems, with urgency and innovation, over a five-year period. Therefore, we present the Results program as a good example or test case to show that interagency performance targets can be successful, allowing public services to understand persistent social problems through collective responsibility for improving intermediate outcomes. It is our hope that sharing these stories will help both the New Zealand public service and other jurisdictions to better understand the dynamics of operating in this context.

Others have described getting agencies to work better together as the *Holy Grail* and the *philosophers' stone*. We might compare it to conquering Mt. Everest. Like New Zealand's adventuring hero Sir Edmund Hilary, it feels like the New Zealand public service "knocked the bastard off." Great things were achieved, innovation and creativity were unleashed, and those involved felt like New Zealand was a better place—in terms of improved lives and a stronger public service. It was a developmental step in working better together, which began with the audacious act of putting a number and a date in the same sentence. It was time for New Zealand to move on to something else.

No matter how successful they are, new ways of thinking in public management have their day and are replaced by something else, having achieved only some of the reformers' lofty objectives. The Better Public Services Results program is no different. The New Zealand government canceled the program in 2018 to pursue different priorities with a different approach to public management. Nevertheless, the legacy of the program remains visible in changes in culture and practice of the public service.

The new government has been working on how to ensure that in the future interagency targets can persist beyond the term of any one government. This has taken the form of setting targets in legislation or of legislating requirements that targets must be set and reported on. Two significant pieces of legislation exemplify this. First, in 2018, the legislature passed the Child Poverty Reduction Act, which outlines several measures to be used for monitoring child poverty and legislates the requirement to set targets for reducing those measures over long-term and intermediate periods (s 21). Second, in 2019, the government passed the Zero Carbon amendment to the Climate Change Response Act 2002, enshrining the Paris Agreement target "to limit the global average temperature increase to 1.5° Celsius above pre-industrial levels" in the purpose of the Act (s 3) and, more specifically, setting a New Zealand target to reach net zero greenhouse gas emissions by 2050 (s 5Q). These new targets have interesting implications for expectancy in terms of the likelihood of program completion and setting targets at the edge of possible.

The governance arrangements developed in the Results program were also retained in many cases and have continued to evolve. For example, the Justice Sector Leadership Board (responsible for Results 7 and 8) was retained, along with its shared secretariat "Sector Group." The groups continue to meet in much the same way, poring over crime and reoffending data, looking for ways to collectively improve performance. There is a direct lineage between the Social Sector governance group responsible for Result 4 and the new government's Social Wellbeing Board, which is the first "interdepartmental board" that reports to a single superordinate minister. The Result 9 Better for Business brand has continued and been strengthened.[2] From Result 10, the Digital Government Partnership remains operational, supported by a secretariat led by the Department of Internal Affairs, to help ensure that government is aligned with its "Strategy for a Digital Public Service."[3] In December 2019, the governance groups that once represented Results 9 and 10 jointly presented an "All-of-Government Innovation Showcase" with the theme "collaborate + innovate = better services."[4]

The State Services Commission collated the different practices used in the Results program as a System Design Toolkit for Organizing Around Shared Problems, using the interagency governance arrangements as exemplars in associated guidance material (also discussed in chapter 13). SSC now uses the toolkit as the basis for its advice to the Cabinet and other agencies on how to effectively organize interagency working. These collaborative governance models were extended with the inclusion of three additional organizational forms in the new foundational legislation for the public service, the Public Service Act 2020. Simultaneous amendments to the Public Finance Act 1989 (also discussed in chapter 6) extend the funding models described in this book, making it procedurally easier to pool resources from budgets held by different agencies.

Similarly, the focus on intrinsic motivation has been retained and expanded under the banner of "a spirit of service to the community," with a real effort to "name and fame" public servants both for their innovation and their commitment (also discussed in chapter 14). The passage of the Public Service Act 2020 means that, for the first time, senior officials will be legally required to preserve, protect, and nurture the spirit of service to the community that public service employees bring to their work.

A third element of this new reform is the intention to create a more "unified" public service, drawing lessons from the work on social identity discussed in chapter 13.[5] Given that individuals are more likely to cooperate, share resources, and extend charity to others they perceive as part of their group, provisions in the Public Service Act 2020 represent a conscious effort by the New Zealand government to foster a shared public service identity.[6] The intention behind introducing common language, purpose, principles, and values across the various agencies that make up the public service is that a unified public service will predispose public servants to working more cooperatively with public servants from other agencies.[7]

Although the Results program has ended, these various elements point to its legacy in New Zealand. The public service learned how to do things it didn't know how to do before. Many of the governance and funding innovations remain and have been cemented with legislative change. Similarly, a reform focus on intrinsic motivation and social identity (spirit of service and unified public service, respectively) are exemplified in the new Public Service Act 2020. These two examples are different approaches to addressing the same problems of improving interagency performance.

The legacy of the program and the lessons it has for others from those who worked so hard to implement it will now also be preserved in this book. We should at this point again note that this cannot be a purely impartial text, because the authors are not impartial. One of the authors, Ross Boyd, worked on the Better Public Services Results program for many years—through design, implementation, monitoring, and refining. But no author who feels compelled to write a book could be truly impartial. The decision to write a book is one to invest countless hours of effort and is not taken lightly. A book is written because an author or authors believe in something they have to say.

In that spirit, it seemed appropriate to give Ross the final word:

> The public service was implored to take action—collective action. We were encouraged to get on with it, try new things and learn from them. Mobilization meant rallying around a common cause, important for New Zealand and New Zealanders. The challenge was to get results—to solve gnarly problems and improve lives, as opposed to "servicing misery." This was more than a public management experiment. It did change people's lives—and that's why people join the public service. It permanently changed how the New Zealand public service operated and organized itself.
>
> The Results program is the most important and most valuable program I have been part of in my four-plus decades in the public service. This sentiment was shared by many others. We were so excited about what had been achieved, and so proud to be part of it, that we had to write this book.

Appendix 1

Results Action Plan Guidelines

The following guidance was issued by Central Agencies (State Services Commission, Treasury, and Department of Prime Minister and Cabinet) to aid each of the ten Results teams to prepare their Result Action Plan. This guidance was issued in March 2012.

Result Action Plan—Guidelines

1. Introduction

  1.1. This guidance should assist with the development of draft Result Action Plans (RAPs).

Expectations

  1.2. Given the diversity of the results (see full set listed at Annex A) and the different stages of associated policy development, there is no standard template for RAPs, and uniformity is not expected.

  1.3. Rather, this guidance proposes several common features and base requirements that should help us deliver a recognizable and credible set of RAPs to ministers. In places, the guidance offers some specific pointers to assist result teams in considering what to include.

  1.4. To ensure an immediate focus on delivering results, draft RAPs are to be developed by March 30 for sign-off by responsible ministers. Drafts can build on the initial material on results produced for the February 7 Cabinet paper. Then, over the next three months until June 30, result teams will be able to further strengthen their RAPs and firm up certain aspects—for example, the precise formulation of targets and stakeholder engagement. RAPs will continue to evolve thereafter as "living" documents.

1.5. Result leaders and their teams are expected to seek advice from Statistics New Zealand as they develop indicators and targets, to ensure performance information is robust, meaningful, and reliable. Result teams should also consider the role the population agencies could play in supporting RAP development.

Purpose of Result Action Plans

1.6. The purpose of RAPs is to determine the actions needed to achieve the government's ten Better Public Services (BPS) Results, establish contributions, and assign responsibilities.

1.7. RAPs will be strategic documents that express a shared vision for success, set a high bar on ambition, and provide a focus for aligning resources and improving effort across agencies. Each result relates to a difficult area in which it has proven challenging to improve outcomes for New Zealanders for some time. Ministers are clear that results therefore represent areas needing new thinking and transformation—business as usual will not suffice.

1.8. By their very nature, the results will require collaboration between agencies, the sharing of knowledge and expertise, and varying degrees of reprioritization. Preparing RAPs provides an opportunity to shape a coherent vision of priorities, review the effectiveness of current approaches, and consider ways to marshal resources for maximum impact.

1.9. This exercise should help foster a results-focused approach across clusters of agencies that aims to:

- *focus* agencies on delivering the government results that are important to citizens and businesses;

- ensure *collaboration and alignment* of resources around results that cross agency boundaries;

- stimulate *innovation and new approaches* to achieve results in difficult areas, based on evidence of what works in practice;

- enhance *system capability* and effectiveness and reduce duplication of effort; and

- increase transparency, *inform continuous improvement*, and bolster public confidence through open reporting of results.

1.10. To ensure RAPs accomplish their intended purpose of supporting the new results-focused approach, each plan will be:

- *owned*—by all contributors and led by one result leader chief executive who is accountable for interagency performance, and each RAP will be signed-off by responsible ministers;

- *clear and simple*—expressed in concise and straightforward language, avoiding unnecessary use of technical terms and jargon;

- *dynamic*—plans will be "living" documents, reviewed and updated regularly as evidence of progress and program evaluations become available, and as new approaches are adopted;

- *informed by a range of perspectives*—drawing on the known views of key stakeholders (using best available knowledge rather than new consultations); and

- *credible*—robust and open to potential external challenge and underpinned by high-quality evidence, research findings, and sound analysis.

2. Suggested Content

2.1. As a minimum, the base content of RAPs should cover the six elements listed below. Under each of these headings are listed several pointers illustrative of the kind of issues you may wish to consider in formulating RAPs.

Leadership and Governance

- How will the lead and contributing agencies create a unified and coherent focus on results, promote collaboration, and closer alignment of activity?

- What governance arrangements or decision rights are needed to support effective delivery?

Result Clarity and Context

- Why is this result important to government and New Zealanders? How would success contribute to the government's overall priorities?

- How are we doing at present? In what direction are trends headed, and what factors explain current performance (for example, what is driving demand and/or costs)? The annex of the February 7 Cabinet paper, "Better Public Services: Results," is a starting point.

- Is the issue concentrated geographically or among certain sections of the population?

Strategy

- Explain briefly the overarching strategy to improve performance.

- What are the major strengths of our current approaches and which areas are priorities for improvement (for example, barriers that may impede better performance)?

- How will the strengths/resources of contributing agencies be aligned or combined to achieve the result?

Actions

- What are the crucial actions needed to achieve the result? Which agency is responsible for these actions, and what are the related timeframes? A detailed work program is not required; rather, focus on a handful of actions with critical milestones.

- Are there clear lines-of-sight between resources, priority actions or programs, and results?

Resourcing

- Are the actions costed out for future years and financially sustainable? What are the sources of funding?

- Are prioritized actions consistent with 4-year Budget plans?

Performance indicators

- How will result performance be quantified? What indicators will be used and in what way will they be reported (for example, as trends against baseline or targets)?

- How regularly will performance information be updated? How will you provide assurance to ministers about the pace of progress?

- How will the data be used to tell the performance story in a way that is accessible to ministers and the public?

- Is the performance information valid/credible (in other words: shows actual performance shifts) and sustainable/reliable over time?

- Is the performance information consistent with Official Statistics (where relevant)?

3. Milestones and Timeline

3.1. The main phases of activity to produce and update the RAPs include:

By March 30   Result leader chief executives to prepare draft Result Action Plans (RAPs) for sign-off by responsible ministers

April   Engagement with Ministers and refinement of RAPs

May   Engagement with Ministers and refinement of RAPs

State Sector Reform Ministerial Group develop proposals for Cabinet on arrangements for communicating progress on BPS Results to the public

June   First quarterly report on Results to SSRMG ministers

First report to Cabinet on progress on Results (half-yearly report)

Specific and measurable targets for each Result agreed and made public

Mid- to late 2012   Public communication of progress of Results and associated actions

Late 2012   Result Action Plans updated

- Develop new actions and test them with key stakeholders

- Adjust organizational arrangements, anticipating legislative change in 2013

3.2. The expectation is that RAPs will continue to evolve over time as live documents, particularly through new and adjusted actions being added and costed out as part of Budget 2013/14.

Appendix 2

BPS Results Reporting—Criteria for Rating Forecast Target Achievement

This rating system for the dashboards was provided as an annex to the Cabinet paper end-year progress reports.

Green *On track*

1   The lead indicator data are reliable and at, or ahead of, the trend-line forecast to meet the target over at least the previous two quarters.

2   All other significant indicator data provide confidence that the target will be met.

3   Actions taken to reach the target are embedded, and there are indications that these actions are successful.

Yellow *On track, but changes not yet embedded*

1   The lead indicator data are at, or ahead of, the trend-line forecast to meet the target over at least the previous quarter.

2   Other indicator data provide some confidence about target achievement.

3   Planning for actions needed to reach the target is advanced, and funding has been committed. Significant action has already been taken, but it is too early to determine success.

Amber *Progress, but issues to resolve*

1   The lead indicator data are:

- not yet showing a trend; or

- unreliable/volatile; or

- below the trend-line forecast to meet the target.

2   Other indicator data do not yet provide confidence that the target will be met.

3   Actions have been planned to reach the target, and some actions are underway, but these are insufficient to reach the target. Significant issues to resolve, particularly around sustainable funding and joint agreement to action.

Red   *Urgent attention required*

1   The lead indicator data are either unavailable or below the trend-line forecast to meet the target.

2   Other indicator data do not provide confidence that the target will be met.

3   External intervention is needed to resolve issues.

Note: Criteria 1 and 2 are based on indicator data that show progress toward achieving the target. Criterion 3 is based on the maturity of actions taken to achieve sustainable progress. All three criteria should be met for the rating to apply.

Source: Cabinet paper: "Better Public Services Results: 2016 End-Year Progress Report" (with Annex), March 8, 2017.

Appendix 3

Snapshot Reporting Artifact

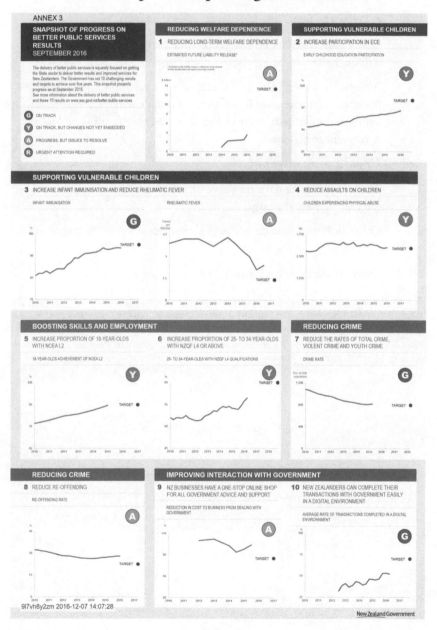

Appendix 4

Case Study Vignette (SSC Website)

Better Public Services Result 1—Case Study: The Other Side of the Desk[1]

Nicole is a Nelson case manager who has been trialing the new approach with clients. She remembers how it feels to be sitting on the other side of the desk at Work and Income.

"I was there once. I know what it is like to feed my kids on cabbage and rice or to send them to school with just homegrown grapefruit in their lunch box. I know how it feels to look at people with good jobs, that it all just seems impossibly far away."

Nicole says there are huge barriers for people in that position: "Even if life is hard, a lot of them are used to it—and that's a big barrier. And then you start thinking about people judging you, not knowing what you can do, organizing care for the kids, transport if you can't drive—and it gets too big for you."

Nicole's role is proactive and solution focused. Every client needs a different approach. Building rapport and gaining trust is important.

One woman, who hadn't worked in years, told Nicole that she had no strengths to bring to a workplace. Yet Nicole saw potential in the woman's warm personality and experience with her own grandchildren. It took time, but Nicole encouraged the woman to consider childcare as an option, to gain a first aid certificate and hand out her CV at the local pool where she took her grandchildren. Several job offers followed, and she now has permanent employment in a working family with three kids. It is her first job in two decades.

Not everyone is thrilled to have Nicole's help. One client, a man who'd just come out of jail, told her bluntly that he wasn't interested in finding work or in having her as a case manager.

"Well," Nicole told him politely but firmly, "work is where we're heading, and until you're there, you're not getting rid of me—ever."

Soon after, a job at the local sawmill caught his attention. It was physical, but he was fit. "He was really excited about it," says Nicole. "He didn't get that job, but it was a turning point. We were on the same team after that, and we started to really work together."

Better Public Services Result 1—Case Study: Work and Income Is Working Differently to Support New Zealanders into Work[2]

Work and Income is focusing on giving more help to, and intervening earlier with, people who have complex problems, to support them off a benefit and into work.

TRADE EMPLOYMENT PLACEMENT (TRADE UP LIMITED, BAY OF PLENTY REGION): The Trade Employment Placement service commenced in January 2014. The service is provided by experienced industry trainers with strong employer networks and delivers highly individualized support to at-risk youth (ages 18–24) Jobseeker Support clients to gain employment in the trades-related sector. The service involves work readiness and job search support along with employment placement and post-placement support, including support into apprenticeships. Eighty-eight clients commenced participation on the service in the six months to June 2014. As at September 30, 2014, a total of 44 (72 percent) of the 61 clients who had completed the service had achieved an employment outcome resulting in an exit from benefit, while one further client had achieved part-time employment. The remaining 17 clients continue to participate in the service, and this year, an additional 22 have commenced participation in the service, which has now been extended from the Western Bay of Plenty to the whole region.

DRIVE2WORK (YMCA SOUTH AND MID CANTERBURY, SOUTHERN REGION): Drive2Work is a Training for Work program delivered in Timaru to clients at risk of long-term benefit dependency. The program comprises up to 13 weeks of skills training including support with driver licensing, employment placement primarily in the transport sector, and post-placement support. As of September 30, 2014, 45 (68 percent) of the 66 clients who had completed the program had achieved employment, and a further six (9 percent) of the clients had achieved part-time employment. The remaining 16 clients continue to participate in the program, while an additional 22 have commenced participation this financial year.

Working with Employers

MASTER PAINTERS: In the 2013/14 financial year, we have had a contract with Morrison McDougall Limited to train youth for Master Painter Association members and allied construction trades. This program began as a trial residential program with the Sir Edmund Hillary Outdoor Pursuits Centre and has since become a regionally based hands-on training program strongly supported by the construction industry, with suppliers providing materials and equipment for the participants. This program continues to be run under variation into the 2015 financial year, completing November 2014. To date, there have been ninety-two participants in the program with thirty employed, and forty-five currently participating from multiple regions.

SUMMERSET (RETIREMENT VILLAGE OPERATOR): Summerset has eighteen villages throughout the country, and after testing listing vacancies with Work and Income in October 2013, five clients were successfully placed with them. At the same time, a Skills for Industry, Industry Partnership program was initiated to assist Summerset and our clients' transition into employment. Summerset has subsequently decided not to make claim under this contract, saying it is appreciative of the free professional recruitment service and the standard of our client referrals. At the end of September, twenty-two clients had been placed with the employer, and ongoing straight recruitment is managed nationally through an Employer Services Account Manager.

Appendix 5

Results Program—Community of Practice Story

Better Public Services: Community of Practice?[1]

Ross Boyd, Results Workstream Leader in the Better Public Services Program team says that "a community of practice is simply sharing ideas about what works—a sort of cross-pollination of information, experiences, and ideas." It's an approach that Ross and others are using in the BPS Results area.

The Better Public Service Program (BPS) is promoting change and is working with colleagues across the Corporate Center, in government agencies, non-government organizations, community organizations, and the private sector to provide better public services.

"To achieve results for New Zealanders, including the ten Results set by government, we need to mobilize all of the agencies that are out there and learn from each other—what works and what doesn't," says Ross.

"One way of doing that is by holding community of practice workshops where people with solutions can explain what they've done. Others can then pick up on that and take what they need into their particular situation."

To some extent, it replaces top-down decisionmaking with a bottom-up approach, one that will bring about public sector change by sharing knowledge and expertise with people who are already doing things.

"The Results Community of Practice Workshops (RCP workshops) came about in response to an earlier request to develop effective BPS Result Action Plans (RAPs)," information that sets out the "how" for achieving Results. "At the beginning nobody really knew what an effective RAP might look like. As people came up with content, format, and design that started to work for decision-makers, ministers, and the public, the RAP writers were pulled together to share what was working. An effective model emerged and everyone followed it, improving as they went." This is innovation in practice, shared for the benefit of all.

Since then there have been two RCP workshops—the most recent one held on Friday, October 19, covering:

- funding for Results—across multiple agencies

- innovation for Results

Ministers have stated that we will only achieve BPS Results by doing things differently. Presenters at the innovation workshop showed how new ways of thinking are being applied. These include, for example, design thinking (in Result 10), use of tools to stimulate innovation (in Result 9), the capability supporting innovation in Christchurch, and an interactive workshop on rapid prototyping.

Other RCP workshops being planned will include:

- engagement of nongovernment organizations for Results (scheduled for 23 November)

- telling the Results story—data and changes for New Zealanders (scheduled for early 2013)

- working across boundaries to achieve Results (also early 2013)[/BL]

"We usually get about 30 people attending each RCP workshop," says Ross, "and that's from over a dozen different agencies and organizations." Each workshop has a planning team and, if possible, a Better Public Services Advisory Group member contributes.

Notes

Introduction

1. A wicked problem is one for which each attempt to create a solution changes the understanding of the problem. See: Rittel, H. W. and Webber, M. M. (1974). "Wicked Problems. Man-made Futures." *26*(1), 272–280.

2. For a discussion of the "craft" of public management, see: Bardach, E. (1994). "Comment: The Problem of 'Best Practice' Research." *Journal of Policy Analysis and Management, 13*(2), 260–268.

Chapter 1

1. "The Treaty of Waitangi" or "Te Tiriti o Waitangi." https://natlib.govt.nz/he -tohu/about/te-tiriti-o-waitangi/.

2. Fischer, D. H. (2012). *Fairness and Freedom: A History of Two Open Societies: New Zealand and the United States.* Oxford University Press.

3. Halligan, J. (2003). "Anglo-American civil service systems: Comparative perspectives." In *Civil Service Systems in Anglo-American Countries,* J. Halligan (Ed.). Edward Elgar Publishing, 195–216.

4. Pollitt, C. and Bouckaert, G. (2011). *Continuity and Change in Public Policy and Management.* Edward Elgar Publishing.

5. The Statistics NZ estimate of New Zealand population in 2019 is 4.966 million people, over a land area of 267,700 km². The United States Census Bureau estimate of Colorado population in 2019 is 5.759 million people, over a land area of 268,431 km². www.stats.govt.nz/topics/population; https://databank.worldbank.org/views/reports/ reportwidget.aspx?Report_Name=CountryProfile&Id=b450fd57&tbar=y&dd=y&inf =n&zm=n&country=NZL; and www.census.gov/quickfacts/fact/table/CO/LND110 210.

6. Pallott, J. (1999). "Beyond NPM: Developing Strategic Capacity." *Financial Accountability & Management, 15*(3–4), 419–426.

7. Vigoda, E. (2002). "From Responsiveness to Collaboration: Governance, Citizens, and the Next Generation of Public Administration." *Public Administration Review, 62*(5), 527–540.

8. See descriptions by John Halligan and Bob Gregory: Halligan, J. (2003). "Leadership and the Senior Service from a Comparative Perspective." In *Handbook of Public Administration,* B. Guy Peters and Jon Pierre (Eds.). SAGE Publications, 98–108. Gregory, R. (2006). "Theoretical Faith and Practical Works: De-Autonomizing and Joining-Up in the New Zealand State Sector." In *Autonomy and Regulation: Coping with Agencies in the Modern State,* Tom Christensen and Per Lægreid (Eds.). Edward Elgar Publishing, 137–161.

9. Kibblewhite, A. and Ussher, C. (2002). *Outcome-focused Management in New Zealand.* OECD. www.oecd.org/newzealand/43513908.pdf.

10. Schick, A. (1996). "The Spirit of Reform: Managing the New Zealand State Sector in a Time of Change," A Report Prepared for the State Services Commission and the Treasury, New Zealand. State Services Commission. Ball, I. (1992). "The New Approach: Financial Management Reform." *The Journal of the New Zealand Society of Accountants, 71*(5), 17–18.

11. Scott, R. (2019). "Service, Citizenship, and the Public Interest: New Public Service and Our Public Service Reforms." SSC Discussion Paper. See also Kettl, D. F. (2006). *The Global Public Management Revolution: A Report on the Transformation of Governance.* Brookings Institution Press.

12. Norman, R. (2007). "Managing Outcomes While Accounting for Outputs: Redefining 'Public Value' in New Zealand's Performance Management System." *Public Performance & Management Review, 30*(4), 536–549.

13. Boston, J. (1996). *Public Management: The New Zealand Model.* Oxford University Press.

14. On August 6, 2020, New Zealand's State Sector Act (1988) was repealed and replaced with the Public Service Act 2020. Among other changes under the legislation, the title State Services Commissioner was replaced with Public Service Commissioner, and the organization the official leads was changed from State Services Commission to Public Service Commission. For consistency and historical accuracy, the terms "State Services Commissioner" and "State Services Commission" are used throughout this book.

15. Rennie, I. (2020). "Quest: New Zealand Public Sector Reform Since 2000," 295. In Berman, E. and Karacaoglu, G. (Eds.). *Public Policy and Governance Frontiers in New Zealand.* Emerald Publishing Limited.

16. Norman, R. (2003). *Obedient Servants? Management Freedoms and Accountabilities in the New Zealand Public Sector.* Victoria University Press.

17. This general diagnosis has been echoed in reports by academics, independent reviews, and departments themselves; see in particular: Boston, J. (1996). *Public Management: The New Zealand Model.* Oxford University Press. Jensen, K. and others. (2014). "The Management and Organisational Challenges of More Joined-Up Government: New Zealand's Better Public Services Reforms." State Sector Performance Hub: Working paper 2014-1. New Zealand Government. DOI: 10.13140/RG.2.1.3115.3680. Schick, A. (1996). "The Spirit of Reform: Managing the New Zealand State Sector in a Time of Change." Report Prepared for the State Services Com-

mission and The Treasury, New Zealand. State Services Commission. https://ssc.govt
.nz/assets/Legacy/resources/spirit_of_reform_all.pdf. State Services Commission of
New Zealand. (2001). "Report of the Advisory Group on the Review of the Centre."
https://ssc.govt.nz/assets/Legacy/resources/review_of_centre.pdf. State Services Commission of New Zealand. (2011). "Better Public Services Advisory Group Report."
https://ssc.govt.nz/assets/Legacy/resources/bps-report-nov2011_0.pdf. Treasury of
New Zealand. (2006). "Review of Central Agencies' Role in Promoting and Assuring
State Sector Performance." https://treasury.govt.nz/sites/default/files/2007-11/tsy
-exgrev-ca-sep06.pdf.

18. This chapter's description of Managing for Outcomes and its various challenges
relies heavily on: Scott, R. J. and Boyd, R. (2017). "Joined Up for What? Response to
Carey and Harris on Adaptive Collaboration." *Australian Journal of Public Administration*, 76(1), 138–144.

19. See: McConnell, A. (2010). "Policy Success, Policy Failure and Grey Areas
In-Between." *Journal of Public Policy*, 30(3), 345–362.

20. The Rt. Hon. Bill English was deputy prime minister and minister of finance
from 2008 to 2016 and then prime minister of New Zealand from 2016 to 2017, at
which point he became the Rt. Hon. Bill English. He was appointed Knight Compan-
ion of the New Zealand Order of Merit in 2018, becoming the Rt. Hon. Sir Bill English. For the sake of historical accuracy, he is referred to throughout this book by the
title that he held at the time of reference.

21. English, B., Speech to the Australia and New Zealand School of Government
in Canberra, August 6, 2014.

22. While Finance Minister, Hon. Bill English gave an annual address to public
servants through the Institution of Public Administration New Zealand. This theme
that improving outcomes would result in a better fiscal outlook was a feature of several
of these addresses, but this quote comes from the 2012 address. https://ipanz.org.nz/
Story?Action=View&Story_id=51.

23. State Services Commission of New Zealand. (2011). "Better Public Services
Advisory Group Report," 19–20. www.ssc.govt.nz/bps-background-material.

24. Ibid, 18.

25. Gray, A. and Hood, C. (2007). "Public Management by Numbers." *Public
Money & Management*, 27(2), 89.

26. Bevan, G. and Hood, C. (2006). "What's Measured Is What Matters: Targets
and Gaming in the English Public Health Care System." *Public Administration*, 84(3),
517–538.

27. John Bohte and Kenneth Meier would classify both as "cheating" and falsifica-
tion as "lying." See: Bohte, J. and Meier, K. J. (2000). "Goal Displacement: Assessing
the Motivation for Organizational Cheating." *Public Administration Review*, 60(2),
173–182.

28. See the following as examples of performance incentives shaping behaviors:
Power, M. (1999). *The Audit Society: Rituals of Verification*. Oxford University Press.
Bevan, G. and Hood, C. "What's Measured Is What Matters." Arnaboldi, M., Lapsley,
I. and Steccolini, I. (2015). "Performance Management in the Public Sector: The Ulti-
mate Challenge." *Financial Accountability & Management*, 31(1), 1–22.

29. It can be difficult to measure corruption directly, and therefore the Transparency International Corruptions Perceptions index is (as the name suggests) based on perceptions of corruption. Over the history of the index, New Zealand and Denmark have consistently ranked as the least corrupt nations, but the order has varied. For previous editions of the Corruptions Perceptions Index, see: www.transparency.org.

30. For a description of the policies and procedures governing the production of Tier 1 statistics, see: www.stats.govt.nz/about-us/legislation-policies-and-guidelines/.

31. See: Bardach, E. (2004). "The Extrapolation Problem: How Can We Learn from the Experience of Others?" *Journal of Policy Analysis and Management, 23*(2), 205–220.

Chapter 2

1. For a detailed analysis of the philosophy of Old Public Administration and New Public Management, see: Denhardt, J. V. and Denhardt, R. B. (2015). *The New Public Service: Serving, Not Steering.* Routledge.

2. Osborne, D. and Gaebler, T. (1992). *Reinventing Government: How the Entrepreneurial Spirit Is Transforming the Public Sector.* Addison-Wesley Publishing Company.

3. For a discussion on the various definitions of coordination and collaboration, see Thomson, A. M. and Perry, J. L. (2006). "Collaboration Processes: Inside the Black Box." *Public Administration Review, 66*(1), 20–32.

4. Bardach, E. (2001). "Developmental Dynamics: Interagency Collaboration as an Emergent Phenomenon." *Journal of Public Administration Research and Theory, 11*(2), 149–164.

5. Bogdanor, V. (Ed.). (2005). *Joined-Up Government* (Vol. 5). Oxford University Press.

6. While "joined-up government" is typically associated with the Blair government, it has also been used to describe a range of initiatives occurring in different jurisdictions at around the same time; see: Ling, T. (2002). "Delivering Joined-Up Government in the UK: Dimensions, Issues and Problems." *Public Administration, 80*(4), 615–642.

7. Peters' seminal 1998 article "Managing Horizontal Government: The Politics of Coordination," *Public Administration, 76*(2), 295–311, is expanded in his 2015 book *Pursuing Horizontal Management: The Politics of Public Sector Coordination.* University Press of Kansas.

8. The 1978 book, edited by Hanf and Scharpf (*Interorganizational Policy Making: Limits to Coordination and Central Control.* SAGE Publications), contains many accounts of the challenges of horizontal management that remain applicable forty years later.

9. Pressman, J. L. and Wildavsky, A. (1984). *Implementation: How Great Expectations in Washington Are Dashed in Oakland; Or, Why It's Amazing That Federal Programs Work at All, This Being a Saga of the Economic Development Administration as Told by Two Sympathetic Observers Who Seek to Build Morals on a Foundation.* University of California Press.

10. Edward Jennings and Dale Krane preferred to think of coordination as the

"philosophers stone," something that would "provide the key to the universe, and, in effect, solve all the problems of mankind." See: Jennings Jr., E. T. and Krane, D. (1994). "Coordination and Welfare Reform: The Quest for the Philosopher's Stone." *Public Administration Review, 54*(4), 341–348.

11. B. Guy Peters described coordination between public agencies as the "Holy Grail" of public administration; see: Peters, B. G. (1998). "Managing Horizontal Government: The Politics of Coordination. *Public Administration,*" *76*(2), 295–311.

12. At the time of writing, Peters' article (cited above) and Bardach's book had each been cited more than a thousand times: Bardach, E. (1998). *Getting Agencies to Work Together: The Practice and Theory of Managerial Craftsmanship.* Brookings Institution Press.

13. See: Ansell, C. and Gash, A. (2008). "Collaborative Governance in Theory and Practice." *Journal of Public Administration Research and Theory, 18*(4), 543–571. Emerson, K. and Nabatchi, T. (2015). *Collaborative Governance Regimes.* Georgetown University Press. Bryson, J. M., Crosby, B. C. and Stone, M. M. (2006). "The Design and Implementation of Cross-Sector Collaborations: Propositions from the Literature." *Public Administration Review, 66*(s1), 44–55.

14. Taylor, F. W. (1914). *The Principles of Scientific Management.* Harper & Brothers.

15. While the idea of contingent approaches to management was developed simultaneously by different authors, the following are indicative of the arguments presented at the time: Woodward, J. (1958). *Management and Technology.* London: Her Majesty's Stationery Office. Burns, T. and Stalker, G. M. (1961). *The Management of Innovation.* Tavistock.

16. Scott, W. R. (1981). *Organizations: Rational, Natural, and Open Systems.* Prentice Hall.

17. Though there are numerous variations on this quote, one discussion can be found in Clevenger, J. (1997). "Collaboration: Why Participate in an Unnatural Act?" *Journal of Chemical Education, 74*(8), 894–898.

18. Thompson, D. F. (1980). "Moral Responsibility of Public Officials: The Problem of Many Hands." *American Political Science Review, 74*(4), 905–916.

19. For a discussion of transaction costs in interagency working, see: Scott, R. J. and Bardach, E. (2019). "A Comparison of Management Adaptations for Joined-Up Government: Lessons from New Zealand." *Australian Journal of Public Administration, 78*(2), 191–212.

20. For a discussion of goal commitment in interagency working, see chapters 12–14 of this book.

21. See: O'Leary, R. and Bingham, L. B. (Eds.). (2009). *The Collaborative Public Manager: New Ideas for the Twenty-first Century.* Georgetown University Press.

22. See: Carey, G. and Crammond, B. (2015). "What Works in Joined-Up Government? An Evidence Synthesis." *International Journal of Public Administration, 38*(13–14), 1020–1029.

23. Behn, R. D. (2001). *Rethinking Democratic Accountability,* 15. Brookings Institute Press.

24. Hood, C. and Dixon, R. (2010). "The Political Payoff from Performance Target

Systems: No-Brainer or No-Gainer?" *Journal of Public Administration Research and Theory*, *20*(2), 281–298.

25. Dixon, R. and others. (2013). "A Lever for Improvement or a Magnet for Blame? Press and Political Responses to International Educational Rankings in Four EU Countries." *Public Administration*, *91*(2), 484–505.

26. Frederickson, H. G. (1992). "Painting Bull's Eyes around Bullet Holes." *Governing*, *6*(1), 13.

27. Jensen, K. and others. (2014). "The Management and Organisational Challenges of More Joined-Up Government: New Zealand's Better Public Services Reforms." State Sector Performance Hub: Working paper 2014–1. New Zealand Government. DOI: 10.13140/RG.2.1.3115.3680.

28. Musheno, M. C. (1986). "The Justice Motive in the Social Policy Process: Searching for Normative Rules of Distribution." *Policy Studies Review*, *5*(4), 697–704.

Chapter 3

1. Bovaird, T. and Loffler, E. (2005). "Lessons from Europe: Innovations in Rural Service Delivery." *Proceedings of the 2005 National Rural Affairs Conference*, Cumbria. February 24, 2005. https://webarchive.nationalarchives.gov.uk/20060818120000/http://www.defra.gov.uk/rural/voice/nrac/2005-february/report.htm (as cited in Behn, 2014).

2. In *The PerformanceStat Potential*, Bob Behn describes -Stat systems as leadership strategies because they depend as much on the behaviors of the leaders as on the performance information itself.

3. The name CompStat has an uncertain origin. According to an account by Bob Behn, it may stand for "Computer Statistics," "Comparative Statistics," "Computerised Crime Comparison Statistics," or nothing at all. Behn, R. D. (2014). *The PerformanceStat Potential: A leadership Strategy for Producing Results*, 324. Brookings Institution Press.

4. Behn, R. D. (2014). *The PerformanceStat Potential: A Leadership Strategy for Producing Results*, 27. Brookings Institution Press.

5. Kohli, J. (2010). "Golden Goals for Government Performance: Five Case Studies on How to Establish Goals to Achieve Results," 8. Center for American Progress.

6. State of Victoria. (2005). "A Vision for Victoria to 2010 and Beyond: Growing Victoria Together." Government of Victoria.

7. As cited in Kohli, J. (2010). "Golden Goals for Government Performance: Five Case Studies on How to Establish Goals to Achieve Results," 9. Center for American Progress.

8. Budget estimates during this period included a section on linkages to the goals and measures of Growing Victoria Together, for example: www.parliament.vic.gov.au/archive/paec/inquiries/budgetestimates_2007-08/3rd_Report/Section%20C%20Growing%20Victoria%20Together.pdf.

9. Kohli, J. (2010). "Golden Goals for Government Performance: Five Case Studies on How to Establish Goals to Achieve Results," 9. Center for American Progress.

10. Commonwealth of Virginia. (2016). "Scorecard at a Glance." Government of Virginia. https://vaperforms.virginia.gov/ScorecardatGlance.cfm.

11. Government of Scotland. (2007). "Scottish Budget: Spending Review 2007." Scottish Government. www.scotland.gov.uk/Resource/Doc/203078/0054106.pdf.

12. Gregoire, C. (2005). "Executive Order 05-02: Government Management, Accountability and Performance (GMAP)." www.digitalarchives.wa.gov/GovernorGregoire/execorders/eo_05-02.pdf.

13. Krzmarzick, A. (2010). "Project of the week: Washington State's GMAP." *GovLoop*, February 17, 2010. www.govloop.com/project-of-the-week-washington-states-gmap.

14. Barrett, K. and Greene, R. (2008). "Grading the States: The Mandate to Measure." *Governing,* March 2008: 30. eRepublic.

15. Barber, M. (2007). "Instruction to Delivery," 335. Politico.

16. Bevan, G., Evans, A. and Nuti, S. (2017). "Reputations Count: Why Benchmarking Performance Is Improving Health Care across the World." Paper presented at the International Health Policy Conference, London, February 16–19, 2017.

17. As noted by both Barber, on page 236 of his book referenced above, and Bevan et al., on page 10 of their paper.

18. Chabrabarti, S. as quoted by Kohli, J. (2010). "Golden Goals for Government Performance: Five case studies on how to establish goals to achieve results," 21. Center for American Progress.

19. Kohli, J. (2010). "Golden Goals for Government Performance: Five Case Studies on How to Establish Goals to Achieve Results," 21. Center for American Progress.

20. "Killer facts" was a term used by Andrew Kibblewhite, director of the Policy Advisory Group at the Department of Prime Minister and Cabinet in the lead-up to development of the Results program. It referred to selecting and using data that would attract attention and prompt action.

Chapter 4

1. Kurtz and Snowden's "Cynefin" framework has been influential in New Zealand's recent public management reforms, and the authors thank Dave Snowden for his generous time during a 2015 visit to New Zealand. For an introduction, see: Kurtz, C. F. and Snowden, D. J. (2003). "The New Dynamics of Strategy: Sense-making in a Complex and Complicated World." *IBM Systems Journal, 42*(3), 462–483.

2. New Zealand authors Jennifer Berger and Keith Johnston related Snowden and Kurtz's use of the Welsh-language word *cynefin* to the te reo Māori word *tūrangawaewae,* meaning a place to stand; see: Berger, J. G. and Johnston, K. (2015). *Simple Habits for Complex Times: Powerful Practices for Leaders.* Stanford Business Books.

3. Le Grand, J. (2003). *Motivation, Agency, and Public Policy: Of Knights and Knaves, Pawns and Queens.* Oxford University Press.

4. Le Grand, J. (2009). *The Other Invisible Hand: Delivering Public Services through Choice and Competition.* Princeton University Press.

5. For a discussion on the limitations of quasi-markets in delivering complex social services, see: Bevan, G., Evans, A., and Nuti, S. (2017). "Reputations Count: Why Benchmarking Performance Is Improving Health Care across the World." Paper presented at the International Health Policy Conference, London, February 16–19, 2017.

6. Fiske, E. and Ladd, H. (2000). *When Schools Compete: A Cautionary Tale*. Brookings Institution Press.

7. Gordon, L. (2003). "School choice and the social market in New Zealand: Education reform in an era of increasing inequality." *International Studies in Sociology of Education, 13*(1), 17–34.

8. For a discussion of how school choice creates positional goods, see: Hirsch, F. (2005). *Social Limits to Growth*. Routledge. For evidence of the effect of schools picking students/parents, see: West, A., Ingram, D. and Hind, A. (2006). " 'Skimming the Cream' Admissions to Charter Schools in the United States and to Autonomous Schools in England." *Educational Policy, 20*(4), 615–639. Whitty, G., Halpin, D. and Power, S. (1998). "Self-managing Schools in the Marketplace: The Experience of England, the USA and New Zealand." In Legrand, J., Bartlett, W. and Roberts, J. (Eds.). *A Revolution in Social Policy: Quasi-Market Reforms in the 1990s*. Policy Press.

9. The "cautionary tale" of quasi-markets in education has been studied many times, notably: Lauder, H., Hughes, D. and Watson, S. (1999). "The Introduction of Educational Markets in New Zealand: Questions and Consequences." *New Zealand Journal of Educational Studies, 34*(1), 86–98. Gordon, L. (1994). "Rich and Poor Schools in Aotearoa/New Zealand." *New Zealand Journal of Educational Studies, 29*(2), 113–126. Fiske, E. and Ladd, H. (2000). *When Schools Compete: A Cautionary Tale*. Brookings Institution Press. Nash, R. (1999). "Social Capital, Class Identity, and Progress at School: Case Studies." *New Zealand Journal of Educational Studies, 34*(2), 267–280. Waslander, S. and Thrupp, M. (1995). "Choice, Competition and Segregation: An Empirical Analysis of a New Zealand Secondary School Market, 1990–1993." *Journal of Education Policy, 10*(1), 1–26. Musset, P. (2012). *School Choice and Equity: Current Policies in OECD Countries and a Literature Review*, OECD Education Working Papers, No. 66. OECD Publishing. http://dx.doi.org/10.1787/5k9fq23507vc-en.

10. See: Ham, C. (2008). "World Class Commissioning: A Health Policy Chimera?" *Journal of Health Services Research & Policy, 13*(2), 116–121. Maarse, H., Jeurissen, P. and Ruwaard, D. (2016). "Results of The Market-Oriented Reform in the Netherlands: A Review." *Health Economics, Policy and Law, 11*(2), 161–78.

11. Laverty, A. A. and others. "High-Profile Investigations into Hospital Safety Problems in England Did Not Prompt Patients to Switch Providers." *Health Affairs, 31*(3), 593–601.

12. Quasi-markets fail in health care for a variety of reasons, too numerous to mention here. One peculiarity of the health sector is "supply-mediated demand," that is, it is health professionals who recommend and refer patients for services and therefore determine the "demand" for these services.

13. Effort substitution is explored more broadly in Bevan, G. and Hood, C. (2006). "What's Measured Is What Matters: Targets and Gaming in the English Public Health Care System." *Public Administration, 84*(3), 517–538. The specific formulation "what gets measured gets managed" is studied empirically in Catasús, B. and others. (2007). "What Gets Measured Gets . . . on Indicating, Mobilizing and Acting." *Accounting, Auditing & Accountability Journal, 20*(4), 505–521.

14. See: Bevan and Hood (2006) above.

15. Sir Julian LeGrand first described governance options in this way and suggested

that the challenge is to identity the "least worst" option for a given situation based on empirical study but suggests further experimentation with quasi-market approaches despite their history of failure in the delivery of complex social services. See Grand, J. L. (2010). "Knights and Knaves Return: Public Service Motivation and the Delivery of Public Services." *International Public Management Journal, 13*(1), 56–71.

16. Interview, senior official.

17. Cabinet paper: "Better Public Services Results: Targets and Public Communication," June 25, 2012.

18. Minutes, Better Public Services Programme Board and Advisory Group, July 17, 2012.

19. The quotations in this chapter by (then) Prime Minister Rt. Hon. John Key, and (then) Deputy Prime Minister and Minister of Finance Hon. Bill English, are from a government media statement, June 25, 2012.

Chapter 5

1. Cabinet paper: "Better Public Services Results: Targets and Public Communication," June 2012.

2. Cabinet paper: "Better Public Services: Results," February 3, 2012.

3. Ibid.

4. Quotations by a Ministry of Education official in this chapter are from an interview held on April 10, 2018, with a senior manager at the Ministry of Education responsible for coordinating the education Results.

5. New Zealand State Services Commission. www.ssc.govt.nz/better-public-services.

6. State Services Commission. (2014). "Better Public Services Result 9—Case Study: One Number Makes It Easier for New Zealand Businesses to Interact with Government." https://ssc.govt.nz/resources/bps-result9-cs4.

7. Cabinet paper: "Better Public Services: Results. February 2012."

Chapter 6

1. Behn, R. D. (2014). *The PerformanceStat Potential: A Leadership Strategy for Producing Results*. Brookings Institution Press.

2. In an interview, Tony Blair remarked, "I bear the scars on my back" from imposing these unpopular reforms on public servants. BBC News. (2007). "Blair: In His Own Words." http://news.bbc.co.uk/1/hi/uk_politics/3750847.stm.

3. The State Sector Act (1988) was repealed and replaced with a new Public Service Act in 2020, which resulted in changes in terminology. The Minister of State Services is now the Minister for the Public Service, the State Services Commissioner is now the Public Service Commissioner, and the State Services Commission is now the Public Service Commission.

4. *Project Independent Quality Assurance Report, Result 10 programme—Better Public Services Digitally*. August 2014. Caravel Group NZ Ltd.

5. Quotations in this chapter are from an interview with Aphra Green, April 12, 2018. Green was general manager, justice sector group at the time of the Better Public Services reform. When interviewed, she was general manager, strategy, evidence, and investment group.

6. "Radical incrementalism" was a phrase used by Hon. Bill English to describe his approach to reform. James, C. (2015). "Bill English Incremental Radical." *Colin James* (blog). www.colinjames.co.nz/2015/07/07/bill-english-incremental-radical/. Grieve, D. (2017). *The Incremental Radical: Bill English Meets the Spinoff.* https://thespinoff.co.nz/politics/15-03-2017/bill-english-spinoff/.

7. Or what Kurtz and Snowden would refer to as "Probe-Sense-Respond"; see chapter 4.

8. See the Public Finance Amendment Act 2020, New Zealand Government.

9. The "Ratana celebrations" refers to an annual gathering in a small rural town to celebrate the birthday of an important Māori leader, Tahupotiki Wiremu Ratana. The Early Learning Taskforce was a group of public servants that used the celebrations as an opportunity to connect with members of a community who might be otherwise hard to reach. The celebrations provided a place where (predominantly Māori) families (whānau) could experience early childhood education for the first time. New Zealanders often use a combination of English and certain words from the indigenous language, *te reo Māori*, in this case *whānau* meaning "family" and *tamariki* meaning "children" (usually in plural).

10. *Poipoia* means "to nurture," and *Mokopuna* are grandchildren.

11. Plunket NZ refers to the Royal New Zealand Plunket Society, a charity that helps families with young children, and Te Tai Tokerau is the northernmost region of New Zealand.

12. State Services Commission. (2014). "Better Public Services Result 1—Case Study: Reducing Long-Term Welfare Dependence through Youth Service." https://ssc.govt.nz/resources/bps-result1-cs1.

Chapter 7

1. Bevan, G. and Hood, C. (2006). "What's Measured Is What Matters: Targets and Gaming in the English Public Health Care System." *Public Administration, 84*(3), 517–538.

2. Nove, A. (1958). "The Problem of Success Indicators in Soviet Industry." *Economica 25*(97), 1–13, P4. As cited in Bevan and Hood (2006) above.

3. PM Jacinda Ardern: "Merit in Target System, but Labour Will Set Its Own." *New Zealand Herald*, 2018, www.nzherald.co.nz/nz/news/article.cfm?c_id=1&object id=11980625&ref=rss.

4. Cabinet paper: "Better Public Services Results Refresh," March 2017.

5. Tham, I. (2018). "Almost All Government Services in Singapore to Go Digital by 2023." *The Straits Times.* www.straitstimes.com/tech/almost-all-govt-services-to-go-digital-by-2023.

6. Rennie, I. (2020). "Quest: New Zealand Public Sector Reform Since 2000," 288. In Berman, E. and Karacaoglu, G. (Eds.) *Public Policy and Governance Frontiers in New Zealand.* Emerald Publishing Limited.

Part III

1. For a more complete discussion of sensemaking, see: Weick, K. E. (1995). *Sensemaking in Organizations.* SAGE Publications.

Chapter 8

1. See: McConnell, A. (2010). "Policy Success, Policy Failure and Grey Areas In-Between." *Journal of Public Policy, 30*(3), 345–362.

2. Bovens M., 't Hart P. and Peters B. G. (2001). "Analysing Governance Success and Failure in Six European States." In Bovens M., 't Hart P. and Peters B. G. (Eds.), *Success and Failure in Public Governance: A Comparative Analysis.* Edward Elgar Publishing, 12–26.

3. Edelman, M. (1977). *Political Language: Words That Succeed and Policies That Fail.* Academic Press.

4. Hood, C. and Dixon, R. (2010). "The Political Payoff from Performance Target Systems: No-Brainer or No-Gainer?" *Journal of Public Administration Research and Theory, 20*(2), 281–298.

5. Dixon, R. and others. (2013). "A Lever for Improvement Or A Magnet For Blame? Press and Political Responses to International Educational Rankings in Four EU Countries." *Public Administration, 91*(2), 484–505.

6. Bovens M., 't Hart P. and Peters B. G. "Analysing Governance Success and Failure in Six European States."

7. Frederickson, H. G. (1992). "Painting Bull's Eyes around Bullet Holes." *Governing, 6*(1), 13.

8. David, O. and Ted, G. (1992). *Reinventing Government: How the Entrepreneurial Spirit Is Transforming the Public Sector.* Prentice-Hall.

9. Kelman, S. and Friedman, J. N. (2009). "Performance Improvement and Performance Dysfunction: An Empirical Examination of Distortionary Impacts of the Emergency Room Wait-Time Target in the English National Health Service." *Journal of Public Administration Research and Theory, 19*(4), 917–946.

10. The data used in measures for Results 1–8 had been collected for some time, and these historical data were included in the Results program reporting for comparison. The measures used in Results 9 and 10 were new and did not have historical data.

11. Cooke, H. (2018). "Bill English Slams Government for Getting Rid of Public Service Targets." www.stuff.co.nz/national/politics/100801792/bill-english-slams -government-for-getting-rid-of-public-service-targets.

12. Ibid.

13. Ibid.

14. Ryan, B. (2012). "Outcomes Matter, Not State Service Tinkering." www.stuff .co.nz/dominion-post/comment/6427188/Outcomes-matter-not-state-service-tin kering.

15. Nielson Company. (2018). "A Social Licence Approach to Trust: A Close-Up on Trust." www.stats.govt.nz/assets/Uploads/Corporate/Measuring-Stats-NZs-social-li cence/a-social-licence-approach-to-trust.pdf.

16. Ryan, B. "Outcomes Matter, Not State Service Tinkering."

17. Ibid.

18. Ibid.

19. Barclay, G. in Cooke, H. (2018). "Bill English Slams Government for Getting Rid of Public Service Targets." www.stuff.co.nz/national/politics/100801792/bill-en glish-slams-government-for-getting-rid-of-public-service-targets.

20. Turrell, J. (2017). "Government Gets an F for Education." www.stuff.co.nz/southland-times/opinion/96565477/government-gets-an-f-for-education.

21. Ibid.

22. Ibid.

23. Johnston, M. (2015). "What's Driving Endless NCEA Pass Rate Rises?" www.stuff.co.nz/national/education/69887908/whats-driving-endless-ncea-pass-rate-rises.

24. Green Party. (2016). "Minister's Target Put above Giving Kids the Best Start." www.greens.org.nz/ministers-target-put-above-giving-kids-best-start.

25. Ministry of Education. (2002). "Pathways to the Future—Ngā Huarahi Arataki." Ministry of Education. In NZEI Te Riu Roa. (2010). *Early Childhood Education—Quality at Risk*, 2. https://nzei.org.nz/documents/MYNZEI/Resources/whats%20on/Annual%20Meeting/2010/ECE%20special%20report_Quality%20at%20risk_web.pdf. Ministry of Education. (2018). *ECE Funding Handbook Updates* (September 2010). https://education.govt.nz/early-childhood/funding-and-data/funding-hand books/ece-funding-handbook-updates.

26. O'Donnell, M. (2017). "Digital Inclusion Is Not Just Good for People But for the Economy." www.stuff.co.nz/business/opinion-analysis/100114589/digital-inclusion-is-not-just-good-for-people-but-for-the-economy.

27. The shift to e-learning, accelerated by the COVID-19 pandemic, brought some New Zealanders' lack of internet access into sharper focus. The government introduced a program to connect student households that had previously lacked internet. See: Ministry of Education. (2020). "Bridging the Digital Divide," *Education Gazette*, *99*(6).

Chapter 9

1. Threshold effects, as well as several other types of gaming using a slightly different framing from the one in this book, are discussed in detail in: Bird, S. M. and others. (2005). "Performance Indicators: Good, Bad, and Ugly." *Journal of the Royal Statistical Society: Series A (Statistics in Society)*, *168*(1), 1–27.

2. Ridgway, V. F. (1956). "Dysfunctional Consequences of Performance Measurements." *Administrative Science Quarterly*, *1*(2), 240–247.

3. Boston, J. and Gill, D. (Eds.). (2017). *Social Investment: A New Zealand Policy Experiment*. Bridget Williams Books.

4. Quotations by this education official are from an interview held on April 10, 2018, with a senior manager at the Ministry of Education responsible for coordinating the Education Results.

5. Elias, S. "Managing Criminal Justice." Address given at the Criminal Bar Association conference, University of Auckland Business School, August 5, 2017.

6. Kelman, S. and Friedman, J. N. (2009). "Performance Improvement and Performance Dysfunction: An Empirical Examination of Distortionary Impacts of the Emergency Room Wait-Time Target in the English National Health Service." *Journal of Public Administration Research and Theory*, *19*(4), 917–946.

7. Bevan, G. and Hood, C. (2006). "What's Measured Is What Matters: Targets And Gaming in the English Public Health Care System." *Public Administration*, *84*(3), 517–538.

8. The phrase "Hit the target but miss the point" has been used informally in New Zealand and UK public services for some time. Gwyn Bevan and Christopher Hood use the phrase in several of their publications, including their 2006 article referenced above.

Chapter 10

1. Eppel, E. and others. (2014). "The Cross-Organizational Collaboration Solution? Conditions, Roles and Dynamics in New Zealand." In O'Flynn, J., Blackman, D. and Halligan J. (Eds.), *Crossing Boundaries in Public Management and Policy.* Routledge, 47–63.

2. Kingdon describes policy entrepreneurs in the context of his Multiple Streams Framework for understanding the organizational context in which policy is developed; see: Kingdon, J. W. (1984). *Agendas, Alternatives, and Public Policies* (2nd ed.). Pearson.

3. The term "social entrepreneur" has been in use since at least the 1980s with varying definitions. For a discussion of the term and its history, see: Dees, J. G. (1998). "The Meaning of Social Entrepreneurship." Kauffman Center for Entrepreneurial Leadership. Stanford University. Further discussion in: Thompson, J. L. (2002). "The World of the Social Entrepreneur." *The International Journal of Public Sector Management, 15*(4–5), 413.

4. Klein, P. G. and others. (2010). "Toward a Theory of Public Entrepreneurship." *European Management Review, 7*(1), 1–15.

5. See page 53 in Eppel, E. and others. (2014) referenced above. "The Cross-Organizational Collaboration Solution? Conditions, Roles and Dynamics in New Zealand," 52.

6. Eppel, E. (2013). "Collaborative Governance: Framing New Zealand Practice." Working Paper No: 13/02. Institute for Governance and Policy Studies, 43.

7. Eppel et al. refer to these people as "fellow-travelers," 53. Eppel, E. and others. (2014). "The Cross-organizational Collaboration Solution? Conditions, Roles and Dynamics in New Zealand."

8. Cabinet paper: "Better Public Services Results 2015 Mid-Year Progress Report," July 2, 2015.

9. Cabinet paper: "Better Public Services Results 2015 End-Year Progress Report," March 9, 2016.

10. Ibid.

11. Quotations by Kararaina Calcott-Cribb in this chapter are from an interview with her on June 7, 2018. Calcott-Cribb was leading the Early Learning Taskforce at the time of the Better Public Services reforms. When interviewed, she was chief executive of Te Kōhanga Reo National Trust.

12. For more information on the partnership with New Zealand Rugby League, see: www.youtube.com/watch?v=0uWj5raxGGI.

13. Cabinet paper: "Better Public Services Results 2015 Mid-year Progress Report," July 2, 2015.

14. From "Rheumatic Fever Film Project," Ministry of Pacific Island Affairs. https://vimeo.com/118680120.

15. Quotations by Linda Oliver in this chapter are from an interview with her on May 23 2018. Oliver was a manager of Better for Business (Result 9) at the Ministry of Business, Innovation and Employment at the time of the Better Public Services reforms. When interviewed, she was senior project manager at the Inland Revenue Department.

16. For case studies on innovations from Results 9 and 10, see: www.ssc.govt.nz/bps-interaction-with-govt.

17. Quotations by Richard Foy in this chapter are from an interview with him on April 12, 2018. Foy was the project manager of Result 10 at the Department of Internal Affairs at the time of the Better Public Services reforms. When interviewed, he was chief archivist at the Department of Internal Affairs.

18. The Result 10 Blueprint can be found at www.ict.govt.nz.

19. Cabinet paper: "Better Public Services Results 2014 End-Year Progress Report," February 16, 2015.

20. Kearney and colleagues provide a useful framework for comparing and contrasting public and private entrepreneurship. The quote in text comes from page 26 of Kearney, C., Hisrich, R. D., and Roche, F. (2009). "Public and Private Sector Entrepreneurship: Similarities, Differences or a Combination?" *Journal of Small Business and Enterprise Development, 16*(1), 26–46.

21. Ibid.

22. Osborne, D. and Gaebler, T. (1992). *Reinventing Government: How the Entrepreneurial Spirit Is Transforming the Public Sector.* Addison-Wesley Publishing Company.

Chapter 11

1. The emic and etic perspectives are described in: Pike, K. L. (1967). *Language in Relation* to a *Unified Theory of the Structure of Human Behavior.* Mouton.

2. The complementarity of emit and etic inquiry are discussed in Morris, M. W. and others. (1999). "Views from Inside and Outside: Integrating Emic and Etic Insights about Culture and Justice Judgment." *Academy of Management Review, 24*(4), 781–796. The application of emic and etic perspectives to the BPS Results program can be found in Scott, R. J. and Merton, E. R. (2021). "When the Going Gets Tough, the Goal-Committed Get Going: Overcoming the Transaction Costs of Inter-Agency Collaborative Governance." *Public Management Review,* 1–24.

3. Scott, R. J. and Bardach, E. (2019). "A Comparison of Management Adaptations for Joined-Up Government: Lessons from New Zealand." *Australian Journal of Public Administration, 78*(2), 191–212.

4. The four evaluations can be found in: Scott, R. J. and Boyd, R. (2016). "Results, Targets and Measures to Drive Collaboration: Lessons from the New Zealand Better Public Services Reforms." In: Butcher, J. R. and Gilchrist D. J. (Eds.), *The Three Sector Solution: Delivering Public Policy in Collaboration with Not-For-Profits and Business.* Australian National University Press, 235–257. Scott, R. J. and Boyd, R. (2016). "Case Studies in Collaborating for Better Public Services." State Sector Performance Hub, working paper 2016-2. DOI: 10.13140/RG.2.1.3232.8081. Scott, R. J. and Boyd, R. (2016). "Collective Impact in the Public Sector: The New Zealand Results Approach."

State Sector Performance Hub, working paper 2016-1. DOI: 10.13140/RG.2.1.2839 .5929. Scott, R. J. and Boyd, R. (2015). "The New Zealand Better Public Service Results: A Comparative Analysis Linking Inter-Agency Collaboration with Outcome Performance." *Proceedings of the 2015 Australia and New Zealand Academy of Management Conference,* Queenstown. An account of the mixed-methods methodology used to combine findings from these three evaluations can be found in: Scott, R. J. and Boyd, R. (2016). "Collaborating for Results: Evaluation Using Mixed Methods and Triangulation." *Proceedings of the International Public Management Network Conference,* St. Gallen.

5. Jennifer C. Greene's book *Mixed Methods in Social Inquiry* (Wiley, 2007) provides an accessible introduction to mixed-methods research.

6. The challenges of drawing inferences from a single case study are considerable; the challenges of drawing inferences between case studies are different but just as significant. For an overview of some of these challenges, see: Yin, R. K. (1981). "The Case Study Crisis: Some Answers." *Administrative Science Quarterly,* 58–65.

7. "Collective Impact" was first described by FSG Directors John Kania and Mark Kramer (2011) in the *Stanford Social Innovation Review, 9*(1), 36–41. Several FSG staff led by Haillie Preskill subsequently published a three-part guide to evaluating collective impact, with developmental, formative, and summative modules. Both Mark Kramer and Haillie Preskill generously reviewed the application of their framework to the Better Public Services Results program in 2015.

8. In addition to the earlier reference by Jennifer Greene, further commentary on the use of methodological diversity can be found in the following texts: Teddlie, C. and Tashakkori, A. (2009). *Foundations of Mixed Methods Research: Integrating Quantitative and Qualitative Approaches in the Social and Behavioral Sciences.* SAGE Publications. Creswell, J. W. (2013). *Research Design: Qualitative, Quantitative, and Mixed Methods Approaches.* SAGE Publications.

9. For a further discussion of the use and benefits of triangulation from mixed methods studies, see: Campbell, D. T. and Fiske, D. W. (1959). "Convergent and Discriminant Validation by the Multitrait-Multimethod Matrix." *Psychological Bulletin, 56*(2), 81–105.

10. For a further discussion of complementarity, see: Rossman, G. B. and Wilson, B. L. (1985). "Numbers and Words: Combining Quantitative and Qualitative Methods in a Single Large-Scale Evaluation Study." *Evaluation Review, 9*(5), 627–643.

11. Scott, R. J. and Boyd, R. (2019). "Determined to Succeed: Can Goal Commitment Sustain Interagency Collaboration?" *Public Policy and Administration.* DOI: 10 .1177/0952076720905002.

Part IV

1. Klein, H. J., Cooper, J. T., and Monahan, C. A. (2013). "Goal Commitment," 67. In: Locke, E. A. and Latham, G. P. (Eds.) *New Developments in Goal Setting and Performance.* Routledge, 65–89.

2. See, for example, Erez, A. and Judge, T. A. (2001). "Relationship of Core Self-Evaluations on Goal Setting, Motivation, and Performance." *Journal of Applied Psychology, 86*(6), 1270–1279. Schweitzer, M. E., Ordoñez, L. and Douma, B. (2004).

"Goal Setting as a Motivator of Unethical Behavior." *Academy of Management Journal,* 47(3), 422–432.

3. The effects of goal commitment on effort and persistence are explored in: Seijts, G. H. and Latham, G. P. (2000). "The Construct of Goal Commitment: Measurement and Relationships with Task Performance." In: Goffin, R. D. and Helmes, E. (Eds.), *Problems and Solutions in Human Assessment.* Kluwer Academic Publishers, 315–332.

4. The effects of goal commitment on creating task-related strategies are explored in: Earley, P. C., Shalley, C. E., and Northcraft, G. B. (1992). "I Think I Can, I Think I Can . . . Processing Time and Strategy Effects of Goal Acceptance/Rejection Decisions." *Organizational Behavior and Human Decision Processes,* 53(1), 1–13.

5. Thomson, A. M. and Perry, J. L. (2006). "Collaboration Processes: Inside the Black Box." *Public Administration Review,* 66(December), 28.

6. Ibid.

7. Imperial, M. T. (2005). "Using Collaboration as a Governance Strategy: Lessons from Six Watershed Management Programs." *Administration & Society,* 37(3), 281–320. https://doi.org/10.1177/0095399705276111.

8. Huxham, C. and Vangen, S. (2000). "Leadership in the Shaping and Implementation of Collaboration Agendas: How Things Happen in a (Not Quite) Joined-Up World." *Academy of Management Journal,* 43(6), 1159–1175.

9. Orange, R. (2016). "New public Passion: Reflections from New Zealand on Public Service Reform." Discussion Paper 08(01). UNDP Global Centre for Public Service Excellence, Singapore, 16.

10. The phrase "The most significant change to how public services are delivered in twenty years" appears in several media articles from 2012 to 2013 in reference to the Results program. See, for example, Shelton L. (2013). "Al Morrison Leaving Conservation Dept, Joining State Services Commission." *Wellington Scoop.* http://wellington .scoop.co.nz/?p=54803.

Chapter 12

1. Vroom, V. H. (1964). *Work and Motivation.* Wiley.

2. Klein, H. J. and Wright, P. M. (1994). "Antecedents of Goal Commitment: An Empirical Examination of Personal and Situational Factors." *Journal of Applied Social Psychology,* 24(2), 95–114.

3. See: Miller, G. A. (1956). "The Magical Number Seven, Plus or Minus Two: Some Limits on Our Capacity for Processing Information." *Psychological Review,* 63(2), 81.

4. The preceding Millennium Development Goals were typically narrower in scope, with the equivalent goal of "maternal health." To read further about the Sustainable Development Goals, see: www.un.org/sustainabledevelopment/sustainable -development-goals/.

5. See: Meadows, D. (1997). "Places to Intervene in a System." *Whole Earth,* 91(1), 78–84.

6. Quotations in this chapter are from an interview with Dr. Chrissie Pickin, May 23, 2018. Dr. Pickin was chief advisor population health and rheumatic fever program

lead at the Ministry of Health at the time of the Better Public Services reform. When interviewed, she was executive director of Health and Wellbeing, Public Health Wales.

7. Hal Rainey and Paula Steinbauer first connected public service motivation with expectancy theory in 1999; a fuller description relating expectancy and mission valence can be found in various later articles by Bradley Wright, Donald Moynihan, and Sanjay Pandey, such as the following: Rainey, H. G. and Steinbauer, P. (1999). "Galloping Elephants: Developing Elements of a Theory of Effective Government Organizations." *Journal of Public Administration Research and Theory*, *9*(1), 1–32. Wright, B. E., Moynihan, D. P., and Pandey, S. K. (2012). "Pulling the Levers: Transformational Leadership, Public Service Motivation, and Mission Valence." *Public Administration Review*, *72*(2), 206–215.

8. The first human landed on the moon in July 1969, less than seven years after Kennedy's famous "We choose to go to the moon" speech delivered at Rice Football Stadium in September 1962. See: Jordan, J. W. (2003). "Kennedy's Romantic Moon and Its Rhetorical Legacy for Space Exploration." *Rhetoric and Public Affairs*, *6*(2), 209–231.

9. Thirty years later, many Australian children still live in poverty, and Hawke has said he regrets the promise. However, Australian Council of Social Service head Dr. Cassandra Goldie credits Hawke with dramatically reducing child poverty. www.smh .com.au/politics/federal/no-child-will-live-in-poverty-30-years-on-bob-hawkes -promise-remains-an-elusive-goal-20170621-gwvdya.html.

10. Bevan, G. and Hood, C. (2006). "What's Measured Is What Matters: Targets and Gaming in the English Public Health Care System." *Public Administration*, *84*(3), 517–538.

11. Julnes, P. D. L. and Holzer, M. (2001). "Promoting the Utilization of Performance Measures in Public Organizations: An Empirical Study of Factors Affecting Adoption and Implementation." *Public Administration Review*, *61*(6), 693–708.

12. "Reducing Long-Term Benefit Dependency." Welfare Working Group report, February 2011

13. Cabinet paper: "Better Public Services Results 2014 Mid-Year Progress Report," July 3, 2014.

14. Cabinet paper: "Better Public Services Results 2014 End-Year Progress Report," February 16, 2015.

15. Ibid.

16. Cabinet paper: "Better Public Services Results 2016 Mid-Year Progress Report *Snapshot*," September 22, 2016.

17. Cabinet paper: "Better Public Services Results 2015 Mid-Year Progress Report," July 2, 2015.

18. Derek Gill, a former colleague of the authors at the State Services Commission, canvasses the issues in an unpublished 2008 manuscript "Managing for Performance in New Zealand—the search for the Holy Grail?" Derek has made the manuscript available online at http://igps.victoria.ac.nz/events/Ongoing_research/M4P/KPMG_ NZ_Chapter_Managing_for_Performance.pdf.

19. For an introduction to logic modeling, see Julian, D. A. (1997). "The utilization

of the logic model as a system level planning and evaluation device." *Evaluation and Program Planning, 20*(3), 251–257.

20. Variations of the "production model" are found throughout (initially) private and (now) public sector texts. A particularly complete version can be found in the doctoral thesis of Wouter van Dooren (2006), titled "Performance Measurement in the Flemish Public Sector: A Supply and Demand Approach." This particular version usefully closes the "loop" between outcomes, problems, needs, and the selection of objectives.

21. For a description for "intermediate outcomes" and "end outcomes" as used in New Zealand, see: Baehler, K. (2003). " 'Managing for outcomes': Accountability and Thrust." *Australian Journal of Public Administration, 62*(4), 23–34. For a broader discussion of short-term and long-term outcomes within logic models, see: McLaughlin, J. A. and Jordan, G. B. (1999). "Logic Models: A Tool for Telling Your Program's Performance Story." *Evaluation and Program Planning, 22*(1), 65–72.

22. Co-production is described in various ways in the literature, and the sense used here is on the margin of the more common uses. Another term might be "voluntary compliance," but this would deemphasise the value created by the public and the active choice to seek out and participate in the service offered. For a general discussion on co-production, see the work of John Alford, in particular: Alford, J. (2007). *Engaging Public Sector Clients: From Service-Delivery to Co-Production*. Palgrave Macmillan.

23. See correspondence in the *Australian Journal of Public Administration* between Gemma Carey and Patrick Harris and the authors: Carey, G. and Harris, P. (2016). "Developing Management Practices to Support Joined-Up Governance." *Australian Journal of Public Administration, 75*(1), 112–118. Scott, R. J. and Boyd, R. (2017). "Joined-Up for What? Response to Carey and Harris on Adaptive Collaboration." *Australian Journal of Public Administration, 76*(1), 138–144.

24. Quote from an Australian public servant involved in the Social Inclusion Agenda, as cited in Carey, G., McLoughlin, P., and Crammond, B. (2015). "Implementing Joined-Up Government: Lessons from the Australian Social Inclusion Agenda." *Australian Journal of Public Administration, 74*(2), 176–186.

25. Carey, G. and Harris, P. (2016). "Developing Management Practices to Support Joined-Up Governance." *Australian Journal of Public Administration, 75*(1), 112–118.

26. Scott, R. J. and Boyd, R. (2017). "Joined-Up For What?"

27. Quotations by Linda Oliver in this chapter are from an interview with her on May 23, 2018. Oliver was a manager of Better for Business (Result 9) at the Ministry of Business, Innovation and Employment at the time of the Better Public Services reforms. When interviewed, she was senior project manager at the Inland Revenue Department.

28. Chou, T-Z., Chen, J-R. and Pu, C-K. (2008). "Exploring the Collective Actions of Public Servants in e-Government Development." *Decision Support Systems, 45*(2), 251–165. DOI:10.1016/j.dss.2007.02.005, 253.

29. For a discussion on engineering artificially high exit costs, see: Cels, S., de Jong, J. and Nauta, F. (2012). *Agents of Change: Strategy and Tactics for Social Innovation*. Brookings Institution Press.

30. Cabinet paper: "Better Public Services Results 2015 End-Year Progress Report," March 9, 2016.

Chapter 13

1. Ingram, H. and McDonnell, B. (1996). "Effective Performance Management—The Teamwork Approach Considered." *Managing Service Quality: An International Journal,* 6(6), 38–42.

2. Rennie, I. (2020). "Quest: New Zealand Public Sector Reform Since 2000." In Berman, E. and Karacaoglu, G. (Eds.), *Public Policy and Governance Frontiers in New Zealand.* Emerald Publishing Limited, 295.

3. "Accountability is complicated" is one of the seven defining characteristics of the New Public Service paradigm. See: Denhardt, J. V. and Denhardt, R. B. (2015). *The New Public Service: Serving, Not Steering.* Routledge.

4. Page, S. (2004). "Measuring Accountability for Results in Interagency Collaboratives." *Public Administration Review,* 64(September), 5.

5. While other authors have focused on legal and accounting standards of accountability, Behn focuses on accountability as it is experience by public servants; see: Behn, R. D. (2001). *Rethinking Democratic Accountability.* Brookings Institution Press.

6. For an account of New Zealand's experience of "Managing for Shared Outcomes," see: Scott, R. J. and Boyd, R. (2017). "Joined-Up for What? Response to Carey and Harris on Joined-Up Governance Practices." *The Australian Journal of Public Administration,* 76(1), 138–144.

7. Romzek and Ingraham's framework for accountability can be found in: Romzek, B. S. and Ingraham, P. W. (2000). "Cross Pressures of Accountability: Initiative, Command, and Failure in The Ron Brown Plane Crash." *Public Administration Review,* 60(3), 240–253.

8. For a discussion on the history of the justice sector, including reference to the "big three," see: Scott, R. J. (2018). *ANZSOG Case Library: Interagency Collaboration to Reduce Crime in New Zealand* (video). Melbourne: Australia and New Zealand School of Government. www.youtube.com/watch?v=GpBNMd9JpUw.

9. Freeman (2011) stresses the resources that other organisations can bring, while Skrtic et al. (1996) emphasize that a broad membership helps others feel included and therefore more likely to be supportive. See: Freeman, J. (2011). "Collaborative Governance in the Administrative State." *UCLA Law Review,* 45(1), 1–77. Skrtic, T. M., Sailor, W., and Gee, K. (1996). "Voice, Collaboration, and Inclusion Democratic Themes in Educational and Social Reform Initiatives." *Remedial and Special Education,* 17(3), 142–157.

10. Broad participation is linked to resource pooling in several prominent papers: Agranoff, R. (2006). "Inside Collaborative Networks: Ten Lessons for Public Managers." *Public Administration Review,* 66(s1), 56–65. Kenis, P. and Schneider, V. (1991). "Policy Networks and Policy Analysis: Scrutinizing a New Analytical Toolbox." In *Policy Networks: Empirical Evidence And Theoretical Considerations.* Campus Verlag, 25–59. Klijn, E. H. and Koppenjan, J. F. (2000). "Public Management and Policy Networks: Foundations of a Network Approach to Governance." *Public Management an International Journal of Research and Theory,* 2(2), 135–158.

11. See: Ingham, A. G., Levinger, G., Graves, J. and Peckham, V. (1974). "The Ringelmann Effect: Studies of Group Size and Group Performance." *Journal of Experimental Social Psychology, 10*(4), 371–384.

12. While the concept had been studied in the 1950s and 1960s in different forms, the term "diffusion of responsibility" and its accepted definition are largely credited to the work of Michael Wallach and colleagues: Wallach, M. A., Kogan, N., and Bem, D. J. (1964). "Diffusion of Responsibility and Level of Risk Taking in Groups," *Journal of Abnormal and Social Psychology, 68*, 263–274.

13. Wegner and Schaeffer studied this phenomenon in the context of the diffusion of responsibility, but earlier research, by Darley and Latané, had noted a similar pattern: Darley, J. M. and Latané, B. (1968). "When Will People Help in a Crisis?" *Psychology Today*, 2, 54–57. Wegner, D. M. and Schaefer, D. (1978). "The Concentration of Responsibility: An Objective Self-Awareness Analysis of Group Size Effects in Helping Situations." *Journal of Personality and Social Psychology, 36*(2), 147–155. For a summary of the early group size research to which Wegner and Schaeffer contributed, see also: Latané, B. and Nida, S. (1981). "Ten Years of Research on Group Size and Helping." *Psychological Bulletin, 89*, 308–324.

14. For a general description of the behavioral consequences of a diffusion of responsibility, see: Fein, K. and Burke, M. (2013). *Social Psychology*. Nelson Education.

15. Quotations by Richard Foy in this chapter are from an interview with him on April 12, 2018. Foy was director, Result 10, and general manager, Digital Transformation at the Department of Internal Affairs at the time of the Better Public Services reforms. When interviewed, he was chief archivist and general manager, Archives New Zealand.

16. Functional leadership was established in specific business or "corporate" functions, as part of the government's Better Public Services program, to build stronger foundations for system-level improvements and unlock system benefits that would not be possible on an agency-by-agency decisionmaking basis.

17. Blackman, D. A. and others. (2012). "Developing High Performance: Performance Management in the Australian Public Service." Crawford School of Public Policy. https://crawford.anu.edu.au/publication/crawford-school-working-papers/9844/developing-high-performance-performance-management.

18. Ibid.

19. Ibid.

20. Thompson, D. F. (1980). "Moral Responsibility of Public Officials: The Problem of Many Hands. *American Political Science Review, 74*(4), 905–916.

21. Downie, R. S. (1969). "Collective Responsibility." *Philosophy, 44*, 66–69.

22. Sverdlik, S. (1987). "Collective Responsibility." *Philosophical Studies, 51*, 61–76.

23. The phrase "governance cascade" was used by Kania and Kramer in their description of "collective impact." Collective impact has been criticized (for example, by Tom Wolff in 2016) as ignoring more formal evidence and contributions from theory. Nonetheless, the language of collective impact has had a significant influence on practitioner concepts of horizontal management. See: Kania, J. and Kramer, M. (2011). "Collective Impact." *Stanford Social Innovation Review, 9*(1), 36–41. Wolff, T. (2016).

"Voices from the Field: Ten Places Where Collective Impact Gets It Wrong." *Global Journal of Community Psychology Practice*, *7*(1).

24. Cabinet paper: "Better Public Services Results 2013 End-Year Progress Report," February 13, 2014.

25. Cabinet paper: "Better Public Services Results 2015 Midyear Progress Report," July 2, 2015.

26. New Zealand's approach to developing a Corporate Center, as described in the following paragraphs, evolved in the decade that preceded the Better Public Services reform and provided a basis for the joint central agency work described in this book. The theory underpinning the Corporate Center was not explicit at the time, but is well described in the work of Deborah Blackman and colleagues: Blackman, D. A. and others. (2012). "Developing High Performance: Performance Management in the Australian Public Service." Research Paper No. 12-09. Crawford School of Public Policy. https://crawford.anu.edu.au/publication/crawford-school-working-papers/9844/developing-high-performance-performance-management.

27. Various members of FSG consulting group have contributed blog posts to the Stanford Social Innovation Review regarding the importance of "backbone" organizations, in particular: www.ssireview.org/blog/entry/measuring_backbone_contributions_to_collective_impact and www.ssireview.org/blog/entry/understanding_the_value_of_backbone_organizations_in_collective_impact_1.

28. The language used in network literature is confusing and inconsistent. This book reflects the usage in influential works of Keith Provan and Patrick Kenis, particularly: Provan, K. G. and Kenis, P. (2008). "Modes of Network Governance: Structure, Management, and Effectiveness." *Journal of Public Administration Research and Theory*, *18*(2), 229–252.

29. The system design toolkit provides a frame for looking at machinery of government questions that is very different from the way these questions have been considered in the past. See: www.ssc.govt.nz/mog-shared-problems.

30. Adam Oliver provides a more comprehensive description of reciprocal altruism: Oliver, A. (2017). "Do Unto Others: On the Importance of Reciprocity in Public Administration." *American Review of Public Administration*, *48*(4), 279–290. DOI: 10.1177/0275074016686826.

31. David Fischer noted that New Zealand culture is preoccupied by the idea of fairness, and therefore the works of Sen and others take on particular relevance: Fischer, D. H. (2012). *Fairness and freedom: A History of Two Open Societies: New Zealand and the United States*. Oxford University Press. Sen, A. (2009). *The Idea of Justice*. Belknap Press.

32. Marin, B. (1990). "Generalized Political Exchange: Preliminary Considerations." In: Marin, B. (Ed.). *Generalized Political Exchange: Antagonistic Cooperation and Integrated Policy Circuits*. Campus Verlag, 60.

33. Behn, R. D. (2001). *Rethinking Democratic Accountability*. Brookings Institution Press.

34. Quotations by Linda Oliver in this chapter are from an interview with her on May 23, 2018. Oliver was a manager of Better for Business (Result 9) at the Ministry of Business, Innovation and Employment at the time of the Better Public Services re-

forms. When interviewed, she was senior project manager at the Inland Revenue Department.

35. English, B. Speech to the Australia and New Zealand School of Government in Canberra, August 6, 2014.

36. Ibid.

37. Quotes in this case study relating to the Gore Kids Hub are from the case study vignette hosted on the SSC website: "Better Public Services Result 2—Case Study: A Shared Place to Play and Learn." https://ssc.govt.nz/resources/bps-result2-cs16.

38. Quotes in this case study relating to Te Kohekohe drop-in centre are from the case study vignette hosted on the SSC website: "Better Public Services Result 2—Case Study: Kaikohe Weaving Together." https://ssc.govt.nz/resources/bps-result2-cs17.

39. Quotes in this case study relating to Poipoia te Mokopuna are from the case study vignette hosted on the SSC website: "Confident, Connected whānau - Poipoia te Mokopuna." https://ssc.govt.nz/resources/bps-result2-cs13.

40. Deloitte for the Ministry of Business, Innovation and Employment. (2013). "Better Public Services for Business Result 9: Programme Health Check Final Report."

41. Quotations by Richard Foy in this chapter are from an interview with him on April 12, 2018. Foy was Director, Result 10 and general manager, Digital Transformation at the Department of Internal Affairs at the time of the Better Public Services reforms. When interviewed, he was chief archivist and general manager, Archives New Zealand.

42. Quotations by Kararaina Calcott-Cribb in this chapter are from an interview with her on June 7, 2018. Calcott-Cribb was leading the Early Learning Taskforce at the time of the Better Public Services reforms. When interviewed, she was chief executive of Te Kōhanga Reo National Trust.

43. Quotations in this chapter are from an interview with Dr. Chrissie Pickin, May 23, 2018. Dr. Pickin was chief advisor Population Health and rheumatic fever program lead at the Ministry of Health at the time of the Better Public Services reform. When interviewed, she was executive director of Health and Wellbeing, Public Health Wales.

44. Deloitte for the Ministry of Business, Innovation and Employment. (2013). "Better Public Services for Business Result 9: Programme Health Check Final Report."

45. Content in this case study relating to Tai Tokerau regional team is drawn from the case study vignette hosted on the SSC website: "Better Public Services Result 4—Case Study: Strengthening Tai Tokerau." https://ssc.govt.nz/resources/bps-result4–cs4.

46. Content in this case study relating to the Ngāpuhi Memorandum of Understanding is drawn from the case study vignette hosted on the SSC website: "Better Public Services Result 4—Case Study: Bringing Ngapuhi Children Back Home." https://ssc.govt.nz/resources/bps-result4–cs1.

47. Content in this case study relating to Family Group Conferences is drawn from the case study vignette hosted on the SSC website: "Better Public Services Result 4—Case Study: Empowering whanau on marae." https://ssc.govt.nz/resources/bps-result4–cs7.

48. To say that the theory of planned behaviour has had an impact on behavioral

science literature would be an understatement. At the time of writing, Ajzen's 1991 paper has been cited more than 50,000 times: Ajzen, I. (1991). "The Theory of Planned Behavior." *Organizational Behavior and Human Decision Processes, 50*(2), 179–211.

49. This is described in group dynamics literature as the "proximity principle." See: Newcomb, T. M. (1960). "Varieties of Interpersonal Attraction." In: Cartwright, D. and Zander, A. (Eds.). *Group Dynamics: Research and Theory.* Harper and Row, 104–119.

50. Kahan's studies provide a selfish explanation for seemingly altruistic behaviors. See: Kahan, J. P. (1974). "Rationality, the Prisoner's Dilemma, and Population." *Journal of Social Issues, 30*(4), 189–210.

51. A version of this continuum appeared in a 1971 article by Cora Marrett, but since then, numerous variations have emerged, of which the following is a partial list: Brown, K. and Keast, R. (2003). "Citizen-Government Engagement: Community Connection through Networked Arrangements." *Asian Journal of Public Administration, 25*(1), 107–131. Eppel, E. and others. (2013). "The Cross-Organisation Collaboration Solution? Conditions, Roles and Dynamics in New Zealand." In O'Flynn, J., Blackman, D. and Halligan, J. (Eds.). *Crossing Boundaries in Public Management and Policy: The International Experience.* Routledge, 47–63. Gadja, R. (2004). "Utilizing Collaboration Theory to Evaluate Strategic Alliances." *American Journal of Evaluation, 25*(1), 65–77. Gregson, B., Cartlidge, A., and Bond, J. (1992). "Development of a Measure of Professional Collaboration in Primary Health Care." *Journal of Epidemiology and Community Health, 46,* 48–53. Hall, C. M. (1999). "Rethinking Collaboration and Partnership: A Public Policy Perspective." *Journal of Sustainable Tourism, 7*(3–4), 274–289. Howarth, J. and Morrison, T. (2007). "Collaboration, Integration and Change In: Children's Services: Critical Issues and Key Ingredients." *Child Abuse & Neglect, 31*(1), 55–69. Huxham, C. and Macdonald, D. (1992). "Introducing Collaborative Advantage: Achieving Interorganizational Effectiveness through Meta-Strategy." *Management Decision, 30*(3), 50–56. Marrett, C. (1971). "On the Specification of Interorganizational Dimensions." *Sociology and Social Research, 56,* 83–89. Sadoff, C. W. and Grey, D. (2005). "Cooperation on International Rivers: A Continuum for Securing and Sharing Benefits." *Water International, 30*(4), 420–427.

52. Scott, R. J. and Bardach, E. (2019). A Comparison of Management Adaptations for Joined-Up Government: Lessons from New Zealand." *Australian Journal of Public Administration, 78*(2), 191–212.

53. State Services Commission. (2014). "Better Public Services Result 9—Case Study: Business.govt.nz—Bringing It All Together for New Zealand Businesses." https://ssc.govt.nz/resources/bps-result9-cs2.

54. Social identity theory, the social identity approach, collective identity, and related fields, constitute a terrain too vast to explore in this book. Two books provide a useful overview: Tajfel, H. (Ed.). (2010). *Social Identity and Intergroup Relations.* Cambridge University Press. Abrams, D. E. and Hogg, M. A. (1990). *Social Identity Theory: Constructive and Critical Advances.* Springer-Verlag Publishing.

55. There are various versions of this saying to be found in all kinds of literature. One early source is Yehudah from 1932, as cited by Marx in 1978: Marx, E. (1978). "The Ecology and Politics of Nomadic Pastoralists in the Middle East." In: Weissleder,

W. *The Nomadic Alternative: Modes and Models of Interaction in the African-Asian Deserts and Steppes*. Moulton, 59. Yehudah, L. H. (1932). *Mishlei' Arav*. Hasefer.

56. Brewer's studies of differentiated and superordinate group identity explore cooperation in the management of common pool resources, where similar work by Chen and Li explore charity, concern, and jealousy in similar contexts: Kramer, R. M. and Brewer, M. B. (1984). "Effects of Group Identity on Resource Use in a Simulated Commons Dilemma." *Journal of Personality and Social Psychology*, 46(5), 1044. Brewer, M. B. (1996). "When Contact Is Not Enough: Social Identity and Intergroup Cooperation." *International Journal of Intercultural Relations*, 20(3–4), 291–303. Brewer, M. B. (2001). "Ingroup Identification and Intergroup Conflict." *Social Identity, Intergroup Conflict, and Conflict Reduction*, 3, 17–41. Chen, Y. and Li, S. X. (2009). "Group Identity and Social Preferences." *American Economic Review*, 99(1), 431–457.

57. Deloitte for the Ministry of Business, Innovation and Employment. (2013). "Better Public Services for Business Result 9: Programme Health Check Final Report."

58. Social identity has been one of the most important interests of sociologists and psychologists for decades and yet has only recently attracted the attention of economists. Akerlof and Kranton's study is a welcome addition to the field; while sociology research tends to be descriptive, economists seem more comfortable with normative or prescriptive conclusions that lend themselves more direction to use in public policy decisionmaking. For the account of social identity in an elementary school, see: Akerlof, G. A. and Kranton, R. E. (2010). *Identity Economics: How Our Identities Shape Our Work, Wages, and Well-Being*. Princeton University Press, 72.

59. All quotes in this case study are drawn from the following paper, unless otherwise indicated: Scott, R. J. and others. (2019). "The Contribution of Narrative Choice to Institutional Memory." Prepared for the 2019 conference of the International Public Policy Association, Montreal, Canada. www.ippapublicpolicy.org/file/paper/5cf59af36312d.pdf.

60. Quotations in this chapter are from an interview with Aphra Green, April 12, 2018. Green was general manager, Justice Sector Group at the time of the Better Public Services reform. When interviewed, she was general manager, Strategy, Evidence and Investment Group.

61. Excerpt from the educational video: Scott, R. J. (2018). "ANZSOG Case Library: Interagency collaboration to reduce crime in New Zealand." Australia and New Zealand School of Government. www.youtube.com/watch?v=GpBNMd9JpUw.

62. Ibid.

Chapter 14

1. See, in particular: Wright, B. E. (2007). "Public Service and Motivation: Does Mission Matter?" *Public Administration Review*, 67(1), 54–64. Wright, B. E. and Pandey, S. K. (2011). "Public Organizations and Mission Valence: When Does Mission Matter?" *Administration & Society*, 43(1), 22–44.

2. Rainey, H. G. and Steinbauer, P. (1999). "Galloping Elephants: Developing Elements of a Theory of Effective Government Organizations." *Journal of Public Administration Research and Theory*, 9(1), 1–32.

3. Mission valence and goal commitment literature use the term valence in slightly different ways. In literature on goal commitment, valence is seen as a contributor to commitment, along with instrumentality and expectancy. In this sense, and the way it is used in this book, valence is defined quite narrowly as the alignment of personal values with mission. In mission valence literature, mostly notably the works of Bradley Wright and Sanjay Pandey, valence is defined more broadly to include instrumentality, expectancy, and meaningfulness. The way in which valence is used in this book is perhaps more closely aligned to Wright and Pandey's "meaningfulness." See: Wright, B. E. and Pandey, S. K. (2011). "Public Organizations and Mission Valence: When Does Mission Matter?" *Administration & Society*, *43*(1), 22–44.

4. Public service motivation means different things to different public servants. Gene Brewer and Sally Selden categorize this desire to make a difference on the basis of four distinct units of analysis. Some people relate to helping individuals (Samaritans), some to helping communities (communitarians), others to improving the country (patriots), and others still to helping all people regardless of place (humanitarians). See: Brewer, G. A., Selden, S. C., and Facer II, R. L. (2000). "Individual Conceptions of Public Service Motivation." *Public Administration Review*, *60*(3), 254–264.

5. A notable example of the application of public choice theory can be found in a memoir by Graham Scott, the secretary of the treasury of New Zealand during the new public management reforms of the 1980s. Scott argues that public servants should be assumed to be acting in rational self-interest and controlled by extrinsic rewards and sanctions. See: Scott, G. C. (2001). *Public Management in New Zealand: Lessons and Challenges*. New Zealand Business Roundtable.

6. Tversky and Kahneman's behavioral economics appears to have been influential on the choices made in the delivery unit. For ideas relating specifically to loss aversion, see: Tversky, A. and Kahneman, D. (1991). "Loss Aversion in Riskless Choice: A Reference-Dependent Model." *The Quarterly Journal of Economics*, *106*(4), 1039–1061.

7. David Hume's collection of moral, political, and literary essays were first published in the 1750s, but the collection used in writing this book was that edited and notated by Eugene Miller: Miller, E. F. and Hume, D. (1994). *Essays: Moral, Political, and Literary*. Liberty Fund.

8. See Le Grand, J. (2007). *The Other Invisible Hand: Delivering Public Services through Choice and Competition*. Princeton University Press.

9. See: BBC News. (2007). "Blair: In His Own Words." http://news.bbc.co.uk/1/hi/uk_politics/3750847.stm.

10. Deci, E. L. (1971). "Effects of Externally Mediated Rewards on Intrinsic Motivation." *Journal of Personality and Social Psychology*, *18*(1), 105. Fisher, C. D. (1978). "The Effects of Personal Control, Competence, and Extrinsic Reward Systems on Intrinsic Motivation." *Organizational Behavior and Human Performance*, *21*(3), 273–288. Eisenberger, R., Rhoades, L., and Cameron, J. (1999). "Does pay for performance increase or decrease perceived self-determination and intrinsic motivation?" *Journal of Personality and Social Psychology*, *77*(5), 1026.

11. See, among others: Perry, J. L. and Hondeghem, A. (2008). "Building Theory and Empirical Evidence about Public Service Motivation." *International Public Man-*

agement Journal, 11(1), 3–12. Houston, D. J. (2000). "Public-Service Motivation: A Multivariate Test." *Journal of Public Administration Research and Theory, 10*(4), 713–728. Perry, J. L. (1996). "Measuring Public Service Motivation: An Assessment of Construct Reliability and Validity." *Journal of Public Administration Research and Theory, 6*(1), 5–22.

12. Orange, R. (2016). "New Public Passion: Reflections from New Zealand on Public Service Reform," 4. Discussion Paper 08(01). UNDP Global Centre for Public Service Excellence, Singapore.

13. Scott, R. (2019). "Service, Citizenship, and the Public Interest: New Public Service and Our Public Service Reforms." SSC Discussion Paper.

14. Scott, R. J. (2016). "The Performance Relationship between Department Chief Executives and the State Services Commission in New Zealand." State Sector Performance Hub, working paper 2016-3. DOI: 10.13140/RG.2.1.4299.4162/1.

15. Bevan, G. and Fasolo, B. (2013). "Models of Governance Of Public Services: Empirical and Behavioural Analysis of 'Econs' and 'Humans.'" In: Oliver, A. (Ed.) *Behavioural Public Policy*. Cambridge University Press, 38–62.

16. Motivational crowding theory arose in literature on management in the private sector and was named by Bruno Frey and Reto Jegen. The theory has been expanded by the work of Samuel Bowles. See: Frey, B. S. and Jegen, R. (2001). Motivation Crowding Theory. *Journal of Economic Surveys, 15*(5), 589–611. Bowles, S. (2016). *The Moral Economy: Why Good Incentives Are No Substitute for Good Citizens*. Yale University Press.

17. Achievement motivation describes a broad field of psychology; some of the motivations described in this chapter are explored more fully by Deborah Stipek in Stipek, D. J. (1993). *Motivation to Learn: From Theory to Practice*. Allyn and Bacon.

18. Orange, R. (2016). "New Public Passion."

19. Julian Le Grand presents an elegant case for why shaming couldn't drive innovation and high performance and suggests quasi-markets as an alternative. While the points relating to the limitations of shaming are well made, there do not appear to be examples of quasi-markets faring better, as discussed in the introduction of this book. For a more sympathetic and optimistic discussion of quasi-markets, see: Le Grand, J. (2007). *The Other Invisible Hand: Delivering Public Services through Choice and Competition*. Princeton University Press.

20. Quotations by Kararaina Calcott-Cribb in this chapter are from an interview with her on June 7, 2018. Calcott-Cribb was leading the Early Learning Taskforce at the time of the Better Public Services reforms. When interviewed, she was chief executive of Te Kōhanga Reo National Trust.

21. Both these quotes are from interviews conducted as part of Scott, R. J. and Boyd, R. (2017). *Interagency Performance Targets: A Case Study of New Zealand's Results Programme*. IBM.

22. Orange, R. (2016). "New Public Passion."

23. Quotations by Richard Foy in this chapter are from an interview with him on April 12, 2018. Foy was director, Result 10 and general manager, digital transformation at the Department of Internal Affairs at the time of the Better Public Services

reforms. When interviewed, he was chief archivist and general manager of Archives New Zealand.

24. Quotations by Kararaina Calcott-Cribb in this chapter are from an interview with her on June 7, 2018. Calcott-Cribb was leading the Early Learning Taskforce at the time of the Better Public Services reforms. When interviewed, she was chief executive of Te Kōhanga Reo National Trust.

25. Quotes by Bruce Ritchie are from the case study vignette hosted on the SSC website: "Better Public Services Result 5—Case Study: Massey High School and the Auckland West Vocational Academy." https://ssc.govt.nz/resources/bps-result5-cs1.

26. Quotes by Liz Hall are from the case study vignette hosted on the SSC website "Ruapehu College Connects the Dots with Vocational Pathways." https://ssc.govt.nz/resources/bps-result5-cs13.

27. Quotes by Shona Smith are from the case study vignette hosted on the SSC website: "Better Public Services Result 5—Case Study: No school Is an Island: Meet the Waitakere Community of Learning." https://ssc.govt.nz/resources/bps-result5-cs16.

28. Tall poppy syndrome has been described since ancient times, appearing in the writing of Herodotus and Aristotle (Rackham, 1944; Peeters, 2003), and is certainly familiar outside of New Zealand. However, several studies report on its particular prevalence in New Zealand (Mouly and Sankaran, 2000; Jackson et al., 2005; Kirkwood, 2007) and also Australia (Meng et al., 2003; Peeters, 2004; Mandisodza et al., 2006). Rackham, H. (1944). *Aristotle in 23 Volumes.* Volume 21. Harvard University Press. Peeters, B. L. (2003). The Tall Poppy Syndrome: On the Re-Emergence in Contemporary Australia of an Ancient Greek and Latin Motive. *Classicvm, 29*(2), 22–26. Mouly, V. S. and Sankaran, J. (2000). "The Tall Poppy Syndrome in New Zealand: An Exploratory Investigation." *Transcending Boundaries: Integrating People, Processes and Systems,* 285–289. Jackson, D. J. and others. (2005). "Exploring the Dynamics of New Zealand's Talent Flow." *New Zealand Journal of Psychology, 34*(2), 110. Kirkwood, J. (2007). "Tall Poppy Syndrome: Implications for Entrepreneurship in New Zealand." *Journal of Management & Organization, 13*(4), 366–382. Meng, Y. K., Ashkanasy, N. M., and Härtel, C. E. (2003). "The Effects of Australian Tall Poppy Attitudes on American Value Based Leadership Theory." *International Journal of Value-Based Management, 16*(1), 53–65. Peeters, B. (2004). "Tall Poppies and Egalitarianism in Australian Discourse: From Key Word to Cultural Value." *English World-Wide, 25*(1), 1–25. Mandisodza, A. N., Jost, J. T., and Unzueta, M. M. (2006). "'Tall Poppies' and 'American Dreams': Reactions to Rich and Poor in Australia and the United States." *Journal of Cross-Cultural Psychology, 37*(6), 659–668.

29. Sabina Nuti and colleagues describe a similar experience in Toscana (Tuscany), Italy. Exceptional management of diabetic patients in the region of Marche was shared with other regions, causing a motivation effect in Marche and an improvement in performance in neighboring regions. See: Nuti, S., Vola, F., Bonini, A., and Vainieri, M. (2015). "Making Governance Work in the Health Care Sector: Evidence from a 'Natural Experiment' In Italy." *Health Economics, Policy and Law, 11*(1), 7–38.

30. Quotations by Kararaina Calcott-Cribb in this chapter are from an interview

with her on June 7, 2018. Calcott-Cribb was leading the Early Learning Taskforce at the time of the Better Public Services reforms. When interviewed, she was chief executive of Te Kōhanga Reo National Trust.

31. Quotations in this chapter are from an interview with Dr. Chrissie Pickin, May 23, 2018. Dr. Pickin was chief advisor Population Health and Rheumatic Fever Program lead at the Ministry of Health at the time of the Better Public Services reform. When interviewed, she was executive director of Health and Wellbeing, Public Health Wales.

32. For the purpose of this book, we have grouped data, feedback, and learning under the general heading of "valence." Much of the discussion in this section could equally be related to "expectancy," in that it provided feedback on progress toward the target, or "instrumentality," in that it allowed public servants to understand the relationship between action and consequence. We ultimately placed it here because public servants interviewed in preparing the book closely linked the use of data about outcomes for New Zealanders with their spirit of service to the community.

33. Quotations by an education official in this chapter are from an interview held on April 10, 2018, with a senior manager at the Ministry of Education responsible for coordinating the Education Results.

34. Quotations in this chapter are from an interview with Aphra Green, April 12, 2018. Green was general manager, justice sector group at the time of the Better Public Services reform. When interviewed, she was general manager, Strategy, Evidence and Investment Group.

35. New Zealand State Services Commission website: www.ssc.govt.nz/better -public-services.

36. Cabinet paper: "Better Public Services Results 2013 End-Year Progress Report," February 13, 2014.

37. Cabinet paper: "Better Public Services Results 2014 End-Year Progress Report," February 16, 2015.

38. Quotations in this chapter are from an interview with Dr. Chrissie Pickin, May 23, 2018. Dr. Pickin was chief advisor Population Health and Rheumatic Fever Program lead at the Ministry of Health at the time of the Better Public Services reform. When interviewed, she was executive director of Health and Wellbeing, Public Health Wales.

39. See: Hughes, P. and Scott, R. J. (2021). "High Autonomy, High Alignment: Coordinating a More Unified Public Service." In: Mazey, S. and Richardson, J. *Policy-making Under Pressure: Rethinking the Policy Process in Aotearoa New Zealand.* Canterbury University Press.

40. The New Zealand public service has focused on intrinsic motivation, under the banner "spirit of service" at key events since 2016. For an account of the use of "spirit of service," see Scott, R. (2019). *Service, Citizenship, and the Public Interest: New Public Service and Our Public Service Reforms.* New Zealand Government.

41. The phrase "spirit of service to the community" was used by Edgar Gladden in a textbook describing the core requirements of the public service: Gladden described the core requirements of the public service to be "impartially selected, administratively

competent, politically neutral, and imbued with a spirit of service to the community." See: Gladden, E. N. (1945). *The Civil Service: Its Problems and Future.* Stapes Press, 35.

42. The idea of a "spirit of service to the community" first appeared in the New Zealand statute book as part of the long title of the State Services Act of 1962. The State Services Act was repealed in 1988, and the phrase was then included in the purpose statement of the new State Sector Act. The State Sector Act was then repealed in 2020 and replaced with the Public Service Act. In this latest legislation, a "spirit of service to the community" took a more prominent position, with its only standalone section (section 11), as well as a new clause requiring senior officials to "preserve, protect, and nurture the spirit of service to the community that public service employees bring to their work." See: Scott, R. J., Macaulay, M., and Merton, E. (2020). "Drawing New Boundaries—Can we legislate for administrative behaviour?" Presented at the Public Administration Review Symposium, London.

43. Scott, R. J., Donadelli, F., and Merton, E. (2021). "Theoretical Paradigms in the Reform of the New Zealand Public Service: Is Post-NPM Still a Myth?" Presented at the World Congress of Political Science, Lisbon.

44. For a recent account of the spirit of service in the context of New Zealand's public service reform program, see Scott, R. J. and Macaulay, M. (2020). "Making Sense of New Zealand's 'Spirit of Service': Social Identity and the Civil Service." *Public Money & Management*, 1–10.

45. The Spirit of Service Awards celebrate public servants motivated by a spirit of service to the community. See: https://ssc.govt.nz/our-work/awards-and-recognition/spirit-of-service-awards/. The awards were first presented in 2019. For a video of award winners, see: https://ssc.govt.nz/our-work/awards-and-recognition/spirit-of-service-awards/spirit-service-awards-2019/spirit-of-service-awards-2019-winners/.

46. The State Services Commission twitter account is frequently used to name and fame public servants who display a spirit of service to their community. See: https://twitter.com/stateservicesnz.

47. Spirit of Service to the Community has been the major theme of the 2018 and 2019 Public Service Leaders Summit, the largest gathering of public service leaders in New Zealand. At the 2018 event, senior officials were asked to reflect on their own spirit of service, and at the 2019 event, they were asked how they might nurture a spirit of service to the community in their teams. The Public Service Leaders Summit is discussed in Scott, R. (2019). *Service, Citizenship, and the Public Interest: New Public Service and Our Public Service Reforms.* New Zealand Government.

Conclusions

1. Quoted in Johnston, A. (2005). *Sir Edmund Hillary: An Extraordinary Life.* Penguin, 73.

2. Better for Business, Business and Government Working Smarter. See: www.mbie.govt.nz/business-and-employment/business/support-for-business/better-for-business.

3. "Strategy for a Digital Public Service." See: www.digital.govt.nz/digital-government/strategy/strategy-summary/strategy-for-a-digital-public-service/.

4. The All of Government Innovation Showcase was held at Te Papa Tongarewa (the national museum of New Zealand) on December 3, 2019. It was jointly hosted by Better for Business and Digital Government Partnership and highlighted collaborative innovations to deliver easy and seamless services to New Zealand. The All-of-Government Innovation Showcase featured exhibits by eighteen groups, including Creative-HQ's GovTech Accelerator, a spinoff from the R9 Accelerator discussed in chapter 10. See: www.digital.govt.nz/showcase/all-of-government-innovation-showcase-december -2019.

5. For a general discussion of social identity and intergroup behaviour see: Tajfel, H. (1974). "Social Identity and Intergroup Behaviour." *Information (International Social Science Council)*, *13*(2), 65–93.

6. This characterization of the New Zealand public service reforms as aiming to establish a superordinate social identity across the public service was first described in Scott, R. J. (2019). "Public Service Motivation and Social Identity." International Research Society for Public Management.

7. The minister for State Services, Chris Hipkins, describes the new reforms here: www.beehive.govt.nz/release/public-service-undergoes-biggest-shake-30-years.

Appendix 4

1. Te Kawa Mataaho, Public Service Commission, https://ssc.govt.nz/resources/bps-result1-cs4/.

2. Te Kawa Mataaho, Public Service Commission, https://ssc.govt.nz/resources/bps-result1-cs6/.

Appendix 5

1. This content is from the New Zealand Treasury's in-house newsletter "The Treasurist" (2013).

Index